HEARTLAND HIGHWAYS

In Search of America

JOHN W. BUTLER

Copyright © 2025
John W. Butler
All rights reserved.
Publisher: Story Road Press
First Edition

All rights reserved. No part of this publication may be reproduced, stored in a retrieval system, distributed, or transmitted in any form or by any means—electronic, mechanical, photocopying, recording, or otherwise—without the prior written permission of the author or publisher, except as permitted under U.S. copyright law.

JB@JohnButlersBuzz.com

Printed Worldwide
First Printing 2025
First Edition 2025

ISBN: 979-8-9993942-1-7 Paperback
ISBN: 979-8-9993942-4-8 Paperback
ISBN: 979-8-9993942-2-4 Hardcover
ISBN: 979-8-9993942-0-0 E-book
ISBN: 979-8-9993942-3-1 Audio Book

Library of Congress Control Number: 2025914034

Interior Book Design by Walt's Book Design
www.waltsbookdesign.com
Cover design by Victoria Davies

Original photographs and illustrations created by
John W. Butler or used with permission.

JB@JohnButlersBuzz.com
John W. Butler
P.O. Box 670903 Dallas, Texas 75367
www.HeartlandHighways.com

For those who sat with me in diners, shared a Sloppy Joe, a laugh, a story, a cup of hot coffee on a cold morning, and told the truth or something close.

Table of Contents

A Note from Me to You 1
01: Breaking News 3
02: Connecting the Dots Forward 9
03: Finding Argo 15
04: Ringing the Liberty Bell 19
05: Big Apple Surprise 27
06: Confronting Steinbeck 42
07: Lobster In The Forest 58
08: Coffee Down 67
09: Memphis Blues 75
10: The Inauguration 85
11: Got No Suitcase 90
12: Kill Devil Hills 101
13: A Dark and Stormy Night 111
14: Bottom's Up 116
15: Off the Grid 122
16: Dead Dog Saloon 130
17: Southern Crab Soup 138
18: Gator Rivers 146
19: Mijammi 151
20: Ninety-Seven Miles South 160
21: Life and Near-Death 171
22: On the Road Again 177
23: Moonlight Madness 182
24: Jazz and Jambalaya 188
25: Pilots, Pine Trees, and the Panhandle 194
26: Texas 207
27: Fields of Oil 217
28: Cadillac Ranch 223

29: Mother Road	227
30: Pueblos of the Southwest	234
31: Canyon Rim	241
32: Night Cometh	245
33: Wall of Sand	251
34: La Jolla Sunset	256
35: La La Land	262
36: Grapes of Wrath, Then and Now	267
37: A Rare Total Eclipse	272
38: Sleepless in Seattle	276
39: Unsheltered	282
40: Border-Busting	289
41: Forced Back	295
42: Roger to the Rescue	301
43: Crease on a Paper Map	307
44: Land of Oz	314
45: Coffee Talk	320
46: Road to Nowhere	329
47: Million-Dollar Water	334
48: Stone-Faced	341
49: Crazy Horse	347
50: Ghost Plane	352
51: Walter's Cross	358
52: Fargo	365
53: Main Street	371
54: Sweet Home Chicago	376
55: Heading East	380
56: All-American State of Mind	385

A Note from Me to You

THIS STORY IS A TRAIL of moments—of small-town diner stops, of strangers who spoke truth in passing, of silence in a snowy forest, of trading screens for scenes, of nights where the stars felt closer than the ground beneath me. It's about getting lost on purpose, chasing questions, finding pieces of yourself in places you've never been.

If you've ever wanted to disappear for a while, to see what's out there—or what's in here —this journey is for you.

I went without expectation, in search of the real America beyond the scare-you-to-death news headlines. It became a journey of self-discovery and a way to connect with the real America.

As America celebrates the 250th Anniversary of the signing of the Declaration of Independence, July 4, 2026, we celebrate not just a nation, but an idea that has endured, evolved, and inspired for two and a half centuries.

From the bold ink on that magnificent document to the countless voices that have shaped this land ever since, the story is one of resilience, revolution, and reinvention. America was born in the spirit of liberty, built on dreams both fragile and fierce, and though the path has never been perfect, the journey has always been pushed forward—through protest, progress, promise, and fire.

I set out with no agenda. I didn't follow itineraries. I was a "detourist." Followed hunches and locals saying, "It's just 15 minutes that way—you can't miss it." Spoiler: I did miss it. But what I found instead was better. My road trip became less about destinations and more about detours: a series of accidental adventures, spontaneous diner stops, and deeply unplanned human connections that made this sprawling, chaotic, beautiful country feel a little more like home. If you're looking for perfect pictures or practical advice, turn back now. But if you're here for the long, strange ride — hop in. Let's take the scenic route on purpose.

This book is something of a tribute to the winding, sometimes bumpy heartland highways that wind their way through the good ol' US of A—and to the freedom fighters and farmers, the dreamers and doers, the trailblazers and truth-tellers. Here's to 250 years of We the People, still working, still wondering, still writing the next chapter of our collective tale.

May these pages remind you that the road is always waiting, whether you strike off for two years, as I did, or just for two hours. And that sometimes, leaving is just another way of coming home.

01

Breaking News

Blow up your TV, throw away your paper
Move to the country, build you a home
Plant a little garden, eat a lot of peaches
Try to find Jesus on your own.

"SPANISH PIPEDREAM," JOHN PRINE

"ROAD TRIP OR RUNNING AWAY?" he asked, stirring his coffee without looking up. "Little bit of both, I suppose," I replied with a grin. A thousand miles from home, I'd pulled off the road a few minutes earlier as the sun slunk low in the sky. I wanted to avoid the twenty minutes of blinding glare I was about to dance with, so I drifted into the parking lot of a diner with a flickering retro sign. Inside, the scent of coffee and bacon hung in the air as I slid onto a stool at the counter.

The guy who'd struck up the conversation had the face of a farmer—rugged, weathered, real. His sweat-stained ball cap was pulled low on his forehead, broken in and comfortable, the kind you don't replace.

"The news," I said.

"The news?"

"Yep," I said with a half laugh. "Running from the doom and gloom that turns you into a hamster on a wheel trying to outrun the apocalypse."

"Mmm," he said, nodding slowly with an expression of a man who had seen his share of storms.

"I'm on the road in search of America," I said. "Kind'a like Steinbeck did back in the 60s."

"Mmm," he said again, his lips perched, as he wasn't sure about me.

Probably because I was dog-tired, that Harry Nilsson song from Midnight Cowboy started looping in my head—the one where the world's a blur of voices and none of them quite reach you. I stared into my coffee like it might offer an answer.

"Well," he said, "most folks out here still know how to listen. Still know how to talk to each other. Still refuse to be afraid." I guess he was reading my mind.

In that moment, something clicked—the road was a promise—like the neon sign blinking over the diner for fifty years. The promise of connection. A chance to not just explore America but to reconnect with what I had misplaced inside myself—hiding in some dark, forgotten corner of my soul, pretending to be okay.

My story is as old as the hills I am passing over, along with the wind and the dust. The long stretches of two-lane roads curve toward the unknown. The open road strips you of the familiar.

And the ghosts speak—the ghosts of those who made the journey before me and those who carved the paths and worked the lands.

As I drove, the landscapes, the towns, and the faces reminded me that everything we love is transient. And what we choose to protect today shapes the future for those who follow.

It didn't happen all at once.

It snuck up on me somewhere between missing an exit in Virginia and accidentally meeting the Wizard of Oz in Kansas. I wasn't lost. I was detouring. And not the kind of detour that slows you down — the kind that sets you free. I stopped chasing destinations and started chasing moments. Weird, beautiful, ridiculous, perfectly unplanned moments.

I became a Detourist. That happened the second I stopped asking, "Is this the right way?" and started asking, "What's down that road?" Turns out, everything.

My road trip began on a typical Texas end-of-the-day in August. The sun hovered at a blistering two hundred sixty-three degrees—well, maybe not exactly that blistering, but once you hit jalapeño-hot, the numbers hardly matter. If you're not familiar with the jalapeño, it's practically the national fruit of Texas, and it's as hot as, well, August in Texas.

Back at my condo high above Dallas, I shed my shoes ... and the weight of the world. I carried a brown paper sack neatly folded at the top—General Tso's chicken, my comfort food.

I sank into the couch, remote control in hand. A few beats of news, and I realized that, based on what the talking heads were saying, my fellow Americans were dividing into tribes and setting each other's hair on fire. "We are in a moment where the sense of community is breaking down," said Mark Shields on PBS News Hour. "And it's leading to a dangerous level of division." Greg Gutfeld on Fox News agreed, "We've become so divided that it feels like we're living in two different countries, each with its own reality." And Chuck Todd, on NBC, declared,

"We're on the brink of a societal collapse."

Not good. Maybe not entirely true, either. How was one to know?

At age fifteen, when I started in the TV newsroom, the reporting process was straightforward. We stuck to the basics—who, what, where, when, and why. The news was concise, objective. Reporters kept their perspectives to themselves and respected the audience's intelligence. Then came the internet, and now the media industry felt like a free-for-all. The truth? Well, it seemed optional.

My better angel all but whispered to me: "Turn it off. Shut this nonsense down."

I thought back to Paddy Chayefsky's *Network*, that unforgettable movie scene where news anchor Howard Beale finally snaps. He rages at the camera, urging viewers to open their windows and shout, "I'm mad as hell, and I'm not going to take it anymore!"

I didn't open any windows that night, but I sure felt like Beale. I swore off the news, polished off my General Tso's, and headed to bed.

◀ ▲ ▼ ▶

Hours later, still wide awake, I climbed out of bed, pulled the drawstrings on the window drapes, and opened the sliding glass doors to the late-night air. From my vantage point, a few stories up, I caught sight of a plane taking off from Love Field. Heading west. I should be on that plane, I thought. I couldn't face another hot Texas day.

In that quiet moment, regret whispered its seductive song. It reminded me of roads I hadn't traveled, dreams I hadn't chased, love I'd left unspoken. I didn't want my last days to be clouded with regret—those "what could have been" ghosts; the chances missed, the dreams faded into inaction's drought.

Coffee in hand, I sat down at my computer and began searching for a last-minute trip. Hours later, I was boarding a plane bound for the Colorado Rockies clad in my trusty red-plaid shirt, faded denim jeans, and nearly new gray running shoes.

As the sun was rising and the plane ascended, leaving the city and heat behind, a thought lingered with me: This restless longing for escape, for connection—was it the road I was truly seeking, or something else instead? Something that beckoned me from so many miles away, where home resided, distant but always calling.

Note to Self

I still have this itchy, annoying feeling that crept in watching the chaos in the news that night. Maybe I need to pay attention. Maybe it's an angel tapping me on the shoulder, going, "Hey, genius, something's off. Time to shake things up."

Maybe the restless discomfort is just the cost of something new wanting to be born. The Swiss psychoanalyst Carl Jung emphasizes the importance of paying attention to these inner signals, saying that they are invitations to transformation.

For once—just once—listen.

02

CONNECTING THE DOTS FORWARD

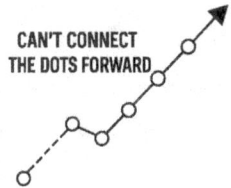

Some people come into our lives and quickly go. Some people stay for a while, and move our souls to dance. They awaken us to a new understanding, leave footprints on our hearts, and we are never, ever the same.

FLAVIA WEEDN

AT THE DENVER AIRPORT, end-of-summer travelers juggled cups of coffee, luggage, and kids. Snaking between them were business professionals glued to their devices, muttering excuse me's without looking up.

I'd made the nearly twenty-five-mile drive to the city center, my patience tested as I'd navigated the frenzied dance of Denver traffic. Once locked onto I-70, the commotion had dissolved as the Front Range came into view.

I'd been pulled forward by the whisper of adventure echoing from the folds of the mountains ahead. A mysterious force was drawing me towards those grandiose fourteeners—the famous fifty-eight peaks proudly soaring fourteen-thousand feet above sea level. For many hikers and mountain enthusiasts, they're an obsession, entries on a bucket list they're determined to check off.

I'd felt like a phoenix rising from the ashes, ready to emerge from the smoldering despair of negative news and fly high above the noise.

◀ ▲ ▼ ▶

My phone rang. I answered the incoming call to find Rickly on the other end. He ran a successful literary agency, with earlier roots in newspaper and magazine publishing. I'd left him a message upon landing in his mountainous home state, inviting him to join me for a day or two of adventure, a last-minute junket among friends. "Hey, buddy," he says, "I can't get away. Just come to my place instead." He was at his retreat on Shadow Mountain Lake, which is connected to Grand Lake, the western entrance to Rocky Mountain National Park. I'll throw steaks on the grill. Have dinner with Debbie and me. I was on my way faster than you could say, "medium rare."

Driving farther into the mountains, I came upon the pristine Lake Granby, ringed with colorful wildflowers and a forest that had seen better days, back before the pine beetle decimated the pines and turned the usually green hillsides brown. Downed trees lay like Pick Up Sticks, and yet there was beauty on a grand scale. As the magnificence of it all washed over me, I was comforted. I exhaled the breath I'd been holding. Steak and camaraderie now on my mind, as Rick, Debbie, and I sat down for dinner.

"Well, we've shared a lot of adventures over the years," I said. "Fly fishing, riding horses to the top of mountains, being stalked by a bear, and…"

"And playing cards," Rick interrupted, "in the tent when those monsoon rains kept us pinned down." Debbie hosted a toast, "To good friends and great meals together!"

"Watching you two combine families has been wild; it was the Brady Bunch—a TV sitcom on steroids." Rickly's three children and Debbie's four gave them a small village to oversee (count 'em, seven!). I recalled when Rick first told me about meeting Debbie. He was so glassy-eyed in love that he didn't pay me any mind, ignoring my sage advice. And so, he made the high dive into the deep end of the marriage pool. Hand in hand, Rickly and Deb bravely embraced the chaos and joy that comes with a grand total of seven children.

After a delicious meal and delightful conversation, I slept harder than I had in some time. The next morning, Rickly and I finished off cups of steaming coffee, headed to his garage, and tugged out two kayaks. Outside, a pair of ospreys dive-bombed trout, and Canada geese bobbed near the shoreline. A tranquil charm hung over the whole area, and Shadow Mountain Reservoir was beautifully unwrinkled and serene, which made my onboarding with that kayak all the clumsier—obnoxiously so.

I plunged my foot into the cold water with a splash, clutching the craft while attempting to stabilize both it and me. With a little effort, I positioned the port side to parallel the shore and then stood between it and the water's edge. It would have been nice to look confident in front of the unyieldingly self-possessed Rickly, but of greater importance in the moment was just getting into the dang boat.

Lifting my right leg over the side, I crouched my posterior down into the cockpit while swinging my left leg up and over. With a little wiggling around, and with the same effort it would take to put on a piece of clothing that's blowing in the wind, at last I wedged myself in, my legs straight under the skin of the bow. Which is when I glanced over to see Rickly ease himself into his boat in one smooth movement, muscle memory of one who lives on a lake.

With our double-bladed paddles, he and I both shoved away from the bank as Debbie waved us off from the living room balcony.

The orange kayak skimmed proudly along, seeming to enjoy the adventure as much as I did. The lean, angular bow cut efficiently through the turquoise water a little faster with each alternating stroke as I feathered my way across the lake.

Eventually, we reached a narrow strait between two islands, and while I didn't admit it, as we slowly drifted our way between the banks, I was grateful for the pause from such vigorous paddling. Seemingly on cue, an eagle landed impressively in one of the towering lodgepole pines that reached toward the sky, an incredible sight.

I'd known Rickly for so long that we now communicated in shorthand about everything from sports and past hunts to family ski trips and thoughts on life. In short order we sounded like two old codgers missing the good ol' days and all too happy to hear themselves declare their answers to the world's most pressing questions. Indulging the reminiscence bump—that's what that was about.

As he and I both have a background in mass-media communications, it was perhaps expected that our conversation would lead to the regrettable state of journalism these days. Or the lack thereof, I should say. Newspapers are failing. TV ratings are down. Biased, 24/7 rants are all the rage, as algorithms spin and smile. "How can you trust any of it?" I said, reflexively shaking my head in disbelief. "I mean, where are things headed? Is the America we grew up in all but gone? Are Americans being warped by the media, which is now nothing but a mouthpiece for one political party or another?"

Rickly took in what I was saying, hurling a harpoon of an idea in reply: "Why don't you stop bitching about it and go find out? Drive around America, interview real people you come across, write about them, see what you learn."

I was like Moses before the burning bush, God messaging me through the flames. "You need to do this, John," Rickly said, as though reading my mind. "And you've got to drive it. You can't do this by plane. Get a camper. Go see what everyone's thinking. Report on it like a real reporter would."

As Rickly continued, I chased back in my mind's eye to a previous era, me at age twelve. "It's impossible to connect the dots forward," Steve Jobs had once said. "You can only connect them by looking backward. So, you have to trust that the dots will somehow connect in your future." I was having a connect-the-dots moment on that lake.

When I was in junior high, I read John Steinbeck's *Travels with Charley*, a travelogue chronicling his 1960 road trip across America with his poodle—that's Charley—as he explored the nation's landscapes, people, and social issues. Immediately, I was compelled to follow suit, to see this country firsthand, to form my own opinions and perspectives, to have an adventure like that. Pretty bold for a boy, but there you have it. Some ideas lodge in your psyche like a grain of sand in an oyster, churning and irritating your imagination until, in time, something meaningful and beautiful results. I was ready for meaning and beauty. I was ready to take to the roads.

Steinbeck departed Sag Harbor, New York, on September 23, 1960, to make a 10,000mile driving trip that took just over two months. He and Charley made a giant loop around America in a brand-new GMC pickup with a camper on the back, and while a few of the details may have been embellished, the work was his personal account. Now, some fifty years later, I was eager to follow suit.

Note to Self

My inner voice was tossing between talking me out of it and urging me on—actually doing it. One part "heck yeah," two parts "what am I, *nuts?*" Sometimes you have to step away from the noise—step forward in faith; worry about the dots connecting later. Hey, what's life without a little leap of faith, right? When the big adventure is calling, is it crazy to just say, "Yes!"

I thought about Joseph Campbell's Hero's Journey — it always starts with the call. And sure, the hero usually hesitates at first ... but eventually, then comes the leap.

03

Finding Argo

Twenty years from now, you will be more disappointed by the things you didn't do than by the ones you did. So, throw off the bowlines. Sail away from the safe harbor. Catch the trade winds in your sails. Explore. Dream. Discover.

MARK TWAIN

ON A WEDNESDAY AFTERNOON IN November, I flew from Dallas to Baltimore, carrying nothing more than a duffle bag packed to the brim with clothes and essentials, ready for whatever lay ahead. A short drive brought me to a place near Chesapeake City, Maryland, where I stood before the gleaming 188-horsepower, six-cylinder Airstream, her sleek tortoiseshell exterior gleaming like a prizefighter preparing for a bout. This was my trusty steed, the one that would carry me on a journey to far-off places, through the fields and forests of this vast, blessed land.

Inside, the Airstream was bigger than I expected. The sofa turned into a bed, the bathroom had a shower, and the kitchen area was simple but enough. I stood up straight, pleased I didn't have to hunch. Outside, I saw the solar panels on the roof and smiled. With them and a good battery, I could disappear from civilization—no hookups, no grid—and live well.

I needed to give her a name. The writer who inspired this adventure, John Steinbeck had chosen the name Rocinante, like Don Quixote's faithful but weary horse, for his journey, but it didn't quite fit this Airstream.

After a lot of thought, I locked in on the name, Argo.

Argo—yes. That was it.

In Greek mythology, Argo was the name of the ship that carried Jason on his quest to retrieve the Golden Fleece, a symbol of courage and adventure. Jason's Argo sailed through danger and uncertainty, much like I hoped mine would. But in the story, Jason's ship was old and rotting. One night, Jason was sleeping on shore, on the ground, when a beam from its hull fell on him, ending his life. I made a mental note: Sleep inside Argo, not on the ground.

Another Argo, a steamship, had made its way around the globe in 1853 under Captain George Hyde's command. It circumnavigated the world in a record 127 days, but on its way home, it wrecked on a reef in thick fog. A second Note to Self: If I encounter fog, I'll settle in and wait it out.

I could not decide whether to head north or south from Chesapeake City. I had no plan. Should I flip a coin? I felt a tug to head to Hwy 1. I saw a sign for Philadelphia. Not that far away.

Within two miles of hitting the road, I chuckled at the absurdity of it all. Here I was, embarking on this great adventure, while America seemed locked in some sort of cultural cage match. Politics and anger had consumed the airwaves, leaving little room for anything else.

Polite discourse had become a distant memory, discarded like yesterday's news.

As the miles slipped by, I realized I wasn't just chasing freedom across the open road. I was chasing something deeper—clarity, sanity, peace. Amid the noise and the madness, maybe, I was seeking respite—breathing space.

I flashed back to that night back in Dallas, watching the world in chaos on the news. The riots. Warnings of shadowy figures—the FBI, the government, the media—all echoing the same refrain: "The Russians are coming!" "The Russians are coming!"

Into this turbulent America, I steered Argo, not away from the storm, but straight toward it. And so, appropriately, I headed to Philadelphia—the birthplace of a nation born out of courage and conviction. It felt right. This was where the grand experiment began. Perhaps, just perhaps, it was the right place to begin seeking the answers I was looking for.

The world outside blurred past along Hwy. 1, and then over to the road tracing the Delaware River like a watercolor painting in motion. I felt the freedom of the open road—it was a chance to find the quiet in the storm, to clear my mind of the chaos. Unless, of course, America really is on fire.

Note to Self

The engine is humming beautifully. The miles are stretching out. But something is there. Quiet. Unseen. Something was creeping up that I hadn't dealt with—the kind that doesn't care if you're speeding down the highway a thousand miles from home. I turned up the radio. Rolled down the window. Tried to drown it out. But it's still there. Lurking. Watching. Waiting. And it would be there until I faced it.

It's like the universe is saying, "Yep, you may be moving, but you're not going anywhere until you figure this out."

Figure it out, I will. And in a blinding snowstorm, no less.

04

RINGING THE LIBERTY BELL

Those who expect to reap the blessings of freedom, must, like men, undergo the fatigues of supporting it.

THOMAS PAINE

AS I DRIVE TOWARD PHILADELPHIA, THE sun has long slipped below the horizon. The dark sky above me is dotted with a smattering of stars. I drove with the window down. The road was long and flat and went on as towns came and went. I kept going.

My first stop in Philadelphia was not something I planned. As if I had a plan. I did not. But picking up Argo near Chesapeake City, Maryland, it was perfect to visit the place not far away where the pulse of the American dream first began to beat. The Liberty Bell, Independence Hall, the birthplace of freedom itself—this is where it all happened, where the United States of America was conceived.

And, as strange as it sounds, something seemed to be guiding me. It felt like a hand was there, not pushing. Not heavy. Just enough to remind me I wasn't alone. You don't question it.

You drive. You follow. You keep going.

I wanted to keep going, but it had been a long day. Up at dawn, a flight from Dallas to Baltimore, then the drive to Chesapeake City to pick up Argo. New vehicle, new buttons, excitement mixing with confusion. Now, I'm fighting exhaustion, barely holding on.

Twenty-five miles from reaching Philadelphia, I'm just outside Clarksboro, New Jersey.

My eyelids begin to droop.

Again, I'm feeling that invisible force swooshing me along. It gives me a sign. And no, it's not a booming voice from the sky. It's an actual sign. Green. Metal. Ordinary. It reads:

Timberlane Campground. It leans just off the road, half-shaded by trees. Tucked away like a secret meant only for those who need it.

I steer Argo into the entrance, pulling up in front of the office. But the moment I cut the engine and step out of Argo, I am greeted by Ms. Brown Sweater, whose weary eyes tell me she's ready to call it a night. It is just past closing time. She has just locked the door to head to her car.

"Any chance I can still get a spot?" I ask, already preparing for a sympathetic but firm refusal.

She looks me over with a quiet resolve, weighing my request. "Well, ah, a minute more, and you'd have been outta luck," she says. I'm immediately thankful for her kindness. There's a softness to her. A gentle spirit. "I'll take care of you. Come on in."

I mentally breathe a sigh of relief. As she is checking me in, I see the bulletin board filled with thank-you notes and photos of celebrities who've stayed at the campground. There's John Davidson, the seventies singer and television host whom I interviewed on the radio after his concert in my early broadcasting days. Another photo shows Matthew McConaughey, the movie star and a fellow Texan, standing next to an Airstream—his Airstream, no less. He had parked it here while shooting a film in Philly. I look back at Ms. Brown Sweater, who catches me eyeing the shots with a grin and a shrug. "Their hideout," she says, making me feel like I'm in good company.

She gives me directions and a printed map of the campground. I drive around the loop four times, but can't find my spot. With my eyes heavy, my mind foggy, in a fit of desperation, I head back to the office, hoping Ms. Brown Sweater is still around to help me. A faint light shines from within, and I knock on the door. Moments later, she emerges, looking just as tired as before but still willing to lend a hand.

"I was just entering your information in the computer before heading out again," she says, her voice carrying the weight of a long day that I made longer. "But follow me. I'll show you where it is."

"I'm sorry to keep you," I say. "This whole thing is new to me. I watched a ton of videos on parking in campsites, but it's not like it looks in the videos."

She nods with a knowing smile. "Yeah, it can be a little intimidating at first. But that's why I'm here. Let's go together, and I'll show you the only spot left. No need to stress."

I'm embarrassed to be causing her more work, especially after she's already gone out of her way to let me check in after hours. But her response is warm, and I sense she's not irritated with me. Maybe she sees something in my nervous unease as I try to navigate the realities of RV camping for the first time.

She has me follow her car through the loop. She points at the space. I take a moment to study it. A tree on one side. A utility pole on the other. Tight fit. She gets out of her car to wave into the spot. After several attempts, I finally park Argo and thank her profusely. A sense of accomplishment floods over me. I did it. First night camping on the road. I awkwardly wedge my 6'2" body onto the sofa bed in the back of Argo with newfound pride in surviving my first day as a "nomad." This is what they call living the dream, right?

There is an old proverb: "A journey of a thousand miles begins with a single step." Well, I have taken the step. And now the road, and every mile ahead, is waiting with its own story to be told.

The next day, a strong coffee works its magic, clearing the fog of sleep as I head toward Philadelphia. I take a detour through a South Philly neighborhood, weaving past endless rows of gray houses. Each driveway bears the scars of countless snow shovels—a testament to the brutal winters.

Philadelphia is the kind of place where the air vibrates with the echoes of the past. I head to Independence Hall.

"There's something surreal," the tour guide says, "about standing where they signed the Declaration of Independence."

"I'm feeling it," I say. "It's weirdly personal. Especially lately. Freedom, equality — those words sound simple until you try to live them. Maybe coming here helps people connect the dots a bit."

A kid in the group says, "There should be sound effects with thunder and dramatic music."

"Ha! Well, no special effects," the tour guy says. "But if you let your imagination wander, walking through Independence Hall, it is impossible not to imagine the scenes that unfolded within its walls about 250 years ago. The debates, the fierce arguments, the triumphs, and the fears. I can almost hear Jefferson changing the line about 'property' to the 'pursuit of happiness' in the list of unalienable rights as the delegates discussed the essence of liberty. The right to seek personal happiness."

The line moves forward. The room where the Declaration of Independence was signed is preserved as it was in 1776, with its large oak table, quill pens, and inkwells. The room stands quiet, unchanged. The oak table is there, heavy and sure. Quill pens lie still beside dark inkwells. It is as it was in '76. You can almost hear the paper move, the scrape of ink. The air holds the weight of old words and decisions that could not be undone.

I picture those fifty-six delegates, maybe some in powdered wigs, others in more casual attire. They were united in their belief that the colonies deserved to be free. They were willing to risk everything and signed their names with the knowledge that doing so could mean their deaths.

But they did it anyway—laying the foundation for our system of values based on moral responsibility we still rely on 250 years later.

"You from around here?" A lady next to me asks.

"No, I'm on a road trip. Philly—this is my first stop. I have no real plan. Intending to drive across America."

"That's the best kind of travel. The kind where you don't know what you're looking for until it finds you. Be sure to eat a cheesesteak while you're here."

After Independence Hall, I am standing before the Liberty Bell. It's a symbol of our struggle—bloody, bitter, unfinished. And yet, there is hope in it. Not loud. Not easy. But real. "Our struggles are what make us who we are," the man standing next to me says. "Funny thing about that crack in the old bell, it's in the cracks where we find our strength."

I nod. He's thinking what I'm thinking. The crack in the bell is a powerful metaphor for the inherent flaws of freedom.

Standing before the Liberty Bell and walking through Independence Hall, I realize something profound: America, at its core, is about people helping one another, about resilience and connection. No matter where we come from, there's a shared spirit among us that binds us together. As long as that spirit endures, America will remain strong—flawed but resilient, just like the Liberty Bell itself.

I had not planned for Philadelphia to be my first stop, but it's perfect, a symbol that I am on the right path. Again, I feel that mystical force, that unseen hand guiding me. As my road trip is starting, it has taken me to the starting place of the nation.

There is freedom in not knowing what's around the bend. The unknown holds its own kind of magic. I vow to take the detours. Flip a coin. Go the way I am led.

Later, when the day fades into night. My eyes are weary. I'm driving, looking for a place to camp overnight. There is nothing till I see Harrah's casino just across the state line in Delaware. They have a parking lot with dedicated RV spaces. It's not glamorous, but there is security. I slept like a rock that night, my body finally at rest. And although I was feeling lucky, no, I don't go inside to gamble with Argo's fuel money.

The next morning, the force points me toward New York.

Note to Self

The Founding Fathers didn't sit around sipping tea, nodding at the Crown's rules—they were like, "Yeah, this whole 'taxation without representation' thing? Big problem. Let's throw some tea in the harbor and see what happens. And, oh, let's sign a Declaration of Independence that could get us all hanged."

I thought of the ones who came after. The ones who fought. Who bled. Who died. They gave everything. For freedom. For justice. For a country built on moral truths. I owe them. We all do.

I also realized you are never too old to start something new. Look at Ben Franklin. He was well into his 40s when he invented bifocals, and in his 70s when he helped write the Declaration of Independence. In colonial times, that was like being 120. He was a printer, inventor, diplomat, author, kite enthusiast, and probably the first person to ever say, "Let's see what happens if I electrocute myself during a thunderstorm."

Moral of old Ben's story? It's never too late to start something epic, weird, bold, or totally new. Or, start a country. Or, go on a road trip. Heck, sometimes it's just about hitting the road—chasing your dreams. Who knows? The next big thing could be waiting on the other side of a random detour sign.

Meanwhile, I'm still uneasy. There's a storm sitting in my chest pretending to be still air. I just can't pin down what it is. Not that I'm trying to.

05

BIG APPLE SURPRISE

I began to like New York, the racy, adventurous feel of it at night, and the satisfaction that the constant flicker of men and women and machines gives to the restless eye.

F. SCOTT FITZGERALD'S "THE GREAT GATSBY"

OF COURSE, NEW YORK would have to be on the list in my search for America. I did not plan to be here in advance of this election day. But, again, I didn't have a set plan.

The city they call the Big Apple promises everything and nothing all at once.

As I walk, I smell the aroma of freshly brewed coffee from a corner cafe—rich, dark, and inviting. It's November 8th, 2016. A

Tuesday. Election Day. The air is sharp. The light has that pale yellow cut of late fall, when the sun starts quitting earlier. It reflects off the city's towering skyscrapers, echoing the power and aspiration of America's Heartland.

A little further, I encountered a hot dog cart on the sidewalk, with the smell of mustard, onions, and sweet, vinegary sauerkraut. Across the street, restaurants range from dirt cheap to "if you need to know the price of your entrée, you can't afford it."

There's a constant stream of humanity moving unabated in every direction. My first face-to-face encounter with a New Yorker came as I walked down the sidewalk, hugging the building closely, dodging oncoming people, and sidestepping the human tide until a nondescript gray service-entry door abruptly swung open in front of me, forcing me to panic-maneuver myself out of the way. From the door, a woman emerges in a rush.

The collision would have sent us both sprawling on the dirty pavement, possibly stomped to death, but to my astonishment, the woman is unfazed by the near miss, giving not so much as a glance in my direction. At first, she seemed aloof, perhaps just distracted by a rough day at the office. Then she abruptly stopped, turned, and said, "Oh my gosh, I am so sorry! Thank you for not getting hurt. I hope I didn't startle you too much. Please accept my sincere apology!"

I was surprised since the stereotype of New Yorkers is portrayed as not being sensitive to a stranger's feelings. But she was. I gave her a big Texas smile, nodded, and said, "No problem, ma'am." So much for the New Yorker stereotype.

New York City is called "The Big Apple" thanks to a nickname that became famous in the 1920s. It was popularized by John J.

Fitzgerald, a sports writer for the New York Morning Telegraph. He used the term in reference to the big prizes or "big apples" that horse racing jockeys could win. The term became a metaphor for the city's grandeur and opportunities. Over the years, immigrants from around the globe have arrived here, filled with ambition and longing for a better life. I can only imagine the millions of stories of hope, and also of disillusionment.

A cooler breeze is now sweeping between the buildings. Walking by the window of an Italian clothing store, I see my reflection and tug the zipper up a notch higher on my weathered, thin, black leather Italian jacket. It holds memories of the cobbled streets of Florence, Italy, where I bought it from a street merchant years ago on a whim while walking to the British Institute. The pedlar would smile as I walked by, repeating, *"Ciao!"* to catch my attention. I'm sure I had the look of an easy mark. *"Mostrare chi sei al mondo,"* he'd said with a nod of his head. To the Italians, dressing well is considered a sign of respect for yourself and those you interact with. Sure enough, I feel better about myself wearing the jacket years later. And I smile, because it costs far less than the one I see in the store window. I straighten my posture and forge ahead.

New York City is home to nearly 8.5 million people. That is more than in thirty-eight other states in America combined. It is possible to hear more than seven hundred languages on the streets of New York City. According to the US Census Bureau, only 51 percent of New York residents speak solely English in their homes.

Tonight is a politically significant night, and New York City is at the epicenter of it.

Obscene amounts of money have been spent on campaigning. Anticipation is in the air.

If the polls and pundits are correct, the first female president, Hillary Clinton, will be elected. If they're wrong, the first non-politician, billionaire businessman, and TV celebrity, Donald Trump, will take the seat. Either way, it will be a historic night for American democracy. Coverage is on every TV screen in every restaurant, in every bar, and on every LED sign in Times Square.

Amid Manhattan's beehive, I make my way from 38th Street toward the pulsing heart of Times Square. The sound of honking cabs and the grinding gears of delivery trucks surrounds me. Ahead, two sleek black Cadillac SUVs glide through the intersection, their dark-tinted windows shielding the occupants from prying eyes. With the assertive burp and hiccuping of police sirens leading the way, they carve through the sea of vehicles. A silent testament to the power and privilege that permeate the city's veins. A fleeting glimpse at the world of VIPs. A big celebration is planned with hundreds of thousands of dollars in fireworks scheduled to be shot off a barge over the Hudson River to celebrate the first female elected to the presidency.

"So, where is the best place to watch the fireworks over the Hudson River tonight?" I ask a street vendor.

"Ah, sorry, no fireworks tonight," he said. "I heard they were cancelled."

"That is disappointing. I would like to have seen the fireworks reflecting over the Hudson with the Statue of Liberty in the background. I have seen it on TV, but it would be exciting to watch it in person."

"Sorry, Bub," he said, "it's not to be…cancelled."

◀ ▲ ▼ ▶

Continuing my walk towards Times Square, it's time to find a place to eat dinner. The smell of meatballs and tomatoes cooked down with garlic, the kind of smell that hits something old in you, something hungry. Through the café window, I see people crowded in at tables close to each other. A good sign. They talked and laughed. Their plates were full of sauce, thick and red, poured heavily over pasta.

I walked into the restaurant, which, judging by the décor, was attempting to be both upscale and vaguely European. The maître d' glanced at me once, a look that combined disdain with the kind of judgment usually reserved for people who don't know a meatball from a Pickleball. With a single, dismissive shake of his head, he said, "No table." That was it. Not even a "Sorry, we're full" or a "Please come back in 30 years when we might have a cancellation." Just, "No table." I stood there a moment until the saucy tomato smell faded into my disappointment.

Undeterred, I pressed on to another haven, its warm glow spilling out onto the sidewalk, a beacon of hospitality.

"I've got one spot left," the maître d' tells me as he points to a high-top tucked in next to the front door. The surface is barely large enough for a plate, but it's the perfect perch for watching the reactions of people gathered at the bar, watching the vote unfold. Two large-screen televisions are high above the bar. Typically tuned to a ballgame, they are showing cable-news pundits banter away. The young professionals are chatting away about their day, except for an occasional glance at the exit-polling graphic.

I finished the last of my spaghetti, dragging the fork through the red sauce until there was nothing left to drag. Paid the bill and stepped back out into the hum of the city.

At Times Square, a quiet crowd was watching the election results crawl across the LED screens above. I stood with them. The air felt heavy, like just before a storm. You could hear people breathing. The screens lit up again. Another state. Then another. Still no winner called.

Then it came: Trump. A few gasps. Some shouts. One woman laughed like she didn't believe it.

A man next to me said, "That's it." Someone else cursed under their breath. Some cheered.

Others stood still. Eyes locked on the screen. Not saying much. No one moved.

Standing next to me, a man in a well-pressed suit and dark tie gazes intently at the LED screens, his eyes fixed on the unfolding spectacle of democracy. "Think we're headed for a recession now?" he asks me, as if I should know.

"Some have predicted that," I said. "Mark Cuban said it would. Guess we'll have to see."

I can't help but notice that the man's expression is that of someone who has just learned of a dear friend's passing. He gets lost in his thoughts and stands there perfectly still, his mind whirring.

Contrary to expectations, the stock market and the economy surged. But, on the cultural side of things, it was more like that cliché coined by the old French journalist, Jean-Baptiste Alphonse

Karr, "Plus ça change, plus c'est la même chose." The more things change, the more they stay the same.

The fabric of society would continue to strain under the weight of polarization and discord. And I'd be driving through this new chapter of American history on the road across the country.

◀ ▲ ▼ ▶

BONE-TIRED, I AM EXHAUSTED after the twists and turns of election night's rollercoaster. In the early morning hours, I make my way back to the New Jersey side of the Hudson River and reenter the familiar embrace of Argo, parked at the Liberty Harbor Marina.

Once inside Argo, I collapse onto the welcoming mattress. A few hours later, I wake up.

Not wanting to rise from the warm nuzzle of my pillow.

After an extra hot dose of strong French-press coffee, a piece of dry rye toast topped with butter, and a sunny-side-up egg for breakfast, I took Argo on a drive. Staying on the New Jersey side of the Hudson, I found a gas station that offered diesel. Argo, being the thirsty beast, eagerly guzzled down the fuel as if at a frat party, and it was the first beer.

I drove to the Vince Lombardi Park and Ride, where commuters park to catch the bus for the fifteen-minute ride into Manhattan. This place is named after him because about twelve miles from here, he taught Latin, algebra, and physics at St. Cecilia's High School in Englewood. He also coached the school's football team, winning six state championships. He went on to become the legendary coach of the Green Bay Packers, winning the first two Super Bowls.

The commuter bus leaves every hour for Midtown Manhattan. The seats were wide and soft. I sat and looked at the city skyline high above the fray of the honking, frustrated drivers in the traffic inching forward in the flowing river of metal. It was a glimpse into the lives of the commuters who make this journey every day.

Some media friends who covered the election invited me to a cocktail party. As I make my way across town, getting a cab is impossible. Traffic is not moving. I walk.

Dressed in a blue sports jacket—chosen not for its fashion-forwardness, but because it was the only one I had with me. My appropriately muted Burgundy tie helped cover a wrinkled white shirt.

At the street corner about to cross, a guy shouts at me.

"Hey, dude, let me give you a ride." It's a pedicab driver straddling his trike seat—a rickshaw powered by a welded-on bike in front—one way to get around between the cars.

"Uh, I think I'll just keep walking," I say.

"If you're in a hurry, you never gonna get there," he says. "Where you headed?" I give him the cross streets and ask how much the fare will be.

"Twenty bucks! And I can get you through all the traffic, and I'm good at it." "Umm, well, if you can get me there fast for twenty bucks, let's do it?" "Of course," he said, and off we went.

Sure enough, we begin darting around yellow cabs—daring pedestrians at stoplights, barely missing a few fast-footed ones. A bit frazzled, but relieved as he pulled in front of my destination.

"Thanks, buddy," I say as I hand him a twenty-dollar bill, which he takes. Then I start to give him an extra ten dollars, thinking I would get a thank you for a fifty-percent tip.

"No, man, you owe me two hundred dollars," my driver says with a conning smile.

"Come again?" I asked. "You quoted me twenty dollars, and I am giving you a ten-dollar tip."

"No, no, it's twenty dollars a *minute*," he informs me. His ruse is in motion with his unsuspecting victim, me. "And it took ten minutes to get you here."

"You were very clear: twenty dollars for the whole trip. You never said *per minute*. And it wasn't ten minutes! It was five minutes, tops."

"You must have misunderstood. You owe me two hundred now!"

His smirk hit my flashpoint, but I held my tongue. It was not easy, but I realized I was just another lame-brained tourist being taken advantage of by a guy who probably does this multiple times daily. While most unsuspecting tourists likely paid up, I wasn't. There was no way I was going to be taken advantage of by this grifter.

"So, here's the deal, my friend," I say softly but firmly. "I'm holding a ten-dollar tip in my hand." He cuts me off.

"You owe me two hundred dollars!" His friendly persona has evaporated. He's mustering his nasty, serious face to intimidate me. I'm thinking of all the lovely folks he's ripped off without any feeling of guilt day after day. I've traveled a lot worldwide, and I've learned that there are always dark hearts that will rip you off. It's part of the cost of venturing out of your hood. But this one hit my hot button and caught me by surprise.

"I have a strong dislike for people who take advantage of other people," I say, still in as calm a manner as I can collect. "You are trying to rip me off like you most likely do all the time. You just lost your fifty percent tip. I paid you in full per the price you quoted me. Now, ride away very quickly, or I'm going to yell over to the cop we can both see just a short distance up the street and file a complaint." He ducked his head and quickly rode away. I did not enjoy the exchange, but I felt good about standing up to him as I watched him ride away.

A bit rattled, I walked inside, attempting to regain a quiet confidence. My friend, Mica Mosbacher, a television news contributor, greeted me. She would often call me after she was on the air for my critique. The cocktail party was fun, featuring people you would recognize. They were still recovering from the intensity of the 2016 election night coverage. Still surprised the poll predictions were so wrong.

It was one of those chic Manhattan gatherings you see in movies—the kind where the lighting is low, the wine glasses are thin, and the conversations hover somewhere between hushed and conspiratorial. It was an "after-party" for some of the newspeople—those exhausted gladiators of election night. It was a reprieve to toss back a few drinks, shake off the intensity of spinning, predicting, analyzing, and, ultimately, misjudging the whole thing.

I stood clutching a whiskey sour in a loose cluster of producers and reporters.

"I can't believe it," said a national news show producer in a rumpled suit as he loosened his tie with one hand. On the other hand, he was still clutching the cellphone. "This is insane. I feel like I'm living in an alternate reality?"

"All the pollsters," someone else chimed in, shaking her head. "All the numbers said Hillary had it. All of them. It was like watching a horse that led the whole Kentucky Derby stumble right at the finish line."

"They were off by so much," said a woman who wrote a syndicated political column.

"Even in the swing states—I mean, this wasn't just wrong—it was laughably wrong."

"I guess people didn't want to admit they were voting for Trump to pollsters," I said. "Or maybe the conservatives just didn't want to end up on someone's target mailing list."

"Or maybe," the columnist said darkly, "the truth is harder to face than we thought."

The whole scene had the dazed air of people stumbling out of a theater after a shocking ending. The signs were all there in hindsight—economic frustration, political tribalism, a growing sense of disillusionment—but no one had believed it would play out this way.

"Well, the polls weren't wrong about one thing," said the producer, finishing his drink. "It was historic. Just not the kind of history anyone expected."

The buzz of the party swelled and carried on. Conversations hummed and ebbed like the fading notes of a jazz number.

After the party, Mica and I grabbed a late-night dinner in a joint that looked like it hadn't been renovated since the Eisenhower administration. The coffee tasted like it had been filtered through a gym sock. But it was open, and we were hungry, so our standards were low. We sat, talking about what her sources had told her about one thing or another. We spoke in hushed tones. I suppose that's because the Russians might be listening. At least according to all the media reports, those pesky Russians were listening everywhere.

"Wow, I guess we'll be trying to figure out the cracks in the polls for years?" I said.

"Maybe there were cracks," Mica said. "Or maybe they just weren't looking, wanting to know what people were really thinking."

"Amazing," I said, "how often the people with the advanced degrees and complex computer models get it wrong. The pollster, economist, and weather forecasters."

We laughed about it and said our goodbyes. I wandered my way toward the transit terminal. Times Square pulsed and flickered with its usual neon heart attack of light. Then I heard it—a low rumble in the distance.

It was a sound that didn't belong to the usual New York symphony of taxi horns and subway groans. It was angrier. Loud. People yelling profanities.

I followed the noise down a side street until I came upon a surge of bodies moving in rhythm. Hundreds of people marching toward Trump Tower, shouting in unison:

"He's not our President!"

"F--- Donald Trump!"

The whole thing had the feel of something impromptu. Spontaneous, except for the preprinted signs. I was witnessing something important in my search for America. Protests have long been a cornerstone of American democracy and a fundamental aspect of free speech.

This had fingerprints on it of Astroturfing—community organizers with bullhorns strategically placed at key intersections, leading the crowd like a conductor leads an orchestra.

Yet, even in their manipulation, protests reveal something about America. They reveal a nation that cannot be easily controlled, a people who will not be silenced.

A twenty-something guy in a hoodie nudged his way past me toward the edge of the crowd. "What's going on?"

"Not sure!" someone in the marching crowd shouted back.

"Cool," he said, "looks fun." He slipped unfazed into the stream of protesters.

I watched the choreography unfold and pass by me. The noise faded down the street.

Then, I caught the last bus back to the Vince Lombardi Park and Ride, where Argo waited.

At the parking lot, I slid my prepaid ticket into the machine. The gate didn't budge. Tried again. Nothing. The machine spat the ticket out like it was personally offended by my presence.

A security guard in a golf cart outfitted with flashing lights pulled into a parking space across the lot. I yelled out to her. She did not see me. She got out of her golf cart and walked over to her personal car. I watched her and waved my arms. I hoped she noticed me.

She didn't.

She did not drive to the exit lane; she drove to the entrance lane, got out, and manually lifted the gate's arm. It clicked into place and stayed up. She slid back into her car and started to drive away as the gate arm lowered behind her car.

"Hey!" I shouted, running behind her, flailing my arms like a castaway on a desert island.

She stopped and grimaced at me as she slowly rolled down her window. "What?" "This exit gate is not working. How am I supposed to get out of here?" "You can do what I just did, go through the entrance gate," she said.

"What if it doesn't stay up for me?" Argo was much longer and taller than her car.

She shrugged. "Figure it out," and drove away.

So there I was—exhausted, irritated, and apparently at the mercy of a malfunctioning parking lot gate. I backed out of the exit lane, drove over to the entrance side, got out, and lifted the gate. But unlike for her, it didn't stay up.

I glanced around the parking lot and spotted a rock. Channeling my inner MacGyver, I wedged it into the mechanism. The arm held. I sprinted back to Argo, slipped behind the wheel, and gunned it through the exit before the rock lost its grip.

Free. Finally.

I drove aimlessly across the bridge and around the edge of the city. I threaded through the traffic like a caffeinated squirrel in a maze. I kept driving. Nothing clears your head quite like cruising into the darkness with no clue where you're going and a half-melted granola bar in your cup holder.

Driving on, into Long Island. I was wiped out, tired. Not just "I need a nap" tired, but "I think my bones are trying to leave my body and file for retirement" tired. I pulled into a marina on the water's edge, found a parking spot overlooking the quiet bobbing of sailboats, and climbed into my bed in the back of Argo. Sleep hit me hard and fast.

If I'd known what was waiting for me the next day, I might not have slept so soundly. But some things are better faced on a good night's rest.

My search for America behind the headlines was far from over.

Note to Self

Presidential elections are basically the super duper bowl of philosophical throw downs—a battle between two opposing visions of who gets to drive and who gets the backseat. And, for a consolation prize, the "backseat drivers" get to criticize every turn the driver makes.

Being there on the night of the big election, amidst all the bustle and excitement of New York City, was a revelation in my search for America. Our American system empowers the people to vote and elect new leaders. It is the heartbeat of our democracy. I watched as a silent witness to the birth of a new era, smack dab in the middle of the hometown of national media, and with representatives from both sides of the political spectrum in town for the event.

On the personal side, in the quiet pauses, the feeling comes back, like I've tucked something away and forgotten where. Something feels off, like I've left a thought unfinished.

If there is no solution to the problem, then don't waste time worrying about it.

If there is a solution to the problem, then don't waste time worrying about it.

THE DALAI LAMA

06

Confronting Steinbeck

Arrived at last in old Sag Harbor, and seeing what the sailors did there, and then going on to Nantucket, and seeing how they spent their wages in that place also, poor Queequeg gave it up for lost. Though he, it's a wicked world in all meridians; I'll die a pagan.

ERMAN MELVILLE, *MOBY DICK*

Note to reader: The dreams we carry from childhood are like seeds planted deep within us, quietly waiting for the moment when we gather the courage to unearth them and watch them bloom. I was about to cross paths with a great writer whose words had once sparked the idea to go on this journey. Though the man himself, John Steinbeck, had long since passed, his spirit lingered, waiting to greet me. It was as if his ghost was there with a quiet affirmation that this trip had a deeper purpose, a spiritual connection guiding me forward. This road trip is touching every part of me, my past, present, with a whisper of what's to come.

WAKE TO THE SOFT GOLDEN HUE of morning sun filtering through Argo's windows. That sounds peaceful and poetic until you realize the sun was aimed directly at my face, as if it had a personal grudge. I am in Sag Harbor. Located in the Hamptons on the eastern end of Long Island.

New York. It is a place steeped in history and maritime lore.

As a sailor and lover of the sea, it is comforting and familiar. The gentle rocking of the boats in the marina is like the steady breath of Father Time. The reflections of the masts stretch long and thin across the water. A single gull lets out a cry from somewhere beyond my line of sight.

Sag Harbor. It's the kind of expensive place where even the seagulls probably need to have real estate agents. As I walk to the water's edge, an old man is standing next to a boat. "You going out?" I asked an old man as he threw a duffle bag onto his sailboat. He moved slowly but with purpose.

"Yep, just for the day," he said. "The wind should be good." His face was leathered from years of squinting into the wind, with lines that ran deep and permanent, as if the wind and salty sea had carved them there. A white stubble covered his jaw, careless but not forgotten. "You a sailor?"

"I've done my share. I know enough to leave when it's calm and come back before it isn't."

"Good advice!"

"Ha! Well, sometimes you just get caught out there," he said, tugging on his faded blue cap that had once been navy. He rolled up his sleeves on his frayed flannel shirt as he stepped onto his boat. It was maybe twenty feet, and looked as weathered as he did — not neglected, just well-used. "Yep, the trick is getting back when you see Mother Nature has other ideas." "Well, God bless you for a beautiful day going and coming back," I said.

He nodded, looked up, checking the rigging with a glance, and muttered something to the boat that I couldn't hear. Then he pushed off, slow and quiet, as if he didn't need the wind — just time.

Sag Harbor is one of those places that still has a foot firmly planted in the past. It's an old town with deep roots, dating back to the seventeen-hundreds, when it was a bustling whaling and fishing port. It was the kind of town where hard men sailed into hard waters, risking their lives for oil and blubber. At its peak, it was one of the largest whaling ports in the country, a key piece of America's early economy. Ships would arrive loaded down with barrels of whale oil, their hulls stained with salt and blood.

The clapboard houses, the uneven cobblestones, the gray weathered shingles on the waterfront—they all carry the imprint of the men who built them. The harbor that once launched whaling ships into the Atlantic's treacherous waters is now lined with million-dollar yachts, bobbing quietly in the morning light. The cobblestone streets that once felt the heavy boots of sailors are now softened under the weight of summer sandals and weekend tourists.

Sag Harbor was declared an official port of entry by the United States Congress in 1789. Back then, ships arrived from across the Atlantic carrying trade goods—timber, spices, textiles. Today, they arrive with fresh lobster rolls and imported champagne. Progress, I suppose. The old customs house still stands on Main Street, although it's now a gallery selling paintings of seascapes and abstract art.

When I walk down Main Street, I swear I can hear the faint creak of the ships and the clang of rigging in the breeze. The smell of salt and fish has faded over the centuries, replaced by the scent of sea air mixed with the aroma of dark espresso from boutique coffee shops. But the bones of the place are the same. The lighthouse still stands at the edge of the harbor, a quiet sentinel keeping watch over waters that have seen centuries of adventure and loss. It's a light that flickers faintly, even in daylight, a heartbeat that connects the past to the present.

Sag Harbor has always drawn writers and artists—something about the light, maybe, or the steady whisper of the water. Herman Melville came here and found inspiration for *MobyDick*, that great American reckoning with the sea and madness and man's endless need to conquer. E. L. Doctorow summered here, sitting by the water as he worked on *Ragtime* and *Billy Bathgate*.

And John Steinbeck wrote here, in his summer home. Sag Harbor; It all feels familiar, though I've never been here before. It's not déjà vu. It's quieter than that. It's like walking into the middle of a sentence you've been hearing your whole life. Then a breeze came off the water, and I felt it—not just the wind, but the shape of something behind it. A hand, maybe. Not a real one. Just the feeling of being nudged, gently but surely, in the direction I was always meant to go.

And somehow, I knew: this place wasn't the end of the road. It was the reason for it.

◀ ▲ ▼ ▶

Steinbeck's summer home in Sag Harbor was on the bay. He wrote *Travels with Charley* in a little hut next to his house, looking out over the water. The book that launched me on this trip. There's something about following the footsteps of your heroes that makes you feel tethered to the larger story. Steinbeck was trying to figure out America in *Travels with Charley*. America, what it had become, where it was going, who was underneath all the noise. I guess that's what I'm trying to do, too.

"How cool would it be to see the very spot where he wrote it," I mumble to myself, already making plans.

But first, coffee. And something sweet.

I fire up Argo and ease down Main Street, which looks like it's been plucked from a Norman Rockwell painting. The houses are white and tidy, with American flags hanging from porch rails. Flower boxes overflow with petunias and ivy. The street is lined with small shops— an independent bookstore, an ice cream parlor, a jeweler that probably sells nothing under four figures. The town is the kind of place where people linger.

On the corner is the *Grindstone Coffee and Donut Shop*. I swing Argo down a side street to park and walk back. The line inside stretches to the door. That's a good sign. You can trust a long line. The fragrance wraps around me immediately—hot sugar, cinnamon, and fried dough. A sweet yeasty promise. Behind the glass, the donuts look almost too perfect. Giant, golden, glossy with sugar and glaze, each one decorated like it belongs in a museum. Peanut butter and jelly. Lemon-poppy-seed. Nutella. Chocolate with popcorn. One that looks like it's been drenched in caramel and rolled in sea salt.

Unknowingly, I line up behind two New Yorkers—Muffy and Buffy, I decide to call them —who are standing next to a thousand-dollar stroller containing a baby that could double as an accessory. Muffy is wearing black yoga pants and a loose sweater that probably costs more than my entire wardrobe in my closet back home. Buffy is dressed in some "I work out" version of bespoke black. They stand stiffly, perfectly postured, exuding the kind of Manhattan coolness that is meant to communicate, *Please don't talk to me.*

But I'm from Texas, and we don't have that rule. So I try.

"Looks like some great donuts," I say, gesturing toward the case.

Buffy looks up from his phone. "Ah … umm … yeah," he says before immediately returning to scrolling.

Muffy snaps a picture of the display case, probably for Instagram. The baby sleeps on. I briefly consider making another attempt at conversation, but decide against it. I know when I'm outmatched. I settle for studying the donuts and inhaling the sugar-saturated air.

When I reach the counter, the selection is thinner but still impressive. I order a carameldrizzled monster of a donut and a double-shot latte with oat milk (because balance). I sit at a small table near Muffy and Buffy. I'm not expecting anything more from them, but then something strange happens.

I hold up the donut. "I'm not sure if I should eat this or frame it."

Muffy smiles. "Ha! They really are works of art."

"Well, next time y'all come down to Texas, I'll introduce you to the joys of Whataburger." "We've never been to Texas," Buffy says.

We start talking. About donuts, about travel, about how we got here. That's the thing about shared sugar—it lowers the barriers. There's something universally human about finding joy in something simple and indulgent. For a moment, we stop being from different worlds.

We're just three people in a coffee shop, trying to figure it out.

Afterward, I wander down Main Street, feeling light from the sugar and caffeine. I poke into shops, chat with clerks, and ask about Steinbeck. Most of them know he lived here, but they don't know exactly where. Finally, a woman in a bookstore points me toward the cove.

◄ ▲ ▼ ►

It's a narrow gravel road lined with cottages. At the end of the lane, I spot it—a gray house with a small dock stretching out into the bay.

I stand at the gate, unsure whether to press forward. Just then, a man in a Jeep pulls up. He sees my Texas plates and rolls down the window.

"Lost?" he asks.

"Well … kind of," I say. "I read *Travels with Charley* when I was a kid. I heard Steinbeck lived here."

He smiles. "You want to see it?"

"Are you serious?"

He nods. "Come on."

He unlocks the gate and waves me through. I step into the yard, heart pounding.

There it is: Joyous Garde. A little green writing hut tucked under the oaks, facing the water. Steinbeck's desk is still there, the windows slightly fogged from the sea air. His chair sits empty, facing the bay. The air smells like salt and pine.

I stood there for a long time, listening to the soft lapping of the water against the dock.

This doesn't feel like the start of a journey anymore. It feels like an arrival.

As I stand in the small yard outside Joyous Garde, the name that Steinbeck himself gave to his writing retreat, I can't help but feel the weight of history, of words written in this very spot. The landscape around me feels so alive with stories—his stories. There's something powerful about knowing that such a significant piece of literary history exists here, in this quiet little corner of the world. The wind in the trees, the creak of the dock underfoot, and the rhythmic sound of water lapping against the shore—it all carries a certain reverence.

I can almost hear Steinbeck's voice in my mind, reading excerpts from *Travels with Charley*, that masterpiece of observation and reflection. He was trying to make sense of America —its people, its landscape, its future. He set out in a truck with his poodle Charley, a companion to guide him through the challenges of travel and introspection. His journey was one of understanding, of reconciliation with the past, and, perhaps, of finding peace with his place in the grand mosaic of America.

And here I am, standing on the same ground. It feels surreal, almost like I've entered the pages of that book, walking in the very footsteps of someone whose work shaped the way I see the world.

I walk slowly around the small house, taking in the view from every angle. The trees sway gently in the wind, and the bay stretches out before me, a vast expanse of water that mirrors the sky above. The house itself is charming in its simplicity—gray, weathered wood that feels like it's been part of the landscape for as long as the trees have stood. It's not grand or ostentatious, but it exudes warmth and a quiet kind of strength.

Next, I wander over to the small writing hut—Steinbeck's sanctuary from the world. The door creaks as I push on it, and a musty, familiar smell fills the air. Inside, the space is small but purposeful. The desk is simple, made of wood that's seen better days, but there's something incredibly intimate about the space. His chair sits beside it, facing a window that overlooks the bay. I can almost imagine him sitting there, fingers hovering over the keys, searching for the right words to describe the country he loved so dearly.

There is stillness around me. The outside world seems far away here—distant, almost forgotten. The only sounds are the whisper of the wind and the occasional rustle of leaves. Time slows down in this place, and I wonder if Steinbeck felt it too, sitting here in his quiet moments, working through the complex thoughts that filled his mind. What was it that kept him coming back to this spot? Was it the solitude? The beauty of the surroundings? Or was it something deeper, a longing to understand the world in a way that others couldn't?

I think about the last few months—the journey I've been on, the people I've met, and the places I've visited. Each place has felt like a chapter in a book, each person a character with a story to tell. And through it all, I've been searching for something—an answer, a truth, maybe even just a piece of understanding that will bring it all together. I don't know what that is yet, but standing here, in this sacred space, I feel closer to it than I have in a long time.

The wind picks up, sending ripples across the water, and I stand to leave the hut. I don't want to stay too long. There's a quiet reverence here that doesn't need to be disturbed by too much presence. The solitude seems to hold a kind of power, one that doesn't need to be overwhelmed by too many footsteps.

Back in the yard, the cool breeze brushed against my skin. The sun is higher now, casting shadows that stretch long across the grass. The whole world seems to breathe a little easier here. There's something about this place that makes it feel like anything is possible—like all the answers are just waiting to be discovered.

I take one last look at the little house, the writing hut, the dock stretching out over the water. I don't know what I was expecting when I came here, but this feeling of connection, of coming full circle, is something I'll carry with me for a long time.

As I make my way back down the gravel path, I hear the Jeep pull up again. It's the man who opened the gate for me. He's smiling, a quiet, knowing look on his face as he watches me approach.

"I figured you'd be taking it all in," he says, his voice friendly but tinged with respect.

"Not many get the chance to come out here. It's a special place."

"Yeah," I say, "it is. I didn't expect to feel so connected to it."

"It's funny how some places just grab hold of you like that," he says. "Steinbeck knew what he was doing when he chose this spot. I think he needed it as much as the world needed his words."

What else can I do but agree? "Maybe that's what it is. This place has a kind of peace to it—like it's been waiting for the right person to come along and understand it."

He laughs softly. "Maybe it's not just the person who comes here. Maybe it's the place itself that shapes the people who find it."

There was truth in that, too. Places shape us just as much as we shape them. The histories they hold, the stories they whisper—if we listen closely enough, we can learn something profound about ourselves.

We talk for a little while longer, but soon it's time to say goodbye. I thank him for letting me visit and head back toward the road where Argo is parked. As I walk away, I feel a weight lifted off my shoulders—like something I didn't even know I was carrying has finally been set down.

I drive through the town once more, my mind still buzzing with thoughts from the visit. There's a deep sense of satisfaction in having stood where Steinbeck stood, where he found the words that would go on to inspire generations. But there's also a quiet understanding that this journey, like his, is only one part of a much larger story. There's more to see, more to learn, more to discover.

Back at the harbor, I park Argo and walk down the dock, the air crisp and fresh. The water is calm again, like a mirror, reflecting the now-clouded sky above. The gulls circle overhead, their cries echoing off the wooden piers. I take a deep breath and close my eyes, just for a moment, allowing the stillness to settle in.

This place, with all its history and meaning, has taught me something important—that the journey is as much about the questions as it is about the answers. And sometimes, in the quiet spaces between, we discover who we're meant to be.

Like Walt Disney said, "All our dreams can come true if we have the courage to pursue them." As I stand looking out over the water reflecting the soft hues of the sky, I realize something profound. The road ahead may be long and uncertain, but it's in these moments of quiet reflection that we truly begin to understand where we've come from and where we are meant to go. Steinbeck's words, his journey, and this place have sparked something in me—a desire to continue seeking, exploring, and questioning.

This visit was more than just a step in my journey; it was a reminder that sometimes, the most valuable discoveries aren't the ones we set out to find, but the ones that find us when we least expect them. The next chapter of my life? Well, turns out, I'm already in it. It's unfolding with every step I take, every person I meet, and every off-the-beaten path I accidentally take that I'll probably write about later.

And so, with a heart full of gratitude and a renewed sense of purpose, I walk away from this great American place, ready to embrace whatever comes next.

From Sag Harbor, I drive Argo to the ferry near Sag Harbor, getting in the queue of cars waiting to cross the Peconic River and heading to Shelter Island. The air carried the sharp tang of saltwater mixed with a hint of diesel fuel from the ferry's engines, creating a sensory cocktail that hinted at the adventure ahead.

I felt a bit of anxiety as the flagman waved at me to drive Argo forward onto the small ferry boat, for it appeared as small as a canoe compared to the mighty Argo. I couldn't help but wonder, would this ferry withstand the Herculean presence of Argo? Would it rise gallantly like a hero or succumb to the weight, disappearing beneath the waves like a submarine in distress?

I pull forward in faith.

After three ferry crossings, the very same ones I am told John Steinbeck took on his journey in search of America, I made landfall in New London, Connecticut. The town greeted me with the familiar embrace of salt air and the promise of a quiet night by the water. I set up camp near the shore, where the horizon stretched wide and uninterrupted, offering a perfect view of the supermoon. The supermoon—a celestial spectacle when the Moon's orbit brings it closest to Earth, resulting in a visually more prominent and luminous moon in the night sky. This breathtaking phenomenon dominates the night canvas with a radiance that casts a gentle, silvery glow across the landscape. It was a sight that stirred something deep within me, a reminder of the world's unspoken beauty.

This supermoon is the closest the moon has been to Earth since January 26, 1948. And it will be another eighteen years before another full moon comes as close to our planet. The next one will be even a little closer to the Earth on November 25, 2034.

After a while, my eyelids drooped over my sleepy eyeballs. I fight back to catch the whole spectacle of the supermoon show. The next morning, with coffee in hand, I head north.

The rumble in my stomach reminds me it's time to eat. Passing through New London, I spot a diner—Nowhere Café. I laugh; it seems fitting. I feel like I'm nowhere, too. I turn ARGO around and pull up, only to find the place shut down, empty. I snap a picture and laugh again as my stomach rumbles, letting me know it is still empty.

I drive on through a neighborhood of old houses and come across a small grocery store— Sonny's Market, marked by a pole sign that tells me the place has been famous since 1968 for grinders and cold cuts. Just like the one my dad owned back in the fifties before supermarkets took over, I muse. The small store with the American flag waving beside it triggers memories of my childhood, of walking down the street to the grocery store near our home back in Fort Worth with my sister, Cathy, for a cold soda or an orange sherbet push-up on hot days. To us kids on a hot summer day, the taste of the tangy, sweet, and tart sun-kissed orange sherbet brought forth a feeling of happiness and contentment. A simpler time.

Standing in front of Sonny's, the smell of fresh grass mixes with the scent of Italian seasoning from inside. I walk in, order an Italian grinder, wrapped in butcher paper with red-andwhite twine, and head back to ARGO to enjoy it in the sun. I'm content, caught between the present and a past that still lingers in my senses.

Afterward, I continue north along the coast, passing through Rhode Island and Massachusetts. In a Boston suburb, I stop to fill my propane tank—peace of mind for the road ahead. I have been to Boston many times over the years and would like to eat at one of my favorites, Antonio's Cucina Italiana, near Mass General. But I want to reach Maine before the weather turns. Route 1 is my path, the scenic one, hugging the Atlantic coastline, from Key West, Florida, at the southern end, north to Fort Kent, Maine.

By the time I arrived in Kennebunkport, Maine, darkness had descended. Only one local sandwich shop still had a light on, so my choice for dinner was easy. Kennebunkport has been the summer home of the Bush family, which includes two U.S.

presidents: George H. W. Bush and his son, George W. Bush. World leaders, from England's Margaret Thatcher to France's Nicolas Sarkozy to Russia's Mikhail Gorbachev and Vladimir Putin, have visited them here. I don't catch sight of nary a single world leader as I eat my sandwich and read their local paper. However, before George W. Bush became governor of Texas or president, our lockers were across from each other at the Cooper Aerobics Center in Dallas. So, we talked frequently as we suited up and worked out in the gym. And yes, I do have stories—all good ones, I should say.

I continued my journey northward, searching for a place to set up camp for the night. The road stretched before me like an unending narrative, each bend and curve holding the promise of adventure along with the potential for calamity.

Note to Self

A road trip helps in shedding illusions, breaking free from routine, and rediscovering who you are. Each mile takes me deeper into the heart of the real America.. The road is long and empty. That's the point. You drive to get away from the noise, but it follows for a while. Then it fades.

Each mile strips something off you. The lies you told yourself. The habits that felt like safety. You lose them one by one. Out here, the country is real. Hard land. Small towns. People who don't talk much unless there's something to say. It feels honest.

I think about old books. Plato, Steinbeck. Even Kierkegaard, though he'd never have taken this trip. He'd have stayed home and thought too much. I bring him anyway. He rides in the back, quiet.

HEARTLAND HIGHWAYS

I left the warm place. The one with soft chairs and routines and names for everything. I'm not sure I want to go back.

It's winter. The trees are black against the sky. The road winds through them. The silence out here isn't empty. It's waiting.

And something in me is waiting too.

07

Lobster In The Forest

One of the greatest moments in anybody's developing experience is when he no longer tries to hide from himself but determines to get acquainted with himself as he really is.

NORMAN VINCENT PEALE

AS I REACH MAINE, NIGHT approaches, and temps are falling rapidly toward freezing. Snow is forecast to start anytime—the first snow of the season for the lower part of Maine.

Looking for a place to camp, I continue driving down a dimly lit two-lane road lined with towering pines, maple, beech, and birch. In Maine, you are almost always in a forest. About ninety percent of the state is forest land. The sky stretches above, inked with an impressive array of stars twinkling against what appears to be snow-impregnated clouds.

Argo's headlights cut through the darkness, illuminating a small roadside market ahead. I stopped looking inside for something to eat for dinner, like crackers and cheese. In the back of the market is a large glass tank filled with water and lobsters.

Two men wearing aprons stand behind the counter as they prepare something for the deli counter. They are deep in conversation about a girlfriend. I am reluctant to interrupt them. But, I do.

"So, are you guys in charge of the lobster tank?" I say.

"Yep," one of them says. Then they both turn around together and say in unison, "We're the lobster wranglers!"

"Ha! Very cool. You made me smile. Well, I came in for cheese and crackers, but guess I'll splurge. How about a lobster big enough for dinner!" The price is less than I paid for a large pizza in Texas, but, of course, lobsters in Maine are more plentiful than pizzas in Texas.

"You pick, or we pick?" One of them says.

"You pick … since you are the trained professionals at this."

"Okay, let's get you the big guy here. You may need a bib and a lifeboat!"

We banter as they pick out a giant lobster for my dinner. They steam it and wrap it in butcher paper, adding it into a sack with a tub of butter and a few fingerling potatoes for my takeaway dinner.

Leaving the Lobster wranglers, I drove, not paying attention to where I was going. I turned into the thick forest. The road curved. I drove slower. The speed of darkness frightens me slightly, giving me second thoughts about being alone, at the mercy of the night.

Lost like a goose in a snowstorm in some God-forsaken place, I stopped. Climbed out of the driver's seat facing the forest. I walked around Argo, shaking my head in disillusionment over my lostness. Lost with my lobster.

The sharp air, heavy with the scent of pine needles and sap, seized my breath, constricting my chest with an icy grip as the exposed skin on my face and my hands twitched and pricked. As I'm prone to do when tired and rattled, I spontaneously erupted into a stupid laugh— a stress-release valve. Call it the gift of a playful, waggish mind. My sixth-grade teacher would've called it something else.

Fat snowflakes fell and whirled around me. It was like being inside one of those Christmas scenes inside a snow globe. The snow starts falling thicker and faster.

My laughter hung in the frosty air like a song of liberation. Looking down on this scene, God must also have been chuckling at the sheer absurdity of a man armed only with a recently purchased steamed three-pound roadside-stand lobster stranded in the sprawling wilderness.

As my laughter stopped, the echo of it faded into the forest. Silence fell all around. Living in a city, I am more accustomed to the background of a constant, steady roar of machinery, the sound of cars, sirens, and the occasional plane overhead. I'm not one to shy away from a bit of peace and quiet, but this is next-level. Who knew tranquility could be so darn eerie? The aloneness began to fold over me like a mysterious cloak, hiding the twists of fate yet to unfold.

Cascading down from the tops of the pine trees towering above me, the snowflakes became larger and larger—the largest I'd ever seen. Dwight Yoakam's A Thousand Miles from Nowhere drifted through my thoughts—its lonesome twang echoing how I felt, all bruised memories and the sense of being lost, with nowhere that felt right. It was a twangy country melody I shared only with the surrounding leggy pines and the descending snow.

Maybe that unseen hand, the strange force I have felt pulling me along on this road trip, had guided me to this desolate road. I had no "why" for it at the moment.

To escape the bone-chilling temperatures, I climbed back inside my polished silverskinned Airstream motor coach, my home on wheels, Argo. I picked up my cell phone and stared at the ghostly glow on the screen. No one had called me for days, and if I'd wanted to call someone now, with the lack of cell service, it would have been impossible.

At the beginning of my trip, my two kids, Will and Tiffany, and my sister, Cathy, had called frequently to check on my progress.

Some friends flung 'round the country had called to check on me. Some feared for my safety, telling me I was nuts for doing this. Others cheered me on as if I were some kind of modern-day explorer. But the novelty had worn off, and life back home had gone on without me. Now I was feeling disconnected—off their grid. And honestly, it stung a little.

Somewhere past the last gas station and the lobster wrangler's roadside market, the trees closed in around me. The light faded fast. Loneliness came over me. The kind of loneliness that doesn't just sit beside you; it sits inside you. Settles in your spine. I didn't cry. Didn't say anything out loud.

My eyelids felt heavy like a curtain falling on a play. No music. It's quiet. It's real. And I'm not sure if that's a good thing or not.

With the world shut out around me, I was transported into a dreamy, black-and-white scene straight out of Frank Capra's movie, It's a Wonderful Life. As in that movie, it was as if I had died alone on this snowy night. Like my soul had left my body. Not in the usual way — not just tired or far from home. No, this was something else. Like I had floated up and out. Watching from above as if I were transcended, floating above, watching below, as an angelic observer. It happened to me once before as a kid at summer camp. Still a vivid memory. All of us boys jumped into the swimming pool in a rush to the water. One of them accidentally landed on my back, knocking the breath out of me. I slipped under and didn't come back up. Everything went quiet. My spirit, or maybe it was my soul, left my body. I remember hovering above, looking down at the water as two camp counselors pulled my limp frame out of the water, working fast to resuscitate me. My friends stood watching in shock. I came back. But something about me stayed up there a little longer.

Tonight felt like that. Now, I was peering down from the Heavens upon my silhouette in the snowy forest. And then I saw more. My grandkids at home, brushing their teeth, bouncing on beds. The soft chaos of bedtime. Friends finishing dinner, turning off lights, and locking up.

Everyone was going about their everyday lives. Just living.

It was like looking down on the world through the eyes of someone already gone. And yet, I wasn't afraid. There was peace in it. Like stepping back far enough to see how it all fits together. Maybe it was a dream. Or maybe not. But for a moment, I was above it all. And it was okay. I found myself strangely at peace for that fleeting moment.

During my grown-up years, people leaned on me and depended on me for one thing or another. In theory, I should be happy that no one needs me now. I should rejoice in the absence of obligations—I am free and unencumbered. Yet, beneath the surface of liberation, a pang of sadness jabs my heart. I guess I was having one of those "be careful what you wish for moments."

It was one of those times when you can no longer run away from what's been gnawing at the dark corners of your heart. The anger. The sorrow. The stuff tucked away, crouching low, out of sight, where no sun ever touched it. But, on this cold, bitter night, with snow falling and the wind beginning to howl through the trees like some forgotten ghost, there was no more pretending. No more running.

It was anger. It wasn't the kind of anger you could shout about or throw a punch at. It was quieter, quieter than that. A private grudge against God. I had kept Him at arm's length for years.

I told myself I didn't need Him — that I could make my way on my own. But deep down, I knew better. I never lost my faith in God, but the anger had always been there, simmering just beneath the surface.

It occurred years ago, on another cold, icy night, as I pleaded with God in my hotel room at the Kahler Hotel in Rochester, Minnesota. Across the street, my wife, Beverly, lay in the hospital recovery room after her cancer surgery at the Mayo Clinic. We were both just past our twenties, into the third decade of life. Our two young children, Will (5 years old) and Tiffany (4 years old), were back in Texas with my parents, waiting for news.

That long night in that hotel room located at the top of the old Kahler, snow and sleet pelted my window as the wind howled and whistled. From the roof just above my room, a constant clanging sound came from the chain whipping against the metal flagpole. It brought back memories of sailing and anchoring off Catalina Island, about twenty-six miles from the California coast. Memories of sitting on the bow of the sailboat, watching the sunset with the halyards clanging musically against the main mast. A more pleasant memory.

How I had begged God to heal her. How I whispered over the bed like I could force a miracle into existence with nothing more than the sound of my voice. The surgeon told me after the surgery that I should get prepared; she would only have maybe six months based on the statistics. But we were fighters. I would help her battle cancer for the next six years. That was a gift of extra life, but in the end, there was no miracle. And I didn't know what to do with that.

The silence that followed, the feeling of being left behind.

My beautiful wife, Beverly—who loved singing in the rain and who always laughed at my terrible jokes, died way too young—leaving me behind to raise Will and Tiffany. They were just young kids then, in elementary school. I didn't have time to grieve. I had lunches to pack, tears to wipe, and homework to check. I had to be both parents. Did the best I could. I kept the kids fed with my backyard grilling skills and an endless supply of love and determination—all I could muster. And guess what? They survived—I dare say they thrived, given that today they're both married with healthy children of their own. And me, I'm a proud grandfather to five, still young at heart, and well, I've got some stories to tell.

Anger and grief have a strange way of waiting. It sits. It waits. It becomes part of your posture, your sleep, the way your voice tightens. I carried it all this time, but I never really looked it in the eye. Tonight feels different. Maybe it's the stillness of the snow. Or maybe it's just that I've finally run out of reasons not to sit with it.

At the insistence of friends who made it their mission to shake me out of my funk, I started dating reluctantly. It was another version of Neil Simon's *Chapter Two*, which I saw in the movie version with James Caan and Marsha Mason. Like the lead character, everything and everyone had only reminded me of what I had lost. Moving forward wasn't easy. I wasn't sure it was for me.

As time passed, new people came into my life. I'd found love and lost love. Basically, it was an emotional rollercoaster ride I hadn't signed up for. Don't you know, love is the ultimate game of hide-and-seek with your heart. And life, well, it is a bit like a sitcom—you laugh, you cry, and occasionally, you spill coffee on your favorite shirt. Life. Each day is a new chapter, blended with joy and loss.

I remembered the old farmer I sat beside at that roadside diner I stopped at. He was a figure carved out of the land itself, with rough hands and a face weathered by years of toil—his eyes squinting at me with a look that seemed to ask with more than just casual curiosity. "Road trip or running away?" he'd said, his voice gruff but with a knowing edge to it, like he understood what people tried to hide in their hearts.

Maybe it was the way he asked it—quiet, like he was speaking the truth of a thousand other souls who had come and gone on those same roads, or maybe it was just my restless thoughts stirring in me. I didn't know at the time, but now, it felt like it was more than just an idle question. It was a fork in the road I hadn't realized I'd come to. Sure, there was an urge to escape, to flee from the things I couldn't face, but there was something else, too. A promise—a promise of finding something I had lost. A promise of reconnection. Not just with myself, but with others, too. The kind of connection that comes when you strip away all the pretense and stop hiding, when you stop pretending that everything is fine and just let things be what they are.

Maybe it wasn't running away at all. Maybe it was about finding a way back, letting go of what should have been. Looking forward to what can be.

Note to Self

This was a turning point for me. The turning point came not with a thunderclap, but with quiet realization. I started listening for what the silence could teach me. That moment in the forest burned itself into my being, not as fear, but as transformation. I had faced my lost years and hidden grief, and walked through it, not around it. What I brought back with me wasn't a trophy or a tale, but a quiet strength, a new way of seeing. I had entered that forest lost and unsure, and left it forever different—reborn in the stillness at the end of the road.

08

COFFEE DOWN

It is inhumane, in my opinion, to force people who have a genuine medical need for coffee to wait in line behind people who apparently view it as some kind of recreational activity.

DAVE BARRY

I WAKE AT FIVE ON a cold, rainy Sunday morning in Scarborough, Maine. The darkness outside the window feels moody and bleak, like the night's still holding onto the land, unwilling to let go just yet. Argo's house batteries are dead, and the inside of this little home-on-wheels is colder than it should be. The damp air clings to me, but I'm comfortable in my blanket cocoon as I groggily reach for the generator toggle. When I hear the satisfying click, I fire it up, and the warm hum of the generator feels like the start of something new. I settle back onto the pillow, the rain tapping softly against Argo's roof, and let out a quiet sigh.

A minute passes, and the rain comes harder, louder. Something isn't right. I remember the leaky window by the passenger seat. And the vent in the bathroom, too—why did I ever think that would hold up in a downpour? I roll out of bed and stumble into the dim light of the camper, grumbling about my lack of foresight. I pull a towel from the drawer, groggy but determined, and stuff it under the window. It's barely enough to catch the trickle, but it'll have to do for now. The pan goes under the vent. I shuffle back into bed, burrowing into the warmth I've created, and close my eyes, hoping to steal another hour of sleep.

But sleep has been dashed. I'm fully awake now. The rain is still pouring, relentless, and the world outside Argo seems to have its own rhythm. I shuffle through the motions—change the towels, dump the pan, boil water for coffee. Breakfast is simple today: English muffins with apricot preserves and cream cheese. It's enough. A sip of coffee, a bite of muffin, and I settle in for a quiet morning of reading, the rain playing its percussion on the roof.

Eventually, I've had enough of my own company and after heading out past a small, humble spot—St. Joe's, on Mussey Road. It's the kind of place that could only exist in a town like this: local, honest, and grounded.

The door swings open with a creak. Ah, the smell of roasted coffee. Inside, the floorboards are well-worn, stained by years of foot traffic. There are only a few tables, but each one seems to tell its own story—of locals stopping in for a bite, of community, of routine. I step up to the counter, where a teenager, his acne at war with him. I remember those days. He meets me with the kind of attitude that can only come from an adolescent still figuring out how to exist in the world. I ordered a latte, but something seems off.

"Coffee's down," he says, eyes cast low. His tone is as flat as the coffee machine he's speaking of.

"Down?" I ask, the word hanging in the air. "Coffee down. So … no coffee?" "No latte," he mutters, his voice a reluctant drawl.

I'm left standing there, confused, wondering what sort of place this is, where the coffee machine has the power to ruin a morning.

I ask for water, and he offers me a choice: tap or bottled. I take tap—the most honest choice. I try to make small talk, asking what the most popular item on the menu is. "I don't know," he says. Not exactly a surprise. Then he says, "Ah, I guess the Bennies."

I smile, politely enough, unsure if he is making a drug reference or something else. I'll figure it out later. I can't help but feel a little amused by the awkwardness between us. It's the teenage ritual, after all, that moment when you're neither here nor there, not quite a kid, but not yet fully into adulthood.

And that, I think, is the beauty of being young—the ability to be ridiculous, clueless, and somehow still believe you've got it all figured out. And the world just lets you do it, like a kind of cosmic permission slip. I could tell the kid was probably thinking the same thing about me.

From looking at the board, I ordered the grilled cheese with bacon. It feels like a choice I'll never regret. And it's not. The sandwich arrives, and I take my first bite—Manchego cheese, smooth and buttery, a sharp contrast to the crisp Honey Crisp apple tucked inside. The combination is unexpected, perfectly balanced. The bacon adds a crunch that brings it all together, like an old friend showing up at a party he didn't know was going on. I chew slowly, savoring the moment.

But I'm not done yet. I have figured out the Bennies by watching other people order them. I have to try the Bennies. It's as if New Orleans and Maine had a little rendezvous, and I've stumbled upon it by accident. I order, receive, indulge, smile, and lick the sweetness from my lips. During the sugar high, it hits me.

I've come to a crossroads. Argo is my constant companion, but even the most dependable machines need their upkeep. Today, it's the window seal, the bath vent, and the radio. Every part of Argo has its demands. It's a slow, steady rhythm of small fixes—beads of silicone to seal leaks, a quick call to a tech to figure out the radio passcode. There's no drama, just the simple work of maintenance. A dance of caring. I feel a strange satisfaction in each fix. The world is full of little lessons, and today, Argo is my teacher.

Argo has a piece of unfinished business: the license plate. Argo's tag has expired, and in the world of road trips, that's a kind of looming threat. The state where I bought Argo, Maryland, won't issue a plate, and the state where I live, Texas, requires an inspection to get a new license.

It's a small but necessary hurdle that will force me to drive to Texas to obtain the required inspection. It has to be done by a certified inspector inside the state line. It's just another chapter in the travelogue.

I leave the café, the rain still coming down. With my thoughts still clear from the caffeine and sugar high, I become philosophical.

Life, like a road trip, is all about finding your way as you go. You make do with the leaks, the imperfections, and the unexpected detours that lead you down a muddy road. You learn, you laugh, and you keep moving forward, because that's what it means to truly travel through life. To live fully. I oddly remember a quote by Lao Tzu, "A good traveler has no fixed plans, and is not intent on arriving." I start the engine and let Argo take me wherever we're supposed to go next.

◀ ▲ ▼ ▶

I roll down the window just a bit, enough to let in the cool, moist air. The scent of rain is still fresh, clinging to everything—pine trees, wet asphalt, the earth itself. It's one of those mornings when the world feels just a little more alive, as if the rain has scrubbed away the dust of the ordinary, making everything seem new again. I drive through the winding streets of Scarborough, my hands on the wheel, eyes flicking between the wet road and the view ahead. Something is comforting in the steady hum of the tires against the pavement, like I'm part of the rhythm of the world itself.

I pass a sign for Old Orchard Beach and think about the history of this place. It's a quiet stretch of coast, the kind of town you'd never expect to find bustling with tourists or overwhelming crowds. It's just a beach—a humble one, in fact—but there's something beautiful in its simplicity. The ocean rolls in gently, the waves licking the shore with a timeless rhythm. Even on a day like today, when the sky is heavy with clouds, it doesn't seem to matter. The beach, in its quiet majesty, holds steady.

I think about the people I met along the way. The characters who show up for a fleeting moment—faces I won't remember in five years, but faces that are etched into the short story of this journey. The waitress with the sharp eyes who serves me a cup of coffee at another roadside diner, the old man sitting by the fire at a truck stop, telling me about the birds he watches from his front porch. They all leave a mark, a small imprint on my soul, and I wonder if they ever think about the passing strangers they've encountered. Do they wonder where I'm headed? Do they ever think about the brief encounter, or does it fade for them as quickly as it fades for me?

There's something beautiful, almost sacred, in these exchanges. The way you can meet someone once and, in that brief moment, share a truth, a laugh, a story. It's fleeting, but it feels like it matters. Maybe it doesn't matter to them, but it matters to me. Each small connection weaves its way into the fabric of this road trip. I guess, if I'm honest, that's what I'm chasing— these tiny, meaningful moments of human interaction that, when strung together, form a kind of patchwork quilt of experience.

I drive past a small farm, its weathered barn leaning at an angle, the roof sagging from age. But there's something dignified about it, like it has stood the test of time and weathered countless storms. I slow down just a bit, my eyes catching the edges of the land as it stretches out before me. The fields are empty now, the harvest long gone, but in my mind, I can see the farmers working through the seasons, their hands in the soil, their hearts bound to the land. There's a quiet pride in that. It's the kind of pride that doesn't need to be shouted. It's the kind of pride that's passed down from generation to generation, embedded in the very earth beneath their feet.

I think about my roots. Not just the literal ones, the family that raised me, but the more abstract roots—the values and lessons, the quiet moments of guidance and wisdom passed down. My parents, who worked long hours but still made time for the important things—teaching me about kindness, about resilience, about the power of stories. And this road trip is becoming one long lesson. Each turn, each encounter, each stop along the way is a teacher, showing me a bit more of the world, about America.

But even as I reflect on these lessons, I know that there's still much I don't understand.

There are questions I haven't answered yet, lessons I haven't learned. And maybe that's okay. Maybe the journey is about asking the right questions, more than it is about having all the answers. I think about the people I've met who have told me their stories of hardship, of triumph, of love, and loss. They don't always have answers. But they are better at asking the questions.

There's a turning point in every journey—when you realize you've gone as far as you can go in one direction and it's time to head back. I start to feel that pull, the urge to circle back, to check on the repairs I've made to Argo. There's a small crack in the windshield I've been meaning to fix. But then again, what's the rush? Maybe there's something beautiful in leaving the imperfections, in letting the cracks stay where they are. It's a reflection of the journey, after all.

The cracks, the repairs—they're all part of the story.

Back at the campsite, I climb into Argo, the familiar creak of the door like a welcome home. I take a moment to sit in the silence, to breathe in the scent of wood and coffee and rain. And for a brief moment, I think about what it means to be here. To be present, in this moment, with all its imperfections and beauty. To be grateful for the cracks, the leaks, the messiness of it all. Because, in the end, it's all part of the journey. And the journey, as it turns out, is the greatest gift of all.

I settle in for the night, the sound of the rain now a steady companion, and I feel at peace. There's something incredibly comforting about the rhythm of travel. The way it teaches you to let go of expectations, to accept what comes, to embrace the unknown. There's a freedom in it that can't be found in any destination. It's a freedom that lives in the space between where you are and where you're going. And that, I think, is the real beauty of the road—its ability to remind you that the journey itself is enough.

My eyes closed, my thoughts now drift like the rain outside. I feel content. The road is still ahead, and I'm still on it. And that, it seems to me, is just the right place to be.

Note to Self

Rain is significant in my life. It mysteriously arrives on important days. It holds deep spiritual meaning in both Christian and Jewish traditions, often seen as a divine blessing and a sign of God's provision.

In the Bible, rain is a symbol of God's faithfulness—Deuteronomy 11:14 speaks of God sending rain in its season as a reward for obedience, nurturing both crops and souls. In Jewish thought, rain is so vital that prayers for rain are central in liturgy, especially during the festival of Sukkot and in the Amidah prayer.

It represents not just physical sustenance but a spiritual outpouring—God's presence descending to nourish the earth and his people.

09

Memphis Blues

The first time that I appeared on stage, it scared me to death. I didn't know what all the yelling was about. I didn't realize that my body was moving. It's a natural thing to me. So, to the manager backstage, I said, "What'd I do? What'd I'd do?" He said, "Whatever it is, go back and do it again."

ELVIS PRESLEY

AS I SET OUT ON my mad dash back to Texas, aiming to get Argo inspected and back in good legal standing, I couldn't help but feel a sense of dread settle in. The long stretch of Interstate 40 loomed ahead, as thrilling as a library full of dictionaries—endlessly monotonous. There's no getting around it: this is the fastest way home, the quickest route to free my trusty van from its bureaucratic bind. So, I resigned myself to the predictable, somewhat soul-sucking drive, trying to find any sliver of excitement to make the journey bearable.

And then, like a gleam of sunlight breaking through the clouds, there it was: Memphis. A beacon on the horizon, a place that called to me like a mirage in the desert. The prospect of pulling into that city—if Argo would just let me push her a little further—by dinnertime, and eating at The Rendezvous was the kind of hope I needed. It was the kind of thing that could make a long, seemingly endless drive something worth enduring.

Charlie Vergos' Rendezvous restaurant is the stuff of legend, its dry rub ribs a perfect blend of smoky, savory goodness. I could already taste them—juicy, tender, with just the right amount of char to seal the deal. Founded in 1948, nestled in an alley across from the famous Peabody Hotel, it's more than just a barbecue joint. It's a time capsule, a testament to history and culture that somehow still draws the same crowds as it did back in its heyday. I'd heard stories of everyone from Elvis Presley to the President popping in for a bite. You can almost feel the weight of that history, still hanging in the air, as you walk through the front door.

But, of course, Memphis is more than just ribs. Memphis is a city with a storied past, full of cultural riches that stretch far beyond the smoky haze of a good barbecue. It's a city that has played a pivotal role in the American Civil Rights Movement, home to Tennessee's largest African American population. It is the home of the blues, and Beale Street—the beating heart of the city—still echoes with the sounds of jazz, soul, and gospel music.

It's a city where history feels alive. A place where, if you listen closely, you might hear the faint melodies of the greats—W. C. Handy, Otis Redding, Isaac Hayes—still playing in the corners of old recording studios. And of course, there's the indomitable force that is Elvis Presley, whose presence still haunts the streets of Memphis in a way few other cities can boast.

Elvis was, in many ways, just a regular guy. He loved peanut butter and banana sandwiches. He had a family that meant the world to him. He was born into humble beginnings and, despite his massive fame, remained grounded in ways that are often lost on the icons of today. He once said, "The first time that I appeared on stage, it scared me to death. I didn't know what all the yelling was about. I didn't realize that my body was moving. It's a natural thing to me. So to the manager backstage, I said, 'What'd I do? What'd I do?' He said, 'Whatever it is, go back and do it again.'"

Graceland, his home, is now a pilgrimage site for fans from all over the world. The place that once housed the King is now a museum, a peek into the life of the man who changed music and culture forever. The modest living room, with its white-and-blue Christmas tree during the holidays, remains just as it was when Elvis was alive. It's hard not to feel something reverent when you walk through the gates of Graceland—like you're in the presence of something larger than life, something that transcends time.

For me, Memphis holds even more personal significance. It was where Beverly and I spent some of our happiest years together, before the whirlwind of raising children. We were young and carefree, building a life in a small, charming suburban neighborhood just outside the city in Germantown. I still remember the excitement on Beverly's face when I came home from work one afternoon and saw the first tomatoes, the first real fruits of our labor, picked fresh from the garden we had planted in the backyard.

Germantown, with its tree-lined streets and strong sense of community, was where we laid down roots, where we began to build our future together. It wasn't just about the house, though. It was about starting something new, something that we could call our own. I recall the thrill of working on that "lazy person's garden," a concept introduced to us by my Uncle Cecil and Aunt Dion, longtime Memphis residents who knew their way around this city and its ways.

What, exactly, is a "lazy person's garden," you ask? The concept sounds like something straight out of a time-saver's dream, and maybe it is. Before the growing season, you cover a plot of ground with black plastic, a process designed to suffocate the vegetation beneath it. The idea is to let nature do the weeding for you. As the season progresses, you poke holes in the plastic where you want to plant tomatoes, corn, squash, and whatever else you desire to grow. You water, fertilize, and let nature work its magic. And while it might sound lazy, it's far from it— there's something deeply satisfying about watching something grow with minimal fuss.

There are so many memories from our time in Memphis— memories of early mornings and long walks, of small victories and quiet moments shared. It wasn't just the garden, though. It was the life we were building together, one day at a time.

I had the opportunity to move to Memphis when Wallace Johnson, an international businessman and co-founder of the Holiday Inn chain, offered me a position as his assistant. It was a job that would lead to countless adventures and business lessons, a job that opened doors I could never have imagined walking through on my own. Together, we worked on projects that spanned the globe, raising millions to help those in need. He introduced me to the intricacies of international business, a world I hadn't known existed before then.

Wallace Johnson wasn't just a businessman; he was a teacher. He taught me how to look for opportunities, how to see what others missed. He often told me that the key to success wasn't necessarily being smarter than the next guy. It was about seeing what others didn't—seeing what was missing, the needs that hadn't been filled.

One day, as we sat on a plane headed to Chicago, I asked him about his humble beginnings. He told me, "I was born into a dirt-poor family in Edinburg, Mississippi. When I was about seven, I earned my first dollar picking cotton. All I had were two hands and a head on my shoulders. That's all. The rest is just work."

He didn't just work—he built something. He became a homebuilder when that was what people needed. He saved up enough money to start his own business, and from there, he began to build homes for families in need. The money came later, but that was never the driving force.

The work, the building—it was the point.

Together with Kemmons Wilson, Johnson helped create Holiday Inn, a hotel chain that would eventually span the globe. They saw a need in the travel industry: a need for standardized accommodation for road-trippers, for families who had no idea what to expect when they pulled into the next town. Holiday Inn solved that problem, offering the same level of comfort and cleanliness no matter where you went.

In those early days, they developed the Holidex system—a revolutionary tool that allowed travelers to find and book rooms with ease, even before the days of the internet and cell phones. The concept was simple, but groundbreaking: a card system that allowed travelers to see the next hotel on their journey and make a reservation from the front desk. It was a small idea with massive implications, and it changed the way people traveled forever.

Through all of this, Wallace Johnson remained grounded. He never lost sight of the importance of family, of the people who helped him along the way. Every time we arrived at our destination, he would call his wife, Alma, just to let her know he'd made it safely. "I love you," he'd say, and then he'd hand me the phone so I could do the same with Beverly. It was a small gesture, but it meant everything.

Traveling with him was like taking a master class in business and life. He didn't need formal education to be successful. He just needed to understand people, understand needs, and work relentlessly to fill them. His legacy—one of hard work, humility, and generosity—is something I carry with me to this day.

But now, as I head toward Memphis, I can't help but think about the history and memories that make this city so special. Whether it's the soulful rhythms of Beale Street or the quiet strength of Graceland, Memphis is a place that stays with you long after you've left. It's a city that tells its stories not just through its music and its monuments but through the people who call it home.

◀ ▲ ▼ ▶

It was in Memphis where I got a real education, one that didn't come from any university. The lessons were passed down like heirlooms—pragmatic, no-nonsense advice from a man who built an empire from nothing. Wallace Johnson's wisdom was something I absorbed like a sponge. But he never made it seem like a grand lecture. His teachings were woven into the fabric of our conversations, which would often flow like a river, shifting course seamlessly between stories of his upbringing and the latest business venture he was considering.

One evening, after a particularly long day of business deals and meetings, we found ourselves at a local restaurant in downtown Memphis, having dinner. Wallace was silent for a moment, tapping the table rhythmically with his fingers as he often did when he was deep in thought. His brow furrowed as he spoke.

"You know, when I started," he said, "I didn't know a thing about running a business.

What I did know was how to work hard, and that's what got me here." He looked me in the eyes. "Don't be fooled by these fancy degrees people hang on the wall. Hard work and looking for opportunities where others don't see them—that's the real key to success."

I nodded, digesting the depth of his words. It's funny how the simplest advice often turns out to be the most profound. Wallace had lived his life with a keen eye for spotting what others missed. It was his ability to see needs before they became apparent to others that made him successful. He didn't wait for an opportunity to fall into his lap—he created them.

And that's how I started thinking about my life differently—finding opportunities to create where others saw only limitations. That's the type of mentality I carried with me every time I turned the key in the ignition of Argo and set off again, whether it was back to Memphis or wherever else life had taken me.

As I drove along, I couldn't help but think of my days in Memphis with Beverly and the sense of nostalgia that hit me like a wall. Those days felt like a lifetime ago. The house we'd built, the garden we planted, the excitement of starting our new life together—they were all etched in my mind like a fading photograph. Memphis, with all its music, history, and charm, was a chapter in my life I would never forget.

The miles I covered, both in business and life, weren't always easy or glamorous, but they shaped me into the person I am. And as I thought about the journey ahead—my literal trek across the country, and the metaphorical journey I had been on for decades—I couldn't help but feel a sense of anticipation. Life, after all, is a series of roads we travel, some smooth, some bumpy, but all of them offering lessons along the way.

Driving through Memphis felt like a full-circle moment for me, like the ghost of my past was riding shotgun, reminding me of where I'd been, what I'd learned, and who I'd become. The city had been a crucible for me, a place where I had learned not only about business but also about relationships, resilience, and what it meant to live life fully.

I think back to those days when Beverly and I lived in our beautiful little house in Germantown, Tennessee. The excitement of building a life from the ground up, the thrill of planting that first garden, and the way it felt to sit in the backyard watching the sun dip below the horizon, knowing that we were part of something bigger than ourselves. Life was ours for the taking.

As I hit the outskirts of Memphis on my way out of town, recollection tugged at my heart. Leaving a place where so many of my formative memories had been made was never easy. But the road ahead was calling, and I had made my peace with the fact that life doesn't always allow you to stay in one place. The journey is the point. The lessons you learn, the people you meet, and the experiences that shape you—those are what matter most.

By the time I pulled into Rendezvous, it was dark, and the smell of dry rub ribs filled the air, making my stomach growl in anticipation. The dimly lit alleyway and the familiar sound of laughter from inside felt like a warm embrace. I could already taste the smoky ribs as I stepped out of Argo, feeling the weight of the road behind me.

Inside, the atmosphere was as electric as I remembered. The old-school charm of the place hadn't changed, and as I sat down, I couldn't help but feel a sense of belonging. The friendly staff, the bustling chatter, and the mouth-watering aroma of slow-cooked meat—it was like a snapshot of Memphis history, and I was a part of it.

As I dug into my meal, I reflected on how much this city had influenced my life. Memphis, with its rich musical heritage, its diverse culture, and its deep roots in American history, had shaped me in ways I hadn't fully understood until now. And while I was only passing through, there was a certain peace that came with revisiting the past, a sense of coming home even if only for a moment.

And yet, even as I savored the last bite of my meal, I knew that the road was calling me once again. Life doesn't stop for anyone. We can reminisce, but the world keeps turning, the miles keep ticking by, and the future waits to be lived. My time in Memphis was a beautiful pause, but it was only that: a pause.

Note to Self

Almost any problem in life can be temporarily solved by standing around a flaming grill, figuring it out with your friends in between arguing about the correct way to smoke a brisket. It doesn't matter if you're in Texas, Carolina, Kansas City, Memphis, or standing perilously on a grated fire escape right in the heart of New York City, barbecuing is a deeply personal, borderline religious experience that is not to be missed.

10

The Inauguration

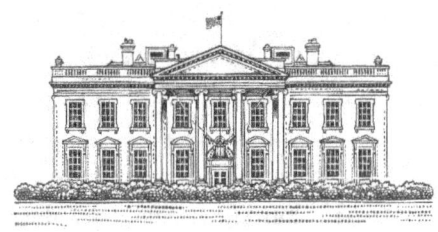

If you cannot beat them...arrange to have them beaten.

GEORGE CARLIN

MY ROAD TRIP ACROSS THE U.S. is turning out to be one of personal and collective transformation. I'm changing. The country's changing. Everybody's changing. It's like a group therapy session.

Many people are convinced that every bad thing in the world can be traced back to politicians, especially to whoever is president. While it gives comedians material, many of them have become angry clowns—angry court jesters—fanning the flames while the proverbial Rome burns. However, the capital of the United States is not burning today, except for a few trash cans set on fire and windows broken by protesters.

I roll into Washington, D.C., in time for the Inauguration. The big ceremony where we swap out one leader for another, like a political game of musical chairs. But instead of music, there are a lot of marching bands and awkward handshakes. This was a crucial stop on my journey in search of America—the transfer of power. One political leader is passing the baton to the next.

Outgoing President Obama packed his things quietly, like a man closing the door on a long chapter. President Trump and his team are moving into the White House to take their turn. The streets were full of noise, but there was a stillness under it all. The country is shifting, slow and heavy, like a great ship changing course. I watched it all, but felt nothing but the weight of the moment.

With temperatures hovering in the thirties, it's almost as if Mother Nature is saying,

"Hey, let's all take a deep breath and chill out for a bit."

The inauguration was a traditional affair, marked by a peaceful transition of power. However, the scene outside the main event was a real circus. The streets were filled with fervent protesters, fortunately not armed with swords. Armed with picket signs and bullhorns. Some were funny, like, "Righties Wrong, Lefties Rule." Some appeared to have been produced in the same print shop. Others, like they were made in kindergarten arts and crafts sessions, only with vile language that would make a salty sailor's parrot blush. Meanwhile, the police watch from the sidelines, scratching their heads. Hopefully, they packed their sense of humor along with their riot gear.

Inside a nearby building, I waited for an elevator to the restaurant above. Two women, who appeared to be in their twenties, walked up, waiting for the elevator. They were discussing their role in the street protest. It was a slow elevator.

"So, where you from?" I asked.

"San Francisco," the brunette answered.

"What do you do back there?"

"Ah, well," they stammered, looking at each other, "we are flight attendants." I didn't get the feel if they were shooting me straight.

"Just curious," I asked, "being from the other side of the country, how did you end up coming here to join in the protest today?"

"Oh, I saw an ad in the community paper advertising a free trip," one of them said. "Really? Wow. So, what did the ad say to get you to travel all this way?"

"Well, it promised a free trip to D.C., with all expenses paid. We talked about it and thought, hey, what the heck. It turned out to be a bus ride. Long ride. But the bus was nice."

"Ah, a fun trip?"

"Yeah," she said. "Our bus leader led us in singing and chanting the whole way. Good times."

"By the time the bus arrived in D.C.," the other one said, "we were ready to party and bring a little mayhem to these bastards!"

Whoever the mastermind was who brought these two, along with other groups from around the country, did a good job summoning the spirits of Che Guevara and Karl Marx for guidance. Their art of rousing people is a strategy from the ancient scrolls of activism. It works whatever the cause. There is nothing like setting a trash can on fire or a police car on fire. Breaking a window at a Starbucks is always good for a photo op, social media posts, and a breaking news segment for the network TV folks.

But here's the thing: despite all the chaos, the pomp, and the circumstance, there's something oddly comforting about watching the transfer of political leadership in America. It's like watching a reality show where, no matter how wild the plot twists, the show must go on.

I was ready to escape D.C., where politics and protests were too hot for me. Leaving behind the chaotic scene where even the clowns say, "Whoa, this is too much," I hit the road like a getaway driver in a rom-com.

I climb behind the wheel of Argo to head south, down the Eastern seaboard, looking for a sane spot to land.

Note to Self

Before the day of the inauguration, my friends called, warning me not to go into D.C. because of fears for my life based on what they were seeing on TV. The scene at the inauguration I saw in person? A different vibe than what the news chose to show. I was there with people holding signs, making their voices heard. But, turn on the TV and it's like, "Breaking News: Society Collapses In Chaos." I half expected CNN to cut to live footage of Godzilla swinging down from the rooftops and stomping through the streets.

When I was in New York, I asked this protester guy who was posted at the same spot every day, "How do you have the time to do this?" And he looked at me like I was the idiot. He told me, "Hey man, it's my job. It's a living."

Later, I discovered that some professional protesters were paid anywhere from a few hundred to several thousand dollars a day. Honestly, if I had known it was that lucrative, I might've grabbed a sign myself.

11

GOT NO SUITCASE

"Suitcase?" Franco tells the agent in Italian. "I got no suitcase. We got nuthin! We had some dirty clothes ... ripped clothes. We didn't have nuthin ... we didn't possess nuthin, you know. And the customs could not believe it. They said, Oh boy, I wish you guys a lot of luck!"

FRANCO NOCERO

I MET FRANCO NOCERO WHEN I stumbled, or rather the wind *blew* me, into the Little Italy restaurant after driving Highway 13 across the bridge across Chesapeake Bay—The Span, so dubbed by locals. It offers a pleasant route, a dance above and beneath the waters, even as the "above" part is a nerve-wracking affair. A sixty-mile-an-hour gust can kiss you perilously close to the icy bay below. Which is precisely what Argo and I encountered on our above-water journey, leaving me wondering if we'd make it across alive.

The Chesapeake Bay Bridge is an automobile bridge-tunnel, twenty-three miles long, that connects Norfolk with the Eastern shore of Virginia. It is technically two bridges laid seventyfive feet above the water, one for eastbound and one for westbound traffic, each with two lanes, no shoulder, and no place to pull off if you have car trouble. Once you are on, you are *on*.

There are tunnel openings at two points, which plunge you under the water for a bit.

Then, you emerge from the tubes above the water and return to the bridge.

It's all fun and games unless you drive it on a day with strong winds, as I did. Then, it's no fun at all.

The winds were variable that day, forty miles per hour with gusts up to sixty. Now, had I known these would be the conditions, I wouldn't have ventured out. But as I said, once you are on The Span, you are on it—no way to turn around.

When wind gusts hit your vehicle (especially a tall one like Argo) from the side, you must instantly correct to stay in your lane and avoid running into the guard rail, possibly going off the bridge into the waters of the Chesapeake Bay. A trucker crossing that day did precisely that. His tractor-trailer rig plunged through the bridge's guardrails into the strong currents and frigid water. With the water temp as frigid as it was, it would have only taken twenty minutes max before his muscles had weakened. He'd have lost coordination and the ability to tread water or swim. I won't tell you what became of that guy because this isn't a sad-sack book.

Exiting the tunnel under Fisherman Island National Wildlife Refuge, I still hadn't made it the entire twenty-three miles across The Span to the Eastern Shore when another sixty-mile-anhour blast of wind whipped against the right side of Argo, forcing me to adjust the wheel to fight back against the wind. Then another and another.

After that white-knuckle drive, I needed a quiet spot to recover. Also, I was starving. A hand-painted sign just off the side of the road gave me hope: *Little Italy Restaurant ahead!*

Steak! Pizza! Seafood! Pasta!

Give! Me! All! That! Food!

Twenty-five miles down Lankford Highway, Little Italy Restaurant is just off the highway in Nassawadox, a town of about five hundred people. Nassawadox translates as "land between two waters," with the Atlantic Ocean on the east and the Chesapeake Bay on the west side.

Looking at a map of the upper East Coast, it's south of the Jersey shore, about five hours past Delaware, and a little more than an hour north of Virginia Beach. Notably, for young readers, it is forty-seven miles from Chincoteague Island, the setting for Marguerite Henry's book *Misty of Chincoteague*, the story of one of the wild ponies descended from a Spanish galleon shipwreck, according to legend, on adjacent Assateague Island. The ponies run wild there still today.

I continued driving Lankford Highway, turning onto Rogers Street, which was lined with cars in front of Little Italy Restaurant. A large banner was nailed across the front entry, proudly announcing its twenty-fourth year in business. It was actually their twenty-fifth year, I'd later learn. They just hadn't updated the sign.

The large parking lot across the street was nearly full. In my exhaustion, my first thought was to go somewhere else since it was so crowded. There weren't many other choices other than a few fast-food places along the highway. I found a spot to park Argo at the rear of the lot across the street.

It was puzzling how such a small town could have so many people in this place. It was a mixture of locals and tourists passing through on their way to the open beaches and staying at the nearby small resorts. It was close to closing time, so I wasn't sure if they would still serve me.

Little Italy wasn't fancy. It was Italian comfortable. And that works since Italian food is the world's comfort food. Travel to almost any country in the world, and ask a local for the best restaurant in town. Invariably, somebody will point you to an Italian restaurant.

A young waitress with brunette hair, wearing a black T-shirt and black pants, and ready to end her shift, seated me at a table in the front dining room. "If you order quickly, I can get it before the kitchen closes," she said, walking away.

"Wait," I said, "I'll order right now. What do you recommend?"

"We still have some clam chowder," she said, "and the lasagna is a house specialty."

"I'll take both of those. Whatever Chianti you have. And a glass of water with a straw." I always ask for a straw with my water glass at a restaurant. It's not because I'm a germaphobe, even as I am indeed a germaphobe. It's just that I think a straw provides an elevated experience, seemingly making the water taste better by providing a barrier between your lips and the invisible lipstick residue from the previous user of the glass.

What's more, straw-drinkers have a sense of control over the act of drinking. And that is true. Ask a race car driver. During and after the race, they drink from a straw to regulate water intake so as not to drink too much at once.

Is it too much to say that the humble straw is a beacon of hope—a sign of civility in an otherwise chaotic world? I don't think so.

I'll never, ever think so.

The ensuing clam chowder was presented as a light broth, not with the creamy base I expected, but it looked good, and it tasted great. Thick with several excellent cheeses, the lasagna also proved to be remarkable. I wanted to eat it all, but wound up returning half the portion to Argo to enjoy as the next day's lunch.

I watched the owner, Franco, make the rounds throughout the several dining rooms connected in what had been three different adjacent buildings dating back to 1889. He was talking to a table of seven people across the dining room in Italian/American English staccato, in sync with his back-handed arm-flaying punctuating gestures to emphasize random points. He spoke with intensity and sincerity, especially when telling a joke.

Franco was the center of attention as he walked up to each table. He obviously had known some of the diners for years.

He repeated stops at each table till he reached mine. He didn't recognize me, so I got the courtesy acknowledgment of a nod, followed by, "How ya doin'?" And he continued walking back to the kitchen. He made a loop through the dining rooms at least six times in the space of thirty minutes.

Franco Nocero and his wife, Cathy, own and run the place. She oversees the kitchen while he rides herd over the dining rooms and front counter.

On the way out, I scanned a map filled with pins showing the hometowns of people who had visited the restaurant. I read a framed newspaper article about his second job. I never would have guessed his second job, nor could I envision him doing it. I decided to hang around Nassawadox to learn more about this fascinating character.

I drive Argo just outside of Nassawadox, finding a place to camp Argo for the night near the water's edge at a nearby marina boat launch. My sleep is long and deep, as my body is starved for rest to replenish.

Returning to the restaurant, I sit at a table with Franco before the dinner rush in the Sinatra Room. Black-and-white photos of the famed Hoboken-born, Italian-American singer Frank Sinatra cover the wall behind him. A life-size statue of Sinatra stands in one corner near the stage where local singers perform on weekends.

"On Friday, October 17, 1964, we came to this country," Franco told me. "And the funny part, when we came to this country, we went to the customs. They asked for da … luggage."

At the time, Franco Nocero had only been seventeen years old, fresh out of an Italian orphanage, stepping off the boat into a strange new country.

"I couldn't understand English; I asked my uncle in Italian, what is he talking about?" I see pain in his eyes, but he tells me about the day with a nostalgic smile.

"He says he wants to know where your suitcase is?" The uncle tells Franco.

"Suitcase?" Franco tells the agent in Italian. "I got no suitcase. We got nuthin! We had some dirty clothes … ripped clothes. We didn't have nuthin … we didn't possess nuthin, you know."

Franco recalls the day vividly. Franco's dad had died, and his mom was dying from cancer. Unable to care for him, she placed him in a Catholic orphanage in Italy before she was taken to New York for a last-ditch effort to save her life.

With the help of the nuns, arrangements were made for Franco to go to New York, where he could see his mother before she died and live with his aunt. His uncle managed to get two steerage class tickets on a ship bound for New York and retrieved him from the orphanage. They didn't have suitcases, because the only clothes they had were the clothes on their backs.

"… and the customs could not believe it. They said, 'Oh boy, I wish you guys a lot of luck.'"

Franco arrived on a Friday. On Monday, he went to work in a coat factory, where the minimum wage was a buck twenty-five.

"I was proud of what I was doing. I had a job. It was good. After taxes, I had forty-two dollars—forty dollars of which I gave to my mother. Two dollars was my pay to go to the movies, you know. A few years later, I went to work for Maxwell House Coffee, General Foods, a big company in Hoboken. I made good pay and benefits and worked there for twenty-five years."

"So, where did you meet your wife?" I asked Franco.

"I met her in Hoboken at a dance. I was president of a soccer club and organized dances for fundraising. I was five years older than her. No way her mother was going to let us go out. But, at the end of 1969, on Columbus Day, I met my mother-in-law for the first time. And that was an experience! Golly! I don't wish that on my worst enemy."

With a lot of perseverance and as much charm as he could muster, Franco eventually won Cathy's hand in marriage. Over time, including three daughters later, the mother-in-law came around.

All was going well till Franco lost his job at Maxwell House due to no fault of his own.

"They told us they were closing. So, what I did was I went to night school to learn cooking and catering. It was a sacrifice because I had to go to work and school."

"You are in Hoboken," I say. "The factory you are working for is closing, so goodbye, job. You go to night school, learn how to operate a food business, and end up opening a restaurant on the Eastern Shore of Virginia in a town of five hundred people. How did that happen?"

"Now," I asked, "how does it feel today sitting here over twenty-five years later, owner of your successful restaurant?"

"Well, the possibility that a little guy like me from Italy can do what I did? I own a beautiful house on the water. I own this restaurant ... da-bank owns the mortgage, but you know, when I look back, I say, who helped me? There was nobody to financially help me except God." "You and God. So you have a strong faith?" I asked.

"My faith ... I lost it ... when my mother died, because she was a very devoted woman ... very Christian woman. And I was mad at God because they took my father away when I was nine years old. Took my mother. I'm twenty-four years old and have two sisters to care for. How much more do you want from me, God?

And I lost it for a while; I stopped going to church. I was bitter ... I was bitter.

But, in the meantime, I bought a house. I got married. What happened was we had a friend, a Yugoslavian friend. They used to go to church, and she begged me to go to that church for years. I kept it away from it.

One night, my wife and three daughters were walking. The church had a Friday night service, and we fell in love with it. The kids liked it. We sat in the back, so just in case it's not right, we could get out.

I got back to my faith. We got up at five on Sunday morning to deliver the newspaper. After delivering the newspapers, we would go to IHOP and the church. Or church and the I-Hop, depending on what time we finish delivering the paper.

We didn't deliver it for the money, 'cause it was only five dollars or something like that for one day a week. I made all three daughters get up to show them what work is. Sometimes, it would snow; we had to push the car. It was an experience." "When we started the business ...,"

"It was both of us," his wife, Cathy, said.

"We cooked, and the kids took care of the cash register. It was fantastic. I was ecstatic. Before I opened this place, I put all my eggs in one basket, and if this didn't work out, I would have been broke down."

Before I left, Franco and I smoked cigars. They were the last two of his La Gloria Cubana cigars in his octagon, bright red Glorioso box. When we finished the smokes and conversation, he gave me the box to keep. It was a symbol of connection and friendship, a memory I cherish and reflect on each time I see the unusually shaped red cigar box on my shelf.

Franco's story is one of hope, determination, and resilience—a story that echoes the dreams of countless immigrants who embarked on a journey across oceans and rivers in search of a brighter tomorrow. His journey is not just his own; it's a reflection of the universal human spirit, a testament to the enduring belief that a better life is within reach for those willing to labor and surmount the hurdles life throws at us.

Note to Self

My conversations with Franco at his Little Italy restaurant in Nassawadox were a highlight of my road trip. Of all the miles I put behind me, of all the towns and faces that passed like windblown dust through my journey, it was the hours I spent with Franco in his Little Italy restaurant that stuck the deepest. There, in the warm clatter of pans and the comfort of tomato and garlic in the air, he told me the old, hard story—a man with empty pockets crossing an ocean, chasing the whisper of a better life.

He spoke plainly, not with pride but with the kind of quiet certainty that comes from someone who has seen hard times. He had worked—God, how he had worked—and what he built, he built himself, with his wife and family. A restaurant, yes, but more than that: a place where his past and future lived together. Franco's enthusiasm for life and work is the soul of the American Dream.

12

KILL DEVIL HILLS

*A person with a new idea is a crank until
the idea succeeds.*

MARK TWAIN

CONTINUING THE DRIVE SOUTH, STAYING as close to ocean roads as possible, I feel the urge to chill out on one of the sandy beaches. There is always something about a beach, with the rhythmic dancing of waves lapping at the edge, that puts me into a hypnotic state.

For a few days, I became a slothful beach bum sitting on a beautiful white sand beach on the North Carolina Outer Banks. My mind, typically a whirlwind of thoughts, mirrors the vast expanse of the sky and sea before me.

The following morning, I woke a little after five from a deep dream with a mental boot to my brain. In this dream, I was transported to the shores of America in the year 1620, right there at Jamestown. It was as if I'd time-traveled back to a time when the world was fresh and wild, the land unforgiving and untamed.

In my dream, I saw the first settlers struggling to make their way, find food, build shelters, and fight to exist. For those early colonists, landing on this new world must have been like landing on the moon—alien and unknown.

As I woke, I couldn't help but ponder the incredible courage of those pioneers who had braved the unknown and carved a future from the wilderness. It was a stark reminder that in the grand tapestry of American history, the journey had always been one of audacity, resilience, and a relentless drive to conquer what hadn't been charted before.

As I continue my modern-day odyssey across this vast and diverse land, I hear the echoes of that dream, a reminder that the spirit of exploration and the quest for new horizons were woven into the very fabric of America's story.

In a groggy haze, my thoughts jump from the first settlers to Americans landing on the moon—maybe because I'm in North Carolina, not far from Kill Devil Hills. At Kill Devil Hills, the first successful airplane flight took place almost two hundred years after the arrival of the Pilgrims. That first controlled, sustained flight of a powered, heavier-than-air contraption for a mere fifty-nine seconds led to commercial aviation across the country and worldwide, and even into space, eventually leading to a human-crewed flight landing on the moon. That moon launch would occur just down the coast, a few hundred miles away, in Florida.

These inspiring thoughts fuel my morning—and all before getting out of bed—before my first cup of coffee. "This is going to be a good day," I say aloud, meaning it.

The rain is falling lightly. You would think that would make me melancholy, but it has the opposite effect. I stand in its embrace, not as a spectator but as a participant in its invigorating waltz. It's a reminder that even amid life's storms, beauty and vitality can be found if one is willing to embrace the drops.

The misty coastal rain is clearing the way for what is forecast to be a beautiful day. If that proves to be an accurate forecast, I will return to the beach to write and then go to the site where Orville and Wilber Wright flew that first airplane.

In the cozy confines of Argo, I set about my morning routine. With a trusty butane stove, I conjure the elixir of life itself: coffee. Its aromatic embrace fills the air, coaxing my senses to life. Meanwhile, the microwave hums to life, preparing a humble bowl of oatmeal—a breakfast of champions. I sit and write for a while and let the words flow onto paper, until an out-of-the-blue craving for a donut overwhelms me. I resist, but the temptation is too strong. With a sigh of surrender, I rise from my writer's perch, leaving behind the world of words for a moment. It's time to chase the promise of that delectable donut, to indulge in the simple joys that life on the road can offer.

I pack up my notebook and the breakfast paraphernalia, fire up Argo, and head for town, driving past the endless row of strip malls of Kitty Hawk until I spy a likely prospect: Duck Donuts.

I walked into the tiny space and looked around. No donuts. Nonplussed, I stood and stared at where the donuts should be.

"Looks like you haven't been here before," the dark-haired girl behind the counter says. "No ... I haven't. I saw the sign for donuts, but I don't see any," I said, "… are you out?" "Ha, looking for a display of donuts," she replied.

"Ah, well, yep."

"So, we're a little different than an ordinary donut shop," she says. "We make them as you order them. That's what we do here at Duck Donuts."

"Okay, sounds good. What's the deal?"

"We only make one kind of donut … our special secret-recipe donut," she says and proceeds to explain the approach. "You tell us how many you want, then pick an icing to roll them in … then choose a topping like nuts or coconut. Then, if you want, pick a drizzle like chocolate or caramel to go on top of it."

"That's a new one. Interesting."

"First one's on me—since you're new to Duck Donuts."

Her soft, patient eyes watched as I scanned the freshly baked donuts, waiting to see my reactions to each choice. Her politeness and kindness were so effortless, like being served by a friend.

It stood to reason. Along my journey, some of the happiest people I encountered worked at shops just like this—people who are glad to have a job and contribute to the world around them. They had a sense of self-worth, a sense of belonging. For many, and some more than others, it seemed to be not just about the paycheck but the feeling of being valued and productive.

Moments later, she presented me with my first Duck Donut, a small, hot ball of fried dough rolled in the one topping I'd picked: powdered sugar.

"Try it," she said with a smile.

I did. And man, what a glorious sensation it was.

I'll be back. Maybe not this trip, but when I'm back this way for sure.

The day is pushing toward the sixties. The sun is shining through a cloudless sky as a pleasant breeze caresses my face. Figuring it would be a sin not to, I traverse the few blocks to the beach.

Walking across the sand, my toes gleefully dug into the warm grit. I find a spot on a bluff, settle in, and allow the rhythmic music of the waves lapping against the shore to offer its serenade. At this moment, my soul becomes still, a natural feeling of respectful gratitude washing over me.

I point my face toward the heavens, looking into a sleep-hued Friday sky. A few cottonwhite puffy clouds with steel-gray bottoms form, drift past as if providing punctuation to the universe's statement of perfection.

After writing and lollygagging on the beach, I retrieved Argo and headed to the site where Orville and Wilbur tested their wings. In grade school, countless millions of children had been told that the first flight took place in Kitty Hawk—"First in Flight," and all that. Actually, it happened at Kill Devil Hills, just four miles south of there. News accounts of the day mistakenly reported that the flights had taken place at Kitty Hawk, likely because the telegraph station where the news was sent was in Kitty Hawk, not Kill Devil Hills.

Either way, we owe our appreciation to those dreamers, those visionaries, those highly intelligent or just lucky ones. All those who stuck to their guns, enduring failure after failure until they succeeded, whether for the time it took simply to fall to the ground or for the fifty-nine seconds that proved controlled, powered flight was possible.

Our thanks are lofted to those Walter Mittys who dared "to slip the surly bonds of earth / And danced the skies on laughter-silvered wings," to quote a favorite poem written by a young World War II aviator, John Gillespie Magee, Jr., in his verse, "High Flight." Although Magee died at nineteen, he is remembered decades later for the words he penned after first flying to an altitude of 33,000 feet.

It's been a little more than a century since man has been able to fly in a controlled, powered aircraft, thanks to brothers Orville and Wilbur Wright, two bicycle mechanics from Ohio.

Working on bikes made them a living, but they were bird-wannabes, extreme dreamers. When not occupied with bikes, they worked in their shop experimenting, building, and testing flying machines in a little wind tunnel they designed. For their vacations, they would pack up the contraptions and head off to test-fly them in a place with steady winds and lots of sand to soften the landings, somewhere with high places for launching their gliders.

The Wright brothers did not invent "the" flying machine; others had already done that. Theirs was a flying machine that could be gas-powered and controlled by a human. To be more exact, they figured out how to take off, fly, and land using a three-axis control configuration on a flying machine they took turns piloting.

Until their success, man's attempts to fly in machines usually resulted only in hopping and bopping erratically or being pushed off the side of a cliff for brief periods of gliding—all at the whim of wind and gravity.

Orville and Wilbur figured out how a pilot could control the three primary critical elements: yaw, pitch, and roll. "Yaw" is nose left or right about an axis running up and down (from ground to sky); "pitch" is nose up or down about an axis running from wing to wing; and "roll" is rotation about an axis running from nose to tail, keeping the plane level. The basic systems they engineered remain in use today.

Their aircraft was the Wright Flyer, built of spruce and muslin, twin wooden "pusher" propellers, and a purpose-built gasoline engine fabricated in their bicycle shop. Gasoline was gravity-fed from the fuel tank mounted on a wing strut into a chamber next to the cylinders, where it mixed with air. The propeller drive chains, resembling bicycle chains, were heavy-duty automobile chains. The Flyer cost less than a thousand dollars to build, equivalent to $28,000 today. The Wright Flyer had a wingspan of just over forty feet, weighed 605 pounds, and possessed a twelve-horsepower, 180-pound engine.

Stones on the beach mark the distance of each of the four flights at Kill Devil Hills on December 17, 1903. The first two flights were from level ground into a headwind gusting to twenty-seven miles per hour. The first flight, piloted by Orville, went 120 feet in twelve seconds at a speed of six-point-eight miles per hour. The following two fights, by Wilbur and then Orville, went 175 and 200 feet respectively, only ten feet above the ground. Orville made the day's final flight, the longest at 852 feet in fifty-nine seconds. Five people witnessed the flight, including John T. Daniels, who snapped the famous "first flight" photo using Orville's prepositioned camera.

Twenty-five years after the Wright brothers' plane left the ground, defying gravity's grasp, for those first four successful powered flights, the place was memorialized by a large boulder with a bronze plaque. Orville was present for the unveiling of the plaque on a cold and crisp December 17, 1928, along with notables such as aviator Amelia Earhart, and witnessed by a crowd of three thousand. Sadly, a void was left by Wilbur not being present, having passed away in 1912 with typhoid fever.

Kill Devil Hills is sacred ground. The story of the Wright brothers is a great American story of possibility, of inventiveness, of perseverance. Here, against the backdrop of endless dunes and the relentless Atlantic winds, the Wright brothers had pursued the dream of flight, transforming it from an ethereal aspiration into a tangible reality.

And as I stood there on that hallowed ground, I knew what I had to do before leaving.

There may not have been a sign expressly permitting it, but the spirit of a place called out to me. And so I retrieved a box from the back of Argo and prepared to launch my very own flying machine, "Air Argo," a drone that would carry my imagination aloft.

As I watch, I'm filled with wonder and awe. The drone moves with a grace that defies gravity, gliding effortlessly on unseen currents. It's as if it possesses a secret language with the wind, a silent conversation that guides its every move.

The view from below is mesmerizing. The drone's silhouette is stark against the canvas of blue sky, a modern-day marvel against the timeless backdrop of nature. It maneuvers with precision, banking and turning as if it were a bird in flight, a creature of the air.

From this vantage point, I can't help but feel a sense of connection to the Wright brothers on this site, marveling at the possibilities of flight. It's as if we're sharing a moment of exploration, a journey into the great unknown.

For a fleeting moment, I soared where they had once soared, above the very sand that had witnessed their dreams take flight. I could almost sense Orville and Wilbur, those pioneers of the sky, smiling down from their celestial perch, giving me a thumbs-up of approval.

As the drone danced in the breeze at that moment, I felt a deep connection to the past and the boundless horizons that beckon to all who dared to dream. The Wright brothers left an indelible mark on history, and now, even in the modern age of flight, their spirit lives on in the skies above Kill Devil Hills.

Just then, a park ranger came into view. "You're standing on history, my friend," he said.

"This is where they did it."

"I've heard about it all my life," I said. "Just didn't know what to expect."

"Well," he said, "this is the place where the two bicycle-shop guys figured out how to get a machine into the air that weighed more than a piano and could carry a grown man."

"And now, we flash across the air at thirty-five thousand feet watching an action movie, sipping on a cold soda, and whiling away the hours."

The wind shifted, kicking up a swirl of sand, as if the past still whispered through this place.

I turned back toward the ranger, but he was already walking away, leaving me alone with history, the sky stretching endlessly above.

Note to Self

One of the things that has always set America apart is our relentless inventiveness. We are a nation that looked at a perfectly good horse and said, "What if it could fly? Wait, what if it had cup holders and Wi-Fi?"

We gave the world the light bulb, the airplane, the internet, and a machine that can fry an entire turkey in under four minutes. That's the American spirit: if it can be built, we'll build it; if it can't, we'll duct-tape some stuff together, give it a Bluetooth speaker, and sell it on late-night television. The same country that cracked the moon landing also figured out how to make a bed that changes positions, gives you a massage, and charges your phone — all at the touch of a remote. This is the country that sent a man to the moon and invented spray cheese, and frankly, I'm not sure which was harder.

13

A Dark and Stormy Night

Many of the things you can count, don't count. Many of the things you can't count, really count.

ALBERT EINSTEIN

DRIVING SOUTH NEAR THE WATER'S EDGE on the Outer Banks of Cape Hatteras, I stop to walk around on the beautiful white sand, listen to the waves lapping at the edge, and breathe the salty Atlantic air. Seagulls wheel and cry overhead, their calls mingling with the rhythmic crash of waves. The expanse of the horizon stretches before me, an unbroken line where sky and sea converge, inviting me to lose myself in the vastness of it all.

As I stroll along, I spot a beam of dark, weathered wood. It and several other pieces of timber dotting the beach appear to be part of an old ship. My curiosity piqued, I decided to have a look.

It was a dark and stormy night—no, really, it *was*—and the year was 1899. The location was right where I stand.

The waters off the Outer Banks of Cape Hatteras are infamously known as the graveyard of the Atlantic Ocean. The list of ships that met their final fate hereabouts over the years is staggering.

The first recorded account I am aware of dates to 1585, with the wreck of the *Tiger*, an English ship that was part of Sir Richard Grenville's expedition. Grenville was the admiral of the seven-strong fleet that brought English settlers to establish a military colony on Roanoke Island off the coast of modern North Carolina in North America. Too large to enter the waters near Roanoke, the *Tiger* was forced to anchor along the coast of the Atlantic, where it was destroyed by volatile weather and high seas, sinking with much of the settlers' provisions.

Hatteras is the sixth oldest surviving English place name in the United States. Grenville named the cape "Hatrask" in 1585, and it was later renamed to Hatteras, after the Hatteras Indians who were native to the place.

It's worth noting that just off the shores of Cape Hatteras, the Gulf Stream's warm waters collide with the Labrador Stream's cold, and like two mighty lions, these currents roar and fight for dominance. They are treacherous enough for all sailors, but add another one of Mother Nature's tricks to the mix, such as a hurricane, and the task of steering a ship through those rocky waters can end calamitously for the poor sailors aboard.

Add another ingredient, such as pesky humans with ill intent, to the Labrador and Gulf collision cocktail, and you get even more doom-laden stories. Pirates such as Blackbeard, as well as events like the American Civil War and World War II, contributed to the demise of more than one thousand vessels off these Outer Banks beaches.

Since 1915, the U.S. Coast Guard has helped to rescue ships in peril in these waters. Before that, volunteers kept a lookout for distressed ships from watch stations on the shore. The first U.S. Life Saving Service was created under the U.S. Treasury's Revenue Marine Bureau in 1871 to train the people who were keeping watch. Life-saving stations were built along the coast from 1874 until 1915, staffed by lifesavers called Surfmen.

Back to that dark and stormy night story, on August 18, 1899, the lone Surfman patrolling the coast in those gale-force winds was Rasmus S. Midgett. At some point, he spotted items newly washed ashore, indicating a shipwreck. He walked two miles on, heard what sounded like sails flapping in the wind, and thought he heard faint voices. Flashing his lantern over the ocean, he saw a ship keeled over some twenty-five feet from shore, its injured sailors clinging to the remaining wood of the boat. They were the crew of the *Priscilla*, a massive, 643-ton vessel bound for Rio de Janeiro, Brazil, and in the hundred-plus-mile-an-hour winds, her once-trusty timbers now were ripping apart as grown men uncontrollably wailed.

The men aboard the *Priscilla* were injured, helpless, and in fear of their lives as wave after wave pulled them into the roiling abyss. Beaten and battered for hours by a churning, angry sea, they saw their ship splinter and rip apart beneath them.

Hearing the injured men crying out, Surfman Midgett had a difficult decision to make: If he went to find help from the next closest Life-Saving Station, it would take him hours to make the round trip, and by then, all lives could be lost. But the other option was no more desirable: he would need to rush into the water alone and save as many lives as he could.

Midgett decided to go into the violent waves and risk his own life to help the injured men to safety. He yelled to the men that when he called, one man should jump off the debris and swim toward shore, where Midgett would pull him from the waters.

That's exactly what one man did, and he was pulled by Midgett from the waves.

Midgett went back to rescue another man.

Then another. Then another. Seven times he did this before his strength and stamina failed. But three men remained on the ship. After yelling for them to stay put, he dragged himself to his beloved horse and raced to the station to summon aid.

Thanks to the heroic efforts of Surfman Rasmus S. Midgett, ten men were saved on that dark and stormy night. He received the Gold Lifesaving Medal of Honor, and the U.S. Coast Guard continues to recognize his courageous actions as one of the most outstanding maritime rescues in history.

◄ ▲ ▼ ►

The Rasmus Midgett House in Waves, North Carolina, was recently restored and turned into a museum, and in 2009, it was listed on the National Register of Historic Places.

Ultimately, the raging sea receded, and the storm abated, leaving behind a transformed landscape. But what remained, etched in the memory of all who bore witness, was the story of one individual who had risked their own life to save others. It was a tale of human courage, an enduring reminder that the indomitable spirit of compassion and heroism can prevail even in the face of nature's most formidable challenges.

Note to Self

When crisis hits, something incredible happens: Americans do what we've always done best: we rally together, roll up our sleeves, and jump right into the fray. Neighbors check on each other. Strangers show up with casseroles, jumper cables, and hope to spare. People donate money, time, and form human chains to rescue flood victims. We turn high school gyms into shelters, turn pickup trucks into supply convoys. It's deeply American.

What's amazing is that all this comes from a country that, under normal circumstances, will have a six-hour argument over the most stupid things they saw on the internet. But in tough times, we forget about bumper stickers and political yard signs and remember that we're all in the same boat.

If there's one thing Americans know how to do, it's face adversity with grit and heart.

14

BOTTOM'S UP

*Innovation is taking two things that
already exist and putting them together in
a new way.*

ELON MUSK

ON MY WAY SOUTH, I find a story of American ingenuity, inventiveness, and can-do spirit tucked inside every twist in the road. Continuing down the East Coast, I pull trusty Argo into the little town of New Bern, North Carolina, a riverfront haven with tales to tell. It was here that I uncovered the curious saga of Brad's Drink.

It reminded me of the invention of several other enduring American drink creations. One was by a friend of mine back in Dallas. In the summer of 1971, Mariano Martinez stood behind the bar of his new Dallas restaurant, where margaritas were popular. It was Texas. It was hot. And they wanted them frozen. His bartenders couldn't keep up, shaking and pouring each margarita by hand. The crowds wanted something faster. The machines broke. The drinks came out inconsistently.

One morning, looking for coffee, he stopped at a 7-Eleven and watched a cherry Slurpee swirl into a cup, cold and smooth and effortless. Mariano bought an old machine, working night and day to figure out how to make it produce frozen margaritas that were creamy and consistent. His customers loved it. Today, restaurants use this process around the world. Mariano's original machine is now in the Smithsonian.

Another super-star drink came from south of Dallas. Waco pharmacist Charles Alderton worked at Morrison's Drug Store. After much experimentation, he created a bold, unique soda flavored with hints of cherry, licorice, clove, and a secret ingredient. Customers loved it, asking simply for "a Waco." Needing a name, Morrison chose Dr. Pepper, perhaps after a real doctor or merely to evoke health and refinement. The name stuck, and the drink spread far beyond Waco. And, of course, from Atlanta came a legendary drink from an Atlanta pharmacist, John Pemberton, in 1886. He created a medicinal tonic for headaches and fatigue. Customers wanted more of the sweet, spicy flavor from a blend of coca leaf extract and kola nut. The name "CocaCola," in flowing script, was penned by the bookkeeper.

And, Brad's Drink? It began where I am now, in New Bern, North Carolina. It was the summer of 1893, a sultry year in New

Bern. The stage was set in Caleb Bradham's modest pharmacy. Old Caleb, a pharmacist with a penchant for experimentation, was on a mission to concoct a digestive potion to soothe the troubled stomachs of his patrons. He combined vanilla, sugar, caramel, kola nuts, lemon oil, a pinch of nutmeg, and a dash of this and that from his pantry.

After mixing and remixing, days turned into weeks, and Caleb mixed and remixed his elixir, sipping each brew with the solemnity of an alchemist. Finally, like a prospector striking gold in the Klondike, he stumbled upon a formula that tickled his taste buds. His customers, ever the curious lot, found it equally delightful. The folks of that little New Bern village swore by it, claiming it invigorated their spirits, aided their digestion, and, to top it all off, it was downright tasty.

He didn't have a name for it; the townsfolk simply dubbed it "Brad's Drink," a nod to the affable man standing guard behind the apothecary counter. The news spread like wildfire. Friends told friends, who in turn told their friends, creating a cascade of curiosity and thirst.

Soon, the clamor for Brad's Drink was so relentless that Caleb Bradham decided to put it in bottles. People were not just buying it by the bottle; they were buying it by the case. Other pharmacies bought it from him, and that year, Bradham sold 7,968 gallons of syrup. The following year, he sold the drink in six-ounce bottles, resulting in a 19,848-gallon increase in sales.

In 1898, Brad's Drink was given a new name: Pepsi Cola—named after two of its main ingredients: the digestive enzyme pepsin and kola nuts.

Celebrities began endorsing the drink, leading off in 1909 with Barney Oldfield, a famous race car driver. He was the first to drive a car at the then-lightning speed of sixty miles per hour. Regarding Pepsi Cola, he described it as "a bully drink ... refreshing, invigorating, a fine bracer before a race." If Barney drank it, people figured, it must be good. Word of mouth spread the drink's fame. The advertising theme "Delicious and Healthful" was used for a full twenty years.

Unfortunately, due to speculating on erratic high sugar prices during World War I and at the bottom of the Great Depression, Bradham's company sank into bankruptcy. He had to sell to an investor who also ran into trouble and was ultimately unsuccessful.

Ah, the saga of Brad's Drink and its wild journey to cola stardom. You see, Brad's Drink had a tough time finding a dance partner. It asked Coca-Cola to be its date not once, not twice, but three times! And every time, Coca-Cola said, "Thanks, but we've got enough drinks to juggle already." Ouch, rejection hurts, even in the soda world.

Charles Guth, the soda's savior, swept in to buy the drink, introducing the world to the twelve-ounce bottle because who on earth can resist an extra gulp of such alluring sugary bliss?

A catchy jingle even came with the purchase: "Pepsi-Cola hits the spot / Twelve ounces, that's a lot / Twice as much for a nickel, too / Pepsi-Cola is the drink for you."

As Brad's Drink started to gain some traction, it became a cash cow. Celebrities lined up to endorse it like it was the hottest ticket in town. Joan Crawford, who was married to the company's bigwig at the time, sipped on it in between takes on the silver screen. Michael Jackson moonwalked his way into the Brad's Drink stardom, and Ray Charles sang its praises—a sweet melody, indeed. The Spice Girls, Britney Spears, and even NASCAR hotshot Jeff Gordon jumped on the Brad's Drink bandwagon.

And so, Brad's Drink, once the underdog, rose to become Coca-Cola's arch-nemesis worldwide. Some folks even dubbed their rivalry: the Cola Wars, which sounds like a battle of fizz and froth that only the soda gods could genuinely appreciate. Cheers to Brad's Drink, the little beverage that could, and did, in a world filled with cola giants.

◄ ▲ ▼ ►

These days, Caleb Bradham's original pharmacy is gone, but across the street from where it was located, there is a Pepsi store commemorating the history of Brad's Drink with displays of Pepsi memorabilia.

"I guess if I'd held onto my grandmother's old Mason jars and soda bottles," I said to the young woman behind the counter, "they'd be worth something today."

"Ha! If I had a nickel for every time someone has come in here," she said, "bringing in an old Pepsi bottle and asking me if it is worth something, I'd have enough for, well, another bottle of Pepsi."

As we both laughed, she pointed me to an odd-shaped bottle in a glass case, displayed like a magic lamp. "Now, the old-school stuff, like this one, is the real treasure!"

"A lot of history of American ingenuity behind that bottle, I'm sure,"

Note to Self

My "not so better angel" is telling me that in my next life, I need to invent a low-cost drink that's sugary and addictive. I mean seriously—forget curing diseases or solving world hunger, just be the guy who sells liquid candy in a can and retires before forty.

You can print money like the U.S. Treasury by satisfying people's caffeine addiction. Don't change the world. Just caffeinate it, carbonate it, and add sugar.

15

OFF THE GRID

Two things everybody's got tuh do fuh theyselves. They got tuh go tuh God, and they got tuh find out about livin' fuh theyselves.

ZORA NEALE HURSTON, THEIR EYES WERE WATCHING GOD

I LEAVE NEW BERN ON Highway 70 and head south toward Emerald Isle, a popular barrier island vacation spot along the coast of North Carolina. I follow the shoreline of the Neuse River, which widens its mouth into the Pamlico Sound.

The sky is getting darker, and my eyelids feel heavy. I want to make it to the next town, but my body tells me I need to find a place to sleep for the night.

Up ahead, I see a sign for the Croatan National Forest campground. That works, I think, as I pass by the sign. I make a U-turn back to the entrance and make my way down the long, tree-lined, narrow road leading to the camping area. It's a bit spooky, but at this point, the desire for sleep is overriding any other options.

Dusk is closing in. I wonder how far I will drive and where I will settle in for the night. I pass a sign for Flanders Beach Campground on the riverside of the road. I should at least check it out, maybe see the water before it gets too dark. I turned down the narrow road leading to the campsite. By the time I reach the street's end at the entrance to the campground, it is dark. Fortunately for me, it is the off-season, and spots are available for the night. The campsites are only eleven bucks a night. Argo and I circle the campground several times to find the perfect site near the Neuse River. Argo and I settle in and rest well.

The following day, with my ceramic coffee cup in hand, I leave the warmth of Argo and step out into the chill of the newly sprung day. Between the caffeine, the brightness of the sky, and the shocking rawness of the Croatan Forest air, my body is now awake, my brain not far behind.

With a nature trail within yards of my camp, it seems like a sin not to explore. I follow a path that winds me through the trees to the water's edge. Then, a walk down wooden stairs descending to Flanner's Beach. The Croatan Forest is the only true coastal forest in the East. It's 160,000 acres of pine forest, saltwater estuaries, bogs, and raised swamps called pocosins that are bordered on three sides by tidal rivers and the Bogue Sound. It is a naturalist's perfect playground. I revel in its diverse, almost primitive beauty.

I was walking back to Argo when I met the Morgans. Bridgette Morgan appears ahead in my path.

"May I help you?" she shouts to me, standing at the edge of her family camping area. The site is decorated with hanging buoys next to a sizable tan tent and a tan motor home. Her help offer is an opening line to size up strangers like me.

"No, just looking around," I shout back as I continue toward her.

"How long have you been here for?" she asks in a modulated voice as I near.

"It's just one night, but after my morning walk to the water, I think this might be a good quiet place to stay until tomorrow and get some writing done. How long have you been here?"

"Several years."

I grin in surprise. "Well, that's longer than a day."

"My husband and I are the camp hosts. We keep an eye on things."

As we continued our banter, I discovered that she and her husband live at the campground full-time year-round with their two sons. They homeschooled the boys until this year, when they wanted to finish high school at a nearby public school that their friends attended.

◀ ▲ ▼ ▶

Croatian National Forest | North Carolina

I wake up. Make coffee and oatmeal. Check KWJB, the radio station in East Texas, on the Internet stream, as I do daily. I especially check closely on Sunday mornings since several church broadcasts air, either live or delayed. If there is a problem, I hear about it from the faithful listeners who tune in for the inspirational messages. Americans are predominantly people of faith, regardless of the attempts to ridicule it from the darker side of life. There are many different faiths practiced, and they give hope and direction to live a better life.

Sunday Sounds with Johnny Stigler playing inspirational music runs on schedule from 5 a.m. to noon with services from Victory Church, Lakeside Church, and others. Still, the Caney Creek Cowboy Church sermon does not air on time, so I try signing in remotely to the station computer via GoToMyPC. With blurry eyes, I mistyped the password and made two more attempts; then, I was locked out. Then, as the blur in my eyes begins to fade, I use TeamViewer and get signed into the Mac computer at the studio. Digital demons combat my efforts, and I finally give up—no Cowboy Church sermon today.

Whenever there is a technical problem on Sunday mornings, I hear about it from numerous people who listen. Some people can't leave their house on Sunday mornings due to health reasons, but they still want to listen to a sermon, reflect, and get inspired.

So I head down to the beach on the Neuses River bank. It looks like a small ocean beach with white sand. Two dogs are running with their owners watching. A big black dog is running into the waves, biting at the foam on top of each wave, and barking. A happy doggie! I was going to leave today, but the forest is such a tranquil setting that I decided to stay one more night and use the day to catch up on my writing and reading.

Later in the day, I strike up a conversation with the camp hosts, Bridget and Ray Morgan.

Curious about their lifestyle, I ask about living off-grid.

"We've been living here coming up on two years," Ray says. "We moved down from Ohio. We bought the camper we live in, basically just to transition from Ohio down to here, hoping to move into a house, and ended up with a camp-hosting gig and just stayed here. That's the way it went."

"Before that, we lived on a sailboat for six years," Bridget says. "We raised our two children on the boat." "I was working at a big distributing company," Ray says. "And Bridget was managing a floor of a bank. It was hectic and a lot of hours. It was seventy-hour weeks regularly, with a relationship with the kids over a cell phone."

"And our children," Bridget adds, "were literally being raised by strangers, and we just had had enough. We bought the boat and found out that people were living this lifestyle off the grid and sailing around, which was appealing. We jumped ship and did it and never regretted it. I ended up getting a job at the local boat yard right next to where we kept our boat, and it was kinda nice 'cause I could drink my coffee, walk across the parking lot, go to work, and walk back home."

"Where did you all go on the boat?" I ask.

"We stayed local for the most part," Ray says. "We did end up trying to make a trip south to Wilmington, and we ended up with some muffler problems and had to turn around and come back."

"We had to work," Bridget explains, "so we stayed pretty local, but we sailed a lot." "So you wanted to get out of the rat race …." I say.

"Absolutely!" Bridget agrees.

"So, we took a chance," Ray continues, "and got rid of a lot of stuff that we didn't need. I kept a few of the sentimental things and stored them at Grandma's house. And then we ended up moving onto the boat. The peacefulness of it, I think, and the simplicity of it, was a great way to just kinda decompress, I think, and it was really good for the kids, too. We switched the kids into homeschooling, and I think it was a good decision."

"The kids were how old at that point?" I ask.

"Noel was five, and Matt was six," Bridgett says. "They were three and four when we bought the boat. They were known as Tom and Huck around our little town. They were very boyish." Bridget laughs. "Fishin' and crabbing, and they had a good time, a real good time. And they had a lot of freedom 'cause the little town was a real safe little community."

"Yeah, and it wasn't cell phones," Ray interjects. "It wasn't television, and it wasn't video games. It was international people, salty sailors, and strange types. And to be honest with you, many of those strange types are the ones that made the best of it, I think."

"Some of our best friends now," Bridget laughs.

"You know," Ray says, "people, when you first meet 'em, you think, oh my gosh, who is this person, or who is this couple, or whatever, you know, only to find out they are some of the greatest people in the world."

"And the little community we lived in," Bridget adds, "was such a tight-knit sailing community. And, even homeschooling the kids, they took French, art, drama, and sailing lessons.

They had so much exposure to different things that it was really neat."

"A lot of people helped," Ray says. "It was a great community."

"When they say it takes a village," Bridget agrees, "they're not kidding. And we had a village."

"Six years living on the boat," I say, "they got to see a lot of things they normally would not have gotten to see, and you did too."

In one sense, I'd been doing a version of what the Morgans were doing, so I could identify with them. However, I was continually moving and unsure if I could camp in one place like they are doing for an extended period. It would be fun for the first seventeen minutes; then it would be "Where's the Wi-Fi?" And, "Is that a bear or a large chipmunk over there?"

I admire the Morgans for making their dreams come true—a lifestyle choice to connect with the earth, be close to nature, and take time to reflect on it all. Living in the great outdoors, surrounded by nature, has to be freeing. Letting go of what man created to embrace what God created. They traded a concrete jungle with the sound of honking horns for the sound of birds chirping, rustling leaves, and nosy raccoons. And, of course, the occasional bear knocking over a trash can.

There are many valuable lessons to be learned from living off the grid, practicing selfsufficiency, and adopting sustainable living practices. You get good at being independent, responsible, and taking care of yourself. That is incredibly rewarding. Minimizing your personal environmental impact and living in harmony with nature is often discussed, but who can take the whole adventure like the Morgans? And by the way, everyone should learn how to build a campfire with wet wood. Ah, spoiler alert based on my experience: the wood is always wet.

Their campsite had pretty much all the comforts they wanted and new stories to share daily as a family sitting around the campfire or at the picnic table. A new story every time they stepped out of the camper door. And, far away from any human neighbors, they didn't have to worry about being judged for their questionable pajama choices. They could live by their own rules on their schedule. Be authentic. Be eccentric.

The whole experience with the Morgans was like a reality show I didn't audition for. And one I'll never forget.

Note to Self

People go off-grid for all kinds of reasons — some want to live cheap, others want to save the planet, and a few are just one HOA letter away from a full-blown Netflix documentary. I mean, nothing screams "peace and freedom" like flipping off your electric bill. Whether you're dodging debt, drama, or just Karen from the neighborhood watch, going off-grid is the adult version of running away from home… with solar panels. But it's not just about unplugging your toaster and calling it a movement — it's a whole lifestyle. It could be a cozy cabin in the woods, a tiny house, or a van parked so far out even your ex can't find you. The whole vibe is basically: "I don't need your rules, I've got enough canned beans to survive the next three pandemics. I'm good."

16

DEAD DOG SALOON

*If there are no dogs in Heaven, then when
I die, I want to go where they went.*

WILL ROGERS

AFTER AN UNEXPECTED FERRY RIDE for Argo and me, *et voila*, we end up on Myrtle Beach to camp near the water's edge. Myrtle Beach, the land of sandy shores, kitschy souvenir shops, and enough sunscreen to protect a small army from a sunburn apocalypse. After sleeping to the sounds of the ocean, I woke hungry for oatmeal. But it wasn't to be. For the second morning in a row, hitting the thirty-second button on the microwave caused all power to go kaput.

Hungry and increasingly annoyed, I hopped into the cab and sped to the nearest RV repair center, where the place was buzzing with RVs being all prettied up for the summer season. I approached the service desk with all the confidence of someone about to tame a wild electrical beast. I was up to this task, I just knew it. My growling stomach insisted it be so.

The RV repair center had no time for me, but the nice guy at the desk made a call to their other service center. Could they work me in? Nope. Not a chance. I stood there, pondering my next move, feeling about as useful as a screen door on a submarine.

As I walked out the door, the service-counter guy hollered for me to come back. As it turned out, the other center could squeeze me in if I could beeline it there right away. Off I went to the 'crosstown center, and after four hours and three hundred bucks, they discovered the problem: me. It turns out that when you plug many, many small, even insignificant things into the same outlet, you can throw your vehicle's power command center into something called "safety mode," which shuts down the whole works. Who knew?

Myrtle Beach, South Carolina

The night brings darkness to a bright, beautiful, beach-worthy Saturday. Wind blows.

Rain falls. And I sleep well to the rhythm of the falling rain.

I wake on Sunday morning to a freezing Argo. Hesitating—but bravely and quickly, I might add—I slide the bed coverings off and arch my body up to reach the heater controller. Say "buh-bye" to the morning chill as my little propane furnace begins blasting it away—a now-cozy rainy Sunday morning.

What does any sane person do on a cold, rainy Sunday morning? I decided to stay put, sipping coffee in bed, reading, snacking on cheese, crackers, and leftovers, and watching an old movie on DVD. That's what you do on a day like this. Just Argo and I exercising our right to be lazy bums.

After four o'clock and having depleted my leftovers, I am beset by the gnawing hunger. I head out to locate a proper meal. Argo and I drive two miles south on Highway 17 to the parade of local dives and fresh-catch restaurants on the marsh bank of Murrells Inlet, South Carolina. Places regale us with names like Drunken Jack's Restaurant & Lounge, Wicked Tuna, Crooked Floor Tavern, Creek Ratz, Lazy Gator, Big Beaver Bar, Marshview, and Flo's Place.

The Dead Dog Saloon hooks me. It's an easy decision: according to the sign out front, live music by a local band starts in thirty minutes.

I see you reading this while drinking coffee with your pinky finger slightly tilted upward off your ceramic mug handle, nose turned uppity at these nonconformist culinary establishment names. You have the impression that the Dead Dog Saloon and the others are low-class, scruffy, ramshackle, and shabby places. But you, my friend, are wrong. These are upscale, scruffy, worn, shabby, classy places with some yummy fish newly sprung from the waters of the Atlantic just a short boat ride down Murrell's Inlet.

Take Dead Dog Saloon, for instance. It's *not* named after the disposition of the owner. It's named after its memorial walls, which commemorate customers' puppies who have departed— the titular dead dogs. Dead dogs are remembered, revered, and esteemed by customers who have brought in framed photos of their dogs to memorialize them on the restaurant wall.

As I look at all the photos of smiling pups, who could have seen this coming? Reggie. I have flashbacks of my little Reggie, my sweet departed little pup. My Reggie is racing back into my mind, panting, happy to see me, with unconditional, sloppy wet love licks.

Yes, I will return one day with Reggie's photo in hand and tack that photo on the wall to honor my best furry-faced friend.

Ah, the Dead Dog Saloon, a legendary establishment nestled along the shores of Murrells Inlet in South Carolina. This iconic watering hole has a history as colorful as its name, steeped in tales of bootleggers, pirates, and rugged sea captains.

Legend has it that the Dead Dog Saloon earned its name from a particularly rowdy night back in the days of Prohibition when a group of thirsty patrons stumbled upon a stray puppy that had met an unfortunate end. In a fit of inebriated creativity (or maybe just plain insanity), they immortalized the poor pup by naming their favorite haunt after it. Thus, the Dead Dog Saloon was born.

Over the years, the saloon has become more than just a place to grab a cold drink and swap sea-faring stories. It's a cultural institution, a gathering spot for locals and tourists alike, where live music fills the air and the seafood is as fresh as the salty breeze blowing in from the inlet.

The Dead Dog Saloon welcomes all with open arms and maybe a few ghostly barks. So I pull up a chair, raise a glass to remember my long-gone Reggie, and prepare myself for a night of revelry at this one-of-a-kind joint.

Still in Myrtle Beach, South Carolina

For the past few days on my journey to discover America, one story at a time, I have stayed in and around Myrtle Beach for two critical reasons. First, it's on a beach. And second, the weather is supposed to be sunny every day. Done and done.

Well, the weather is reasonably good, albeit rainy. I am about ready to move down the road toward the south; then, I make the mistake of watching a TV weathercast. The weathercaster is excited, frothing at the mouth, talking about the big storm that could wipe out civilization on the East Coast. Sure nuff, using the latest in TV weather forecast computer modeling, the TV guy demonstrates with stunningly effervescent 10D color graphics that the end is surely near, and, after a twelve-and-a-half-minute commercial break, he continues in more vivid, scare-your-pants-right-off detail.

I can see from the radar that the storm is worse to the south, in the direction I would be heading, and to the left, which is west, and even worse to the north. So, what I astutely deduce amid the stay-tuned TV hype and thumbing of my iPhone is a little pocket of a not-so-bad storm in Myrtle Beach, right where I am parked.

With the wind blowing and raining outside, I stay inside with time on my hands. You know what happens when I have time on my hands? Yep, I start thinking. It's always a dangerous thing.

I started asking the "why" questions. For example, why would anyone decide to name their beach Myrtle? If you owned a beach, would you call it Myrtle? Would it even be in your top ten? It would only make my top *hundred* if my wife were named Myrtle and merited the appellation.

It turns out that "Myrtle" wasn't the first choice of earlier settlers. One of the first suggestions was Long Bay, but a hurricane turned it into Short Bay, and that name didn't carry quite the same punch.

One of the local families came up with an apt name: Withers Town. Go figure. Withers Town would not have been in my top ten either, but the local people loved it. It turns out they were all named Withers. For the locals, the Withers name had a familiar ring, and it was effortless to remember.

As time marched on, the Withers withered or moved away (at one time, eighteen Withers had been drowned in a house during a storm, causing the others to abandon the coastline after that). The time came when the remaining non-Withers who lived in Withers decided they needed a new name for this beautiful beach town that wasn't nearly as limp as its name.

Local legend has it that the locals were discussing new names while partaking of ninetyproof home-brew libations around a campfire on the beach. There was conflict over each of their favorite titles, and they were on the edge of giving up for the night when a whole new line of thought was presented from an unlikely participant.

Billy Bobby June Augustus (his actual name) had yet to contribute much to that point. When he did speak, it was apparent he was a few drinks over his limit. Slurred out with finger waving in a different rhythm to his face, he said, "Hey, wurn't dar people air' fore us ... dem dang engines? What wuz dey culled dem selves?"

Now, that was a particularly long speech for Billy Bobby June Augustus, and at the end of it, he did a wobbly face plant into the sand right next to it. Fortunately, he *just* missed the fire.

Okay, all kidding aside, after a bit of research, I found out Myrtle Beach got its name from a contest held about 1900 by the developers who owned much of the land. Mrs. F.E. Burroughs suggested **"Myrtle Beach"** because of the many wax myrtles (also called southern wax myrtle or bayberry) growing wild along the coast. The name stuck.

Note to Self

The Dead Dog Saloon was not as dark as it sounds. It's not a bar where dogs go to cash in their chips. It's a super sweet tribute to all the good boys and girls who've climbed the Stairway to Heaven. Tons of photos of pups in their prime, just chillin', looking like they're one belly rub away from running for president.

Now, it was a happy place, but man, also kind of a gut punch. Like, the kind of place where you're smiling one second, then next thing you know, you're trying not to ugly cry into your nachos. Because yeah, it reminded me of my old doggies, back when there were no leash laws. The real MVPs of my childhood and beyond. First, there was Reggie. A total mixed mutt, but the good kind—like, the dog version of a classic rock station. A little of everything, and all of it awesome. Then came Dante, who had the attitude of a biker but the heart of a therapy dog. And Spotty… oh man, Spotty was basically my furry therapist with a tail. Loyal, loud, and always knew when I needed him most, usually around dinner time.

They were more than dogs; they were family. And even though they're gone, walking through that saloon was like catching up with them one more time. Just a bunch of legends, frozen in their best moments. Pretty sure if dogs could text, they'd have group-chatted me from heaven with a "We miss you, ya big sap" followed by an obnoxious string of emojis.

17

Southern Crab Soup

First, we eat. Then we do everything else.

M . F . K . F I S H E R

IT'S ONE OF THOSE MORNINGS. I wake from a profoundly deep sleep, having no idea where I am or what day it is.

It's a case of geographical amnesia, and as I stumble around in search of clues like a detective in a slapstick noir film, I can't help but marvel at the absurdity of it all. I rise in a groggy state, and for the life of me, I can't fathom where in this vast American expanse I've washed up.

I must have checked off each sleep stage quickly, diving into Stage 4 REM sleep for longer than usual. Slowly, like the lifting of a heavy fog, my mind begins to stir. Looking out the window, it's the reality beyond the dream. I am deep in a forest.

I recall that evening drive down Highway 17, a highway flanked by towering sentinels of the woods, their branches reaching out like skeletal arms. In the cloak of night, I saw a sign that read "National Forest campsite." So, like an intrepid explorer, I turned my trusty Argo down a narrow trail, the headlights piercing the darkness like a lighthouse in a storm. With a longhandled flashlight, its beam piercing the black night like a spear, I sought out a suitable spot, parked Argo, and with the exhaustion of a weary traveler, I quickly surrendered to the night.

It all comes back to me now; I'm in the deep embrace of the Francis Marion and Sumter National Forest.

The Francis Marion and Sumter National Forest is a place on Earth where Mother Nature went all out, decorating it with more trees than you can shake a stick at, so to speak. But it's not just about the greenery; I hear the birds chirping like they're auditioning for a starring role on Broadway. So, in the heart of the Francis Marion and Sumter National Forest, it's a wild world where trees rule, vines are the acrobats, and the critters throw a party. The only unwelcome guests are the blood-sucking mosquitoes.

With the enigma of my whereabouts unraveled, hunger sets in. This hunger won't be curable by the few cans of edible items I have remaining in the Argo's cupboard. Typically, I wouldn't flinch at the prospect of cracking open a can of whatever, regardless of the expiration date. But the cupboard doesn't give me any real choices, so a creeping sense of unease began taking root in the depths of my forest-surrounded location.

With my mental fog dissipating like morning mist, the mission at hand is crystal clear:

find food. *Now*. In short, I fire up Argo to head out on the hunt. A more manly man might have foraged for berries, roots, or squirrels, but the city-dwelling side of my brain prompts me to drive until a restaurant appears, sit down, and order. Besides, if I must keep moving, Charleston isn't too far away.

Sure enough, I don't have to wait too long. A restaurant of sorts squats in the forest on the side of the road. A nailed-together wood shamble with a screen door bearing a sign that reads, "Open." My gut pipes up with a growl: *Go for it.*

The Seewee café, I learn it's called. I assume they misspelled "sea" and "weed," but I am wrong. The place was named after a Native American tribe. The structure is an old general store with a rickety plank floor, turned into a diner. It's not just a diner; it's a Southern diner with a capital "S."

The unassuming, well-handled, smudged menu at Seewee lists an array of offerings, from fried pickles to She Crab soup with sherry. When the servers do the seating and order-placing routine, there is no standard Southern grits charm. No, this is more of an order, eat, and get the hell out kind of place. It is all about the food here at the Seewee Cafe.

I'm told that this unassuming eatery, nestled in the heart of the Lowcountry along South Carolina's coast, has become a legend. It's the kind of place where you walk in, and the aroma of Southern comfort food wraps around you like a warm hug from a long-lost friend. You'll hear the sizzle of the grill and the friendly banter of locals, making you feel like you've stumbled upon a hidden gem.

Now, when it comes to the menu, The Seewee Cafe doesn't mess around. They've got all the southern classics cooked up with passion. Whether it's the crispy fried catfish that practically melts in your mouth or the shrimp and grits that'll make you question every other version you've ever had, this place gets its cuisine *right*.

My lunch of fresh-caught something was delicious. Served with collard greens, the type of coleslaw I like, and a basket full of heavenly hushpuppies—crispy on the outside and fluffy on the inside—my meal thoroughly satisfied.

Before leaving the place, I picked up a pamphlet, learning that the national forest is named after the Revolutionary War hero Francis Marion, known to the British as the Swamp Fox. Marion used irregular methods of warfare against the British, as he and his troop of men attacked from the swamps, did their damage, and then faded back into the swamps, where the British could not track them or discover their hideouts. He's considered one of the fathers of guerrilla warfare and is credited with the lineage of the United States Army Special Forces, the Green Berets. Walt Disney Productions had a television mini-series called *The Swamp Fox* from 1959 to 1961, starring Leslie Nielsen. Mel Gibson's character in *The Patriot* was based on Marion. He's a man of legend in the South if little known elsewhere.

With the mysteries of the night behind me and a belly well-fed on the delights of Southern cooking, I stand ready to embark on the next leg of my adventure. Ahead of me is Charleston, South Carolina, with its charm and history waiting to be explored. Beyond that, Savannah, Georgia, promises its unique treasures. The road stretches before me like an old friend, with more places to see and taste.

Florida beaches are some of my favorite places. Water and boats have captured my imagination since my earliest memory, and standing at the ocean's edge, next to a winding river, or on the banks of a lake, I feel a connection to the water. Just looking out over the water brings me a sense of deep-seated calm.

That may be why the first thing I bought with my hard-earned money—mowed lawns, a paper route, and washing dishes at the Dairy Queen—was a yellow canoe. My mother always said my savings, combined with what I made at the radio and television station, were "burning a hole in my pocket." Maybe so. But the moment I saw that canoe gleaming in the sporting goods store on Valley Mills Drive in Waco, I knew I had to have it.

Old Yeller, as I named her, carried my friends and me on countless adventures across Lake Waco and the Brazos River. The Brazos, that great Texas river, begins humbly in the high plains of New Mexico and meanders its way through the heart of Texas before spilling into the Gulf. Dams along its length, including the one at Lake Whitney, tame its floods, most of the time.

One summer afternoon, Clark Robertson and I set out on the Brazos, paddling upstream under a wide, sunlit sky. It was easy going, the water calm and slow-moving. When dusk crept in from the east, we turned back, figuring we had plenty of time to get home for dinner.

That's when we heard it.

A deep, rolling thunder that wasn't thunder. The water at the banks swelled, lifting Old Yeller beneath us. Then we saw it—

charging toward us around the bend, a wall of roiling, frothing water.

"They've opened the dam at Whitney!" Clark yelled.

"Keep her straight!" I hollered back. If we got turned sideways, we'd be flipped like a pancake.

The wave caught us, lifted us high, and sent us hurtling forward like two surfers in a yellow torpedo. We dug in our paddles, straining to stay upright as the river took over. Our launch point flashed past.

"We gotta get to the bank!" Clark shouted.

"There!" I pointed to a break in the brush. We paddled hard, but the current had its plans. The opening rushed past in a blur. We tried again. And again. The river swatted us away each time, laughing in the way only rivers can.

Darkness fell. The floodwaters settled at their new height, no longer raging but still swift.

Finally, we found a low-hanging branch and seized it, pulling ourselves and Old Yeller to shore.

We stumbled out, soaked and shaking, and collapsed onto the muddy bank, breathing hard.

For a long moment, we just sat there, listening to the river's deep murmur. We knew we'd been lucky. Another few miles, another missed branch, and we might have been nothing more than a couple of names in the newspaper, lost to the Brazos.

Clark broke the silence. "My mother is going to kill me."

"We gotta find a phone."

This was before cell phones, when payphones cost a quarter and mercy was up to the store clerk. We hiked barefoot through the brush, dodging whatever slithered in the dark, and finally reached a 7-Eleven. Neither of us had a dime, but the clerk took pity and fronted us a call.

Clark was right—his mother wanted to kill him. So did mine. Funny thing about parents: after the relief of knowing their kid survived, they want to strangle them for making them worry.

Lately, I've been talking with my friend Craig Clemmer about another adventure—sailing to Cuba. He's in Dallas, but we swap sailing stories like old sea dogs. A Florida sailing club has permission to enter Havana's Marina Hemingway, a rare diplomatic gesture from the Cuban government.

It's a big deal.

And the more I think about it, the more I feel that same pull I felt years ago in the sporting goods store, staring at that yellow canoe. Some things, once seen, cannot be unseen.

Some journeys, once imagined, must be taken.

Florida awaits.

NOTE TO SELF

You know, thinking back on the best part about being a kid—*besides* the dogs and all the cereal bowls with added extra sugar—was the big adventures. And by "adventures," I mean the completely insane stuff I did with my friends. They only sound cute in hindsight because we survived. Like my canoe ride down the Brazos River.

Those moments—those "What was I thinking adventures- are where you meet yourself. You confront the limits of life, and somehow, despite the odds and terrible canoe steering, you come out the other side with a story.

And maybe a scar or two. And probably the fresh revelation, *Ohhh, so this is why Mom and Dad had rules.*

18

GATOR RIVERS

Heaven is under our feet as well as over our heads.

HENRY DAVID THOREAU

ARGO AND I DRIFTED INTO Savannah, settling near Thunderbolt Marina on the city's edge.

That marina—perched along the Wilmington River like a patient old dog—felt like an old friend. I'd docked my boat, *Memory Maker*, there more than once on my East Coast jaunts, lured back each time by a simple ritual: every morning, the dockmaster delivered a dozen fresh donuts to your boat. A sweet little bribe that kept boaters coming back.

With our spot secured, I turned Argo toward the heart of Savannah. Now, Savannah, well —she's got a way of clinging to you, like honey on a warm biscuit. You can put miles between yourself and those moss-draped oaks, but she lingers. That city gets in your bones. You don't just visit Savannah; you let her work on you. And I was ready to be worked on once again.

Savannah is stately, genteel, and just a little haunted. The kind of town where history and mystery hold hands. The fountains stand tall, statues watch like silent sentries, and Spanish moss hangs from the trees like the veil of a widow with stories she's not ready to tell. You walk her squares and feel the past pressing in—saints and specters, gamblers and soldiers, all mingling in the sticky Southern air.

Charleston is just a stone's throw across the river, but Savannah has its own rhythm, its own ghosts, and I let them lead me. Strolling through the historic district, I let the city pull me into its stories—some etched in bronze plaques, some whispered through the leaves. I found myself at the Wilkes House, a place of quiet fame. It's been feeding folks since 1943, when Sema Wilkes turned an old boarding house into a lunch-only restaurant that still draws crowds like bees to molasses. I took that as a challenge and headed straight there.

The line snaked down West Jones Street, up to a red-brick townhouse with wrought-iron railings and a modest sign that simply read, "The Wilkes House." Inside, the air was thick with the scent of collard greens, cornbread, and fried okra—Southern cooking just like my mother's. A matronly woman in a faded blue dress and apron guided me to a long wooden table, already filled with strangers who felt like family within minutes. I took my seat, the same one, I was told, where President Obama once dined.

Across the table sat a man who looked like he'd seen his share of stories. Muscular, with graying charcoal hair and a quiet authority, his polo bore the words: "Unforgettable Bakery and Café—Healthy Cooking with Southern Sweetness." He introduced himself, but I didn't quite catch the name. He was surrounded by family, nodding and grinning at the regulars who stopped to greet him. The food kept coming—mashed potatoes, cucumbers, a pitcher of sweet tea—and before I knew it, we'd eaten our way to the sweet potato pie.

As we finished up, he came over to me. Shook my hand. "Larry Gator Rivers," he said. The name clicked the second time around. You don't forget a name like Gator. And you sure don't forget Gator Rivers.

A legend in Savannah, Gator made his name with the Harlem Globetrotters—a team that spun magic on the court, blending basketball wizardry with a showmanship that transcended the game. Born in the streets of Chicago during segregation, the Globetrotters played not just for points, but for something bigger—breaking down barriers, proving that talent and heart could bring people together when the world wanted to keep them apart.

Gator had set his sights on that team at just seven years old. And like any good Southern story, his was one of grit, talent, and an unstoppable dream.

Gator and I made an instant connection. Since our meeting, I've shared his story countless times. Gator inspired me, as he has so many others over the years.

After lunch, Gator invited me to his office, where he helps young people prepare for life. The building is filled with wood, construction items, and the like, with Gator's office towards the back. He leans back in a swivel desk chair to talk with me, surrounded by papers, books, nicknacks, and memorabilia from his world tours with the Harlem Globetrotters.

"I saw the Globetrotters in a movie my mom took me to when I was seven years old," he told me. She was nineteen."

"Wait a minute," I interrupted. "Your mom was nineteen, and you were seven? That means your mom was twelve when she had you … when you were born."

"Yes, my mom was twelve when I was born."

"And you were her only child?"

"Yes, my mom and I grew up like brothers and sisters around Crawford Square. Crawford Square was the square that we played in; during Jim Crow, it was the only park that blacks were allowed to congregate in downtown Savannah."

"Is that when the fire got lit?"

"Yes. It changed my life. I saw something I felt I could do, and I thought I would like to do it.

Gator Rivers's story of how he set the goal of becoming a Harlem Globetrotter at the age of seven, worked every day towards that goal with fire in his belly, and then achieved success is inspiring. Equally inspiring is that upon retirement from all the world tours and excitement of being part of the Globetrotters, Gator returned to live in the community where he grew up in Savannah, devoting his time to helping young kids in his old neighborhood dream big and make something of their lives.

"What's the difference between when you grew up here and now?" I asked him.

"When I was growing up, our attitude was, we're gonna show you—we're gonna show you what we got, man. Now, the kids say, 'You show me what you got … what you gonna do for me,' and that's a different attitude. That's hard to work with."

His comments, a reflection of our culture's ever-shifting tides, echoed the sentiments of the new generation. The world is changing, constantly changing, and with it, the aspirations and ideals of those who will shape its future.

The next morning, Larry Gator Rivers invited me to meet him at his favorite morning spot, owned by a friend of his, the Unforgettable Bakery. The coffee, the baked goods, and the place lived up to its name. And so was my morning conversation with Gator Rivers. Gator had a way of helping things and people live up to their name.

Savannah had once again cast her spell. And as Argo and I walked back through her misty streets, I knew I'd be back. You don't shake off a city like this. Not when she's got hold of you.

Note to Self

I will never forget what Gator Rivers' story means to me. The guy wasn't just a Harlem Globetrotter—he was a walking legend, a basketball superstar, still inspiring everyone around him. A reminder that magic is real and dreams do come true. He set his sights on that dream of his when he was seven. Gator was eyeing a jersey, seeing his future, and saying, "That's gonna be me." And it was. His journey was everything a Southern tale should be: grit, grind, and a dream that refused to stay quiet. That kind of focus, that kind of heart—it's rare.

I want to be like Gator: smile big, move fast, and never forget that greatness isn't just about winning—it's also about why you play.

19

Mijammi

Miami is a melting pot in which none of the stones melt. They rattle around.

TOM WOLFE

SO THERE I AM, CRUISING south on Highway 1, leaving Georgia, passing the big, bold sign that screams, "Welcome to Florida—The Sunshine State," when I realize I simply can't let the Kodak moment slip away. I pull an expert U-turn on par with that of a seasoned getaway driver in a 1970s heist flick, ease up next to the sign, and snap the pic. Florida—it's a cultural gumbo, a mishmash of people and places you won't find anywhere else on this planet. With more flavors than a bag of Skittles, it dances to the beat of its sweltering drum.

As I continue my journey southward, I spot not one but two more of the prehistoric reptilian giants native to this wild land. They've figured out that the canals along the road are prime real estate for gator-watching and lurk there, basking in the Florida sun, eyeing up the smorgasbord of brightly dressed tourists passing by. It's like a real-life version of *Jurassic Park,* but with sunburned tourists instead of dinosaurs. Florida is already amazing me, and I've only just crossed the state line.

◄ ▲ ▼ ►

I realize, as plentiful signs and scenes pass by, that had I opted for the more trodden I-95 thoroughfare, I would be missing so many sights. Mom-and-pop motor lodges scattered along my path harken back to the era of family road trips following World War II, when soldiers returned home and the baby boom began. These war men ignited a passion for exploration, manifested in automobiles, steering families toward boundless horizons on family vacations to explore the country they risk their lives to save in fiery battles on foreign soil. "See the U.S.A. in your Chevrolet" wasn't just an ad slogan; it was a challenge.

Argo and I make our way to Fort Lauderdale, where their annual boat show is underway.

It's a show I've attended many times over the years, as I kept my boat at a marina nearby. Rowboats to some of the largest luxury yachts in the world are featured, a candy store for those who yearn for hardy adventures on the high seas. Had I not sold my own craft years prior, I'd still be high-adventuring out there, too.

I gain entry to the show and happen to run into some old friends from past boating trips, including Bob Stella. Soon after acquiring my boat, *Memory Maker,* I captained it on several trips to the Bahamas that Bob had organized, those early jaunts giving me the confidence to make crossings from Fort Lauderdale to Bimini and on eastward on my own. If you're familiar with the area, you know that to get there, you must sail through the infamous Bermuda Triangle, the enigmatic stretch of sea that holds a mystique as thick as the salty air that hangs above its waters. It beckons with tales of vessels that ventured forth but never returned, swallowed whole by the depths that shimmer under the Caribbean sun. I didn't want to be one such boat! Formed by the points of Miami, Bermuda, and Puerto Rico, stories abound in science and folklore of ships and aircraft vanishing without a trace have left behind questions that echo in the calls of distant gulls. Theories swirl like the currents—magnetic anomalies, rogue waves, even tales of extraterrestrial intervention. Do we know what happened to each fated ship? We don't.

And maybe that's part of the allure. The sea, in all its vast and mercurial beauty, has never owed us answers. It only offers the adventure—one that calls some of us back, time and again, no matter the risk.

Reaching Miami, I feel as though Argo's wheels are rolling into a sun-kissed vacation postcard. The sun shines overhead through a crystal blue sky, highlighting a tapestry of brightcolored buildings and signs that compete with each other like boys on a sandlot of old. Florida beaches, especially Miami's South Beach, are some of the most inviting in the world. The beachgoers move in a rhythm only they can discern, a dance of bronzed-skinned, nearly naked bodies devoted to the art of doing absolutely nothing. We freshly arriving tourists do stand out, don't we, with our crimson-splotched lily-white hides, vivid evidence of the sun's zeal and its unforgiving embrace.

Not far from South Beach, cruise ships, the floating steel titans of exploration, await by the dock to take thousands of new holiday wanderers out across the boundless sea and back again, now sun-kissed and more laden with trinkets. Those colossal ships depart weekly via the busiest cruise port in the world, second only to New York as a central stop in the United States for international globetrotters.

Miami hums with a half-million souls, a crossroads where voices from every corner of the world weave together in an unbroken symphony. It's a city of contrasts—bikinis by day, business suits by necessity, and a banking empire nestled between sand and surf. They call it the "Capital of Latin America" for good reason; the Cuban and South American influences are evident in the food and music. The very air itself.

But Miami's history isn't all sun-drenched glamor. The Wise Guys knew a good racket when they saw one, and Florida—ripe for deals both real and imagined—welcomed them in the Roaring Twenties. Charlie Wall, Joe Silesi, Meyer Lansky—their names still linger like cigar smoke in the alleyways they once ruled. The Five Families of New York operated here too, whispers of their meetings folding into the city's humid nights.

I'm reminded of this because of the radio. Two local hosts chat about a body found floating in Biscayne Bay.

"What, only one this weekend?" one of them cracks, laughing.

Dark humor, maybe. Or just reality. The mob mystique still clings to Miami, as it does to Vegas, to Jersey, to the island I'll soon be sailing toward—Cuba. Ninety-seven miles south of Key West, a place once tangled in the same web of power, money, and men who thought themselves untouchable.

Still, I love this place. The ocean. The people. The feeling that the whole city is a front porch facing the sea. A local tells me Miami is just a small town with a big reputation, a mirage built by land developers and sun-seekers desperate to escape northern winters. Maybe he's right. But when the breeze rustles the palm trees—those hurricane-tested poets of the shoreline—you can't help but believe they're whispering something worth hearing.

Miami's Little Havana

I steer Argo through the rhythmic heart of Miami, turning onto 8th Street—Calle Ocho, the pulsing artery of Little Havana. On a street corner, in front of a modest shop called Ranger Seat Covers—Tapiceria de Autos—a small congregation gathers. Eight people, holding signs and Cuban flags, their presence unwavering. Week after week, year after year, they return, an unbreakable signal fire for a homeland lost but never forgotten. Each face carries a story, a past stitched together with memories of a place left behind.

From that corner, the air thrums with Cuban rhythms, the beats sharp and insistent, an echo of voices that refuse to be silenced. A man, armed with a megaphone, pours his spirit into a metallic, tinny invocation of freedom—a plea to break the chains that still bind a nation across the sea. Near him, a woman with silver-threaded hair, her years written in the lines of her face, holds a sign with a young girl's photo pasted above a single word: FREEDOM.

She wears all white. It is not just a choice of clothing—it is a declaration. The *Damas de Blanco*, the Ladies in White, stand in defiant remembrance of Cuba's *Black Spring* of 2003, when seventy-five journalists, librarians, and human rights activists were arrested and sentenced —some for up to twenty-eight years. Their crime? Seeking truth unvarnished, a life unshackled, hearts beating in time with the idea that change is worth the cost.

A banner flutters on the bushes next to the upholstery shop: TODOS MARCHAMOS. A man in a black newsboy cap and white linen shirt sits on a metal chair, holding a sign: EL SILENCIO NOS HACE. Beside him, a dark-skinned Cuban man grips a long white pole, the Cuban flag unfurling above him. A woman in jeans and black boots stands nearby, her sign stark in its demand: LIBERTAD A LOS PRESOS POLÍTICOS. Others hold hand-painted messages:

HUMAN RIGHTS FOR CUBA. CUBANS ARE HUMAN TOO. SIN UNIDAD, NO HABRÁ LIBERTAD.

In their voices, their faces, their signs, I see not just a plea but a promise—that the fire of liberty will not be snuffed out, that hope will not be buried beneath the waves, and that the human heart will always reach toward a brighter dawn.

Calle Ocho is the epicenter of Miami's half-million-strong Cuban American population. Across the street from the protest, Versailles Restaurant stands, its green-and-white facade legendary, its claim bold: *The World's Most Famous Cuban Restaurant.* Since 1971, its walls have absorbed decades of conversations—whispers of exile, shouts of celebration, the unshakable pulse of a community unwilling to forget.

I park Argo around the corner and step into the sunlit buzz of waiting patrons—twentyfive, maybe thirty people, their names in a queue, their stomachs attuned to the promise of what's to come.

While I wait, I drift over to the ventanita, the small walk-up window, and order a café con leche with two shots of espresso. When the girl hands me the cup, warm and weighty, it feels like holding Cuba itself—a blend of energy, memory, and resilience in a single sip.

The people around me are dressed in the effortless comfort of Miami: linen shirts, floral dresses that speak of tropical dreams, sandals tapping lightly against the pavement. I glance down at myself—khaki cargo shorts, a solid yellow Tommy Bahama shirt hanging loose over a verdant t-shirt, my sockless feet settled into shoreline shoes. I might blend in. Or maybe I don't.

Either way, I don't care.

Inside, Versailles hums with life. The chandeliers glint off mirrored walls, reflecting tables filled with steaming plates of ropa vieja, lechón asado, and yuca con mojo. I take a seat and strike up a conversation with the waiter, a friendly man with a Cuban accent thick as molasses and a smile that makes a traveler like me feel at home.

I ordered Churrasco Versailles—a skirt steak grilled to perfection, served with moros rice, sweet plantains, and a chimichurri sauce of finely chopped parsley, garlic, and chili flakes. It arrives, an edible masterpiece. The only thing missing is someone to share it with. But I don't dwell on that. Instead, I raise a bottle of Cerveza Hatuey, toasting to the Cuban spirit—and, in a way, to Hemingway, who kept a supply of Hatuey on his boat *Pilar* and wove it into his novels.

A beer fit for revolutionaries and writers alike.

When the waiter returns, I give in to temptation. Tres leches, the ultimate indulgence. As he sets the plate before me, he reads me like an open book.

"A Cuban espresso to go with it?" he asks.

I grin. "Why not?"

The espresso arrives, dark as night, bold as the voices outside. I take a sip, then lean forward, curious about my next journey.

"Hey, maybe you can give me some pointers about Cuba," I say. "I'm sailing there soon—"

His face shifts. The warmth drains away. "Oh," he interrupts, his voice clipped, his shoulders stiff. "Sorry. Can't help you."

I start to explain, but he cuts me off with a sharp shrug, turning on his heel. He never comes back. Someone else drops the check at my table, a silent closing note to a conversation that never began.

Later, I learn why. Many Cuban Americans in Miami won't support tourism to Cuba— not while the same regime that drove them into exile still holds power. To them, spending money there is propping up the system they want to see crumble. To them, the embargo isn't just a policy—it's the principle. It's tough love.

I sit with that thought as I polish off my espresso, the bitterness lingering. This exchange —this cold shoulder—isn't just about me. It's history, pain, defiance. It's a reminder that Cuba isn't just an island on a map. It's a story still being written, and every encounter—warm or cold —is another sentence in its unfolding narrative.

I'll feel the cold shoulder again soon, but for different reasons. And I'll be reminded that in places like Little Havana, even silence speaks volumes.

Note to Self

Little Havana didn't just serve up the strongest espresso this side of the equator; it served up a life lesson. I finally get why so many Cuban Americans in Miami won't support tourism to Cuba. It's about principle. You don't feed the hand that forced you to flee, and you don't vacation where your family lost their voice. For them, the embargo isn't some dusty relic—it's tough love with a side of justice. And every dollar kept out of Havana is one more way of saying, not until the house is clean.

I sat with that truth while the *cafecito* bitterness lingered on my tongue—and honestly, that bitterness felt earned. The cold shoulder I got from the waiter wasn't rude. It was a living, breathing reminder that history doesn't die. But that's the thing about places like Little Havana—even the quiet has something to say. So next time I feel iced out, I'll remember this: not all walls are built from bricks. Some are built from memory. And respect means recognizing the difference.

20

NINETY-SEVEN MILES SOUTH

The world breaks every one, and afterward, many are strong at the broken places.

ERNEST HEMINGWAY, *A FAREWELL TO ARMS*

MOST OF MY ADVENTURES AT sea—or on a lake or river—have seldom matched the wild, heart-pounding ride of that Brazos River flood, a surf-ride escapade I once shared with my friend Clark. My life on the water is a tapestry of rendezvous: mornings of serene calm in a Bahamian cove with coffee in hand, contrasted by moments when giant waves rise from the deep, crashing over my boat's bow, drenching me in their ferocity.

Some storms make my fifty-four-foot vessel dance like a puppet on an angry sea—a mere cork amid the tempest. Buzzy Trent was right when he said, "Waves are not measured in feet or inches; they are measured in increments of fear." In those maelstroms, I switch to an intuitive state, partnering with the wind and waves for survival. Yet, when the chaos subsides, my mind replays each harrowing moment like a film reel—a dark theater where every frame is dissected in the quiet aftermath. It is in these crucibles of nature that a sailor's true measure is revealed.

Throughout my life, I have navigated both under sail and engine along the coasts of the United States—from hidden coves to busy harbors. I've ventured among the islands: the Bahamas in the Atlantic, Hawaii in the Pacific, and even parts of Europe, where old-world lands whisper their secrets. Asia, too, beckoned, though mostly from a cruise ship's deck rather than amid the clamor of sails and halyards. In truth, my journey has been a symphony of horizons, a constant pursuit of the unknown.

I have always loved the salty tang of the sea air and the thrill of adventure, and I relish sharing and hearing tales of life on the water. On every dock around the world, I meet people with stories—like the older gentleman at a Charleston marina who once lamented, "I had nothing to tell my grandkids until I bought a boat and set sail." He explained that every day out on the water unveiled a new story, a daily renewal of life's wonders.

My sailing adventure to Cuba began in the most unexpected place—a gym in Dallas. My friend Craig Clemmer and I often crossed paths there, not only for exercise but for connection beyond the iron and sweat. One afternoon, after a workout, I asked him, "So, how are those sailing lessons in Florida coming along?"

"You inspired me with your tales," Craig replied, his eyes alight with enthusiasm.

"Captain Vinny is patient, showing me the ropes."

I teased him, "Just remember, those 'ropes' are called 'lines' on a boat. Out there on the deep blue, you see life for what it is—raw and honest. I still dream of sailing to Cuba one day."

As fate would have it, Craig mentioned that Captain Vinny knew a fellow sailor who'd secured the proper permissions from both our government and Cuba's for a small group trip to Cuba. "Count me in!" I declared, recalling past attempts thwarted by political winds and fickle seas. I envisioned a raw Hemingway freedom—sailing to a Cuba of old cars, colonial streets, and Cuba Libres savored at the 1930s Hotel Nacional, where shadows of mob bosses and celebrities linger.

As we swapped stories between sets, our conversation naturally veered toward destinations painted in salt and sky. Sailing from Key West to Cuba had always been a siren call. Since 1960, a human rights policy and economic embargo had kept Americans at bay—except, perhaps, during the Ernest Hemingway International Bill Fishing Tournament. I once nearly sailed to Cuba for that tournament, but fate and foul weather intervened. Still, with Craig's news of an organized armada, a new opportunity beckoned, promising a glimpse of Cuba under socialism—a land of sugar, rum, cigars, and an undying passion that survives dictatorships and hurricanes alike.

Then came an unexpected twist. Over the phone, while discussing my detour to Cuba, my friend Rickly surprised me. "I want to go with you," he declared, his excitement clear. Our shared exploits—horseback rides in the Colorado mountains, fly-fishing escapades, and even close encounters with bears—had forged a bond strong enough for another grand journey. Rickly, ever the steadfast companion, would join me on this crossing from Key West to Cuba. I scrambled to get him legally cleared for the trip, expediting the necessary paperwork through a well-placed contact in the government office.

Soon enough, Rickly flew in from Colorado, and my son Will and his wife Annie arrived too, ready to babysit Argo while I was away. Within an hour of each other, we were gathered at Fort Lauderdale airport, then en route to Key West to meet Craig Clemmer and Captain Vinny. They arrived aboard *Island Time*—a sleek, forty-seven-foot Beneteau with a polished white fiberglass hull trimmed in brown teak. With a beam just over fourteen feet and a draft of five feet seven inches, *Island Time* demands about sixty feet of clearance under bridges along Florida's intricate intercoastal canals.

Out on the stern, the red, white, and blue stars and stripes of Old Glory dance in the breeze, alongside a Life Sling bag ready to spring into action should any soul fall overboard.

Below deck, a galley equipped with a stainless-steel sink, refrigerator/freezer, propane stove, and oven stands ready for the long voyage. The boat is powered by a sixty-three-horsepower diesel engine—humble yet dependable when docking or when winds leave you "in irons," drifting on a mirror-like sea.

I recall a Thanksgiving Day in Newport, California, with Dr. Tucker—an old friend who'd introduced me to the perils of the sun. As we sailed, he'd laugh at my inexperience, especially after I mistakenly hoisted the spinnaker upside down. His long-sleeved shirts and wide-brim hat were warnings I took too lightly in my youth. Now, his memory and wisdom echo each time the sea calms.

Little did I know that this sail to Cuba might be my final voyage—a black swan song to my mortality. Although *Island Time* has room for only a handful—Craig, Rickly, Captain Vinny, and me—the cramped quarters are filled with determination and hope. As I boarded with my duffle bag, a searing pain shot through my back—a sharp reminder of a careless lift. I kept quiet, masking my discomfort with determination, though back stretches from Craig provided only temporary relief.

We set sail before sunset, bidding farewell to Key West as rain clouds gathered from the east and thunder muffled the dying light. Without a radar to warn us of oncoming vessels, the thought of massive cargo ships—four hundred feet behemoths—lurking unseen in the waves was enough to chill any sailor's heart.

Then the storm hit. Wave after relentless wave battered *Island Time*. I fought nausea and back pain, clutching a small piece of ginger root—a humble remedy that staved off the worst of the motion sickness and kept me from embarrassing myself in front of my steadfast crew.

Amid the tempest, a colossal oil tanker loomed in the distance, its lights cutting through the dark. We were deep in a central shipping lane, vulnerable and exposed. I shouted over the roaring wind, "If I survive tonight, I'm sticking to the two-laner blue highways for the rest of my road trip!" I meant every word.

As the pounding continued, my internal torment faded into a determined focus on our destination. I conjured images of Cuba—a vibrant isle where sugar, rum, cigars, and a fierce passion coexist, where even the ghosts of past dictators and revolutionaries whisper through colonial streets.

At sunrise, the sea finally calmed to a gentle roll. We edged closer to Cuba, the bow slicing through the gentle swell toward Havana Harbor. With careful charting and steady GPS guidance, we maneuvered *Island Time* between buoys and sharp rocks until we reached Marina Hemingway—a tribute to the writer who once found solace in these waters.

Serious-faced Cuban navy and customs officials greeted us. They secured our bow and stern lines, inspected our boat registration, passports, visas, and other paperwork with clinical precision. The scene evoked a Casablanca-like intensity, underscored by an odd request: "You'll need to take some bribes," they advised. I recalled my puzzled response when they clarified that these "bribes" were really goodwill gifts—essential items like toiletries, toilet paper, and children's toys, rare in Cuba but deeply appreciated by the officials. Their wide smiles as they received our humble offerings softened the formalities of our inspection.

Stepping onto Cuban soil, I became an unwitting observer of socialism in action—a reality far different from the romantic notions often held by naive American students. At the Marina Hemingway bar, an array of characters mingled: locals, small fishing boat captains, and the crews of large yachts. They sipped Cuba Libres and traded tales, the air thick with the island's inimitable blend of hardship and hope.

Cuba Libre: Free Cuba!

Cuba Libre isn't merely a drink—it's a toast to Cuba's freedom since the 1895 uprising against Spain. Today it's made with Cuban rum, Coke, fresh lime, and ice, though long before Coca-Cola arrived in Cuba, water and brown sugar held that role.

I met Phil Thompson over a Cuba Libre at Marina Hemingway. An American now living in Cuba, Phil had penned *97 Miles South*—a nod to the distance from Key West to the Cuban shore. "I started coming here in 1993," he recalled, during the hardship of the 'Special Period' when Cuba had little. Living in Key West, he'd crossed by boat under the Clinton administration —not just to enjoy himself but also to bring supplies, food, medicine, vitamins ... everything we take for granted. Fishing the Hemingway Marlin Tournament, an event started by Ernest Hemingway and held three times a year during Clinton's era, became a habit. "Back then, you couldn't find a cat in Havana—they'd all been eaten," he added with a wry smile.

"Reality is reality," I said. "People do what they must," I noted the scarcity: no toilet paper in most bathrooms, not even proper seats. "Funny you mention that," Phil laughed. "They finally got toilet seats at the club, but paper remains a prized commodity—you ask the bartender before you go in."

Curious about the marina's history, I pressed him further. Marina Hemingway was developed by Batista before the revolution. Afterward, Castro dismissed yachting as a bourgeois sport. At the revolution's height, Cuba boasted 118 yacht and sailing clubs; today, this is the sole

private club—a lifeline between America and Cuba for 25 years now." I then asked, "What's the biggest change you've seen here?"

"Free enterprise," Phil replied. "Cubans can now start and run their own businesses, they're taxed and complain just like we do. Tourism is trickling down—farmers, fishermen, even those raising chickens and eggs, are prospering. In Balta, for example, people are redoing their houses, dreaming again."

"Tell me about the little home restaurants," I prodded.

"Paladares," he said simply. "A taxi will drop you off at what looks like a home, but inside is a fine restaurant. They were underground for years, now they're legal. Similarly, the casa particular offers bed and breakfast comforts with a personal touch. And the Americans— tipping, for instance—bring a freshness to service here."

I recalled our boat parade in Havana Harbor. "Seeing the locals wave and smile—like a family reuniting—was astonishing. I half-expected it to be as surreal as a Russian flotilla in New York Harbor."

Phil nodded. "They've allowed four or five parades now—the largest being this one. Cuba has finally opened up; everyone wants to see this phenomenal city."

Our conversation turned to politics and change. "Castro always said the embargo wasn't the fault of the American people but of the government and, as he put it, the Miami Mafia. Many Cubans have relatives in the States—'Everybody has a cousin in Miami,' as Jimmy Buffett quipped. Phil described how a Cuban word, "resolver," embodied the local spirit—if your wheel falls off in the country, someone will fix it. "Here, if one person has a problem, it becomes everyone's concern. And despite the past, we feel safe—arguably, the safest destination in the world. There are no drugs or guns here; accosting a tourist carries penalties five times greater than for a policeman."

When I asked about business, Phil explained that while foreign businesses run in Cuba, they cannot own land. Cubans seeking a license face mountains of paperwork—the government, steeped in socialism, still struggles with capitalism. "Raul Castro took the first step by allowing private enterprise, but he's stepping down in 2017. Whether Miguel Diaz-Canel will continue this change remains to be seen." He added that the Port of Mariel, the most significant development in fifty years, would soon affect everything—from the price of a toaster in Houston to easing the embargo, more than any politician or rights group could.

"You've seen Cuba from both sides," I observed. "Back in Miami's Little Havana, many were still angry about expropriated property."

"True," Phil agreed. "At the beginning of the revolution, 70 percent of the land belonged to foreigners. Castro reforested vast areas; now 20–25 percent of Cuba is protected land. It's a strange kind of environmental legacy."

As we talked, he explained that Cubans don't use "Gringo" for Americans—they call us "Yuma," a nod to the old film *3:10 to Yuma*. And they abide by the "four P's": no pedophilia, pornography, pot, or politics. One of the best stories came from Joe, a bartender who once endured American cartoons before the revolution, then Russian cartoons as punishment—a relic of the past now softened by time. The Russians, he noted, never quite blended with Cubans; now the Chinese fill that void—buying buses, even scooping up the first run of Cohiba Behike cigars, hailed as the best in the world. "I smoked one," I said, still impressed. "They sell for up to $125 a pop," Phil confirmed.

The soul of Cuba is revealed in music and poetry—over a strong cafecito, one feels the pulse of José Martí, a national hero whose simple verses became the stirring "Guantanamera." His words—drawn from his fight for independence—still echo in every corner of this island.

The next morning, Rickly, Craig, Captain Vinny, and I set *Island Time* in motion. After clearing the Hemingway Marina, we hoisted the mainsail and jib, steering toward Key West under a sky dotted with cotton-candy clouds. The return voyage was a smoother dance with the sea—a welcome respite after the tempest that had taken us to Havana. In those calm moments, time seemed to pause, leaving only the steady wind, gentle waves, and our shared camaraderie.

Beneath the peace, pain still stabbed my chest and back like lightning—a grim reminder of my mortality. A small, insistent voice urged, "See a doctor when you reach dry land." But stubbornness, that old companion of mine, prevailed. After docking in Key West and bidding farewell to the crew, I climbed back into Argo and set off once more. With every bridge spanning the turquoise Keys, I left behind that serene haven, venturing westward on the relentless asphalt —each mile a quiet defiance of my aching body.

Alligator Alley stretched before me like a living incision through Florida—a sun-baked ribbon through marshes and sawgrass, the Everglades unfolding in a hazy mirage. The air was thick with humidity, the horizon blurred as if nature itself challenged me to push on. At the end of that endless road, Naples beckoned like a siren. With my pain intensifying, I knew fate was nudging me toward caution.

With Easter weekend looming, I left Argo parked at Naples airport—a quiet farewell, as if her stillness foretold that our parting might be more permanent than I dared hope."

Outside, palm trees swayed, whispering welcome to arriving travelers, as the scent of saltwater mingled with jet fuel. Inside the terminal, the energy was palpable—a bustling hive that replaced the solitude of Alligator Alley with a vibrant human traffic jam. Boarding the plane was its own kind of chaos, a reminder that after days on open roads and amid gator sightings, a little disorder can be just what the doctor ordered. And, as fate would have it, I had a date with one— once I landed in Dallas.

Note to Self

Those prehistoric tanks taught me something: stay calm, stay low, and don't waste energy chasing everything that moves. Gators don't run around trying to impress the pond—they wait, they watch, and when it's go time, they strike with purpose. That's not lazy—that's efficient. That's Florida, baby. Bottom line? In the swamp of life, don't be the guy splashing around trying to go viral.

Be the gator. Quiet. Focused.

21

LIFE AND NEAR-DEATH

*Some people are so afraid to die that they
never begin to live.*

HENRY VAN DYKE

LEAVING NAPLES BY AIR, THE steady hum of the plane engines soothed the chaos in my mind. I couldn't tell if it was lulling me into peace or simply drowning out the agonizing screams from my back and chest. Easter, with its promises of resurrection and renewal, should have sparked hope, yet here I was feeling like a deflated balloon—a burden I'd long refused to address.

Touching down in Dallas, the familiar embrace of home offered a reprieve. Memories of the past, the comfort of family, and the promise of the holiday kindled a spark of optimism. Clutching that hope like a drowning man grasps a life preserver, I trudged my reluctant self to see a doctor. It was high time; the pain persisted like an unwelcome telemarketer, refusing to take a hint.

My friend and primary care physician, Dr. Boyd Lyles, referred me to Nathan Walters, a renowned specialist in spine and pain management. Dr. Walters explained, with a wry tone that matched my own, that my pain was likely rooted in my back—perhaps a bulging disc or merely the side effect of spending too many days at sea, trying to channel Captain Jack Sparrow, minus the charm and rum. As if dismissing pain was ever "no big deal."

He scheduled a CT scan—a modern marvel that reveals the hidden landscapes of our bodies, one cross-sectional image at a time. Lying there as the machine whirred and clicked, I felt as though it was mapping my inner world, exposing secrets long kept in shadow. I was told to expect the results in a day or so, and with a spare few days for Easter with family, I found solace in clearing out dusty memory boxes.

Sifting through old photographs, college notes, and faded love letters from my late wife, Beverly, I was transported back to moments I once thought would be preserved only for a distant future—an image of me in a rocking chair, recounting these tales to an intrigued grandchild. Instead, the past enveloped me in a musty nostalgia, each artifact a whispered echo of a life that had once been vibrant and whole.

Amid my reminiscence, my cell phone rang—an unknown number flashing "No Caller ID." I hesitated; was it just another telemarketer or perhaps something more important? When it rang again, curiosity prevailed, and I answered. On the other end was the familiar, trusted voice of Dr. Walters.

"Okay," I managed, half-joking, "how long do I have to live?"

There was a brief pause—a moment where our shared humor met the gravity of the situation. "Well, John," he began, "I have good news—and bad news." I played along. "All right. Good news first." "Your back isn't the problem," he said.

I exhaled a shaky breath. "And the bad news?"

He grew stern. "Bad news is, you must go to the hospital immediately. You have a pulmonary embolism. Do not drive yourself—get someone to take you straight to the emergency room."

For a moment, my humor faltered. "You realize, of course, I don't have time for this," I replied, still not fully grasping the reality.

"John, you know about the widow-maker," he warned. "This is serious. You could die on the way. Do not delay."

His words echoed in my mind—a stark reminder that some battles leave no room for laughter. In that heavy silence, I realized that while my back was not the culprit of my pain, something far more sinister was at work.

I called out for my son, Will, who soon became my lifeline, driving me to Presbyterian's ER. On the way, I phoned my daughter, Tiffany; her concern added weight to the situation. The ER, with its chorus of coughs and the unsettling clatter of blood draws, felt like a roulette of germs—a place where fate danced dangerously with chance.

The doctors and nurses worked swiftly, their white coats a stark contrast to the gravity of my condition. They explained that a blood clot had journeyed from my right leg through my heart and lodged in my right lung—a discovery that ushered in a new, chilling chapter of my life. More tests followed, each step measured against the precarious balance between life and death. The prognosis was a mix of hope and warning: my heart, though battered, was holding on; my right lung was the battleground where the clot had made its stand. With medication to dissolve the clot, I was given a second chance.

The doctor's advice was clear: no more long, uninterrupted drives across America. Instead, he laid out simple measures—stay hydrated, take frequent breaks to walk, and keep the blood moving—to prevent another such fate. It was a wake-up call that pierced through my stubborn resolve, a reminder that life's twists can be as unpredictable as they are unforgiving. In that moment, as the absurdity of life gave way to its fragility, I recognized that near-death experiences force us to confront what truly matters. They strip away petty grievances and remind us to live with passion and gratitude—love hard, forgive easily, and seize the day. And so, with a heart heavy yet hopeful, I prepared to embrace life's fragile gift, ready to continue my journey with renewed purpose.

Second Visit to the ER

A few days after my hospital release, fate dealt a cruel hand. I collapsed outside my front door, clutching my chest in raw agony, sprawled on the hallway floor—a moment of stark vulnerability. In that desperate instant, my vigilant neighbor became an unsung hero, swiftly dialing 911. Soon, an ambulance—a quirky SUV adorned with flashing lights—raced to the scene. Its bumpy, jolting ride was a distraction from the mix of dread and hope swirling inside me.

We arrived at the hospital's receiving dock—a sort of VIP entrance that bypassed the waiting room and hurled me directly into the heart of the emergency room. There, the staff in crisp white uniforms moved with determined purpose, their reassuring smiles and gentle touches acting as balm amid the chaos. In this exclusive club of the unwell, a nurse—a constant, caring guardian—became a familiar presence by my side, her check-ins a quiet testament to the compassion that sustained me.

Not long after, déjà vu struck with a second ER visit. My long hours behind the wheel had conspired with my sedentary ways, birthing a blood clot that had crept from my right leg into my lung. Fortunately, there was no damage to my heart; the clot would dissolve under a course of blood thinners over the next six months. I vowed, however, never to join the ER club again. Determined to return to Argo in Florida and continue my cross-country journey, I embraced Dr. Boyd Lyles' advice: stop every hour to stretch, walk around, wiggle your toes—anything to keep the blood moving. He prescribed blood-thinning medication, a necessary risk with its hazards, but life is a gamble every day, and I was not about to let mortality end my pilgrimage across this vast land—a journey of self-discovery and communion with America's very heartbeat.

I flew back to Florida, where Argo awaited, with a renewed sense of purpose and a dream igniting my veins. I resumed my drive along Florida's west side, reminded that a goal can light a fire deep within and propel us forward, no matter the odds.

Note to Self

Life's short, man. Like, very short. One minute you're sipping coffee, the next you're wondering why your back hurts—and it turns out to be a blood clot. So here's the deal: live like there's no tomorrow—because there might not be. Not to be dramatic, but let's be honest: nobody's promised anything past today. So, tell the people you love that you love 'em. Take the trip. Eat the good food. Chase the dream, screw the excuses. Because when the clock runs out, it won't be the risks you regret—it'll be all the times you played it safe and waited for the "right moment." Spoiler alert: the right moment is now.

Bottom line? Burn the fancy candle. Wear the shoes. Laugh loud, cry hard, love bigger. If today's all you've got, make it count. And if tomorrow does show up? Great—do it all again, just louder.

22

On the Road Again

I can't wait to get on the road again;
Going places that I've never been; Seeing
things that I may never see again.

WILLIE NELSON

MY PLANE TOUCHED DOWN AT Ft. Myers/Naples airport a full fifteen minutes ahead of schedule—a rare stroke of luck in the unpredictable world of air travel. I hopped aboard the remote parking shuttle bound for the green lot reserved for trucks like my trusty Argo. Amid a sea of oversized, dually-wheeled pickups, Argo stood out—a lone wolf among overgrown hounds.

Argo was parked here just before Easter, with plans for a brief flight home. Now, thirty-three days later, I return. The moment my hand grasped the cold handle of Argo's door, a shiver ran down my spine—as if an ice cube had slid beneath my collar. My mind raced with the thought of my near miss with that treacherous blood clot of a bullet that had traveled from my heart to my lung.

Then I took a deep breath and chuckled at the absurdity of it all: a cross-country road trip interrupted by a hitchhiking blood clot on the road less traveled within my own body. Inside Argo, I felt an almost sentient welcome. I put away my carry-on bag and checked the gauges. Argo cranked to life with a heavy growl and a whirr, then settled into a brassy, diesel purr. Soon, I was driving toward the water, crossing a sunlit bridge from the mainland to Pine Island. Boats sailed in all directions below, and I couldn't help but break into a wide smile. I was on the road again.

Along Pine Island Road near Matlacha, I encountered a string of weathered shanty huts— a scattering of rambling wooden structures, some dating back to the twenties, now transformed into restaurants, shops, B&Bs, and homes. Driving through this old fishing village, where Elvis once filmed *Follow That Dream* and soldiers from nearby bases once spent their weekends fishing, I noticed a swarm of cars gathering around Bert's Bar and Grill. That's where the people are, and to me, always a good sign.

I pulled Argo in front and strolled to the back deck, claiming a small table. The sun was slowly descending, bathing the scene in a warm, golden glow. From my vantage point, I could see the meticulously maintained docks, a party barge promising future merriment, and a sleek speedboat poised on its lift. It all merged into a serene masterpiece of art. I leaned back, letting the quiet beauty of the moment settle in.

No sooner had I ordered my meal than the wind began to stir. The temperature dropped to a chill. A sudden, mischievous cloud—one that hadn't been there a minute before—unleashed a drizzle of water over the deck, the menus, and me. A tall waitress in tiny jean shorts rushed out with a blue canvas umbrella, urging, "You might want to go inside." I nodded, remarking, "Probably a good idea, huh?" She replied, "Yeah, when it comes, it comes fast 'round here." And true enough, within moments, the rain pounded down, sending me along with the other outdoor patrons scurrying inside.

Meanwhile, Scotty Brian, the bar's local troubadour, kept the energy high—strumming his electric guitar as he belted old tunes, his voice competing with the clamor of a lively crowd. I settled at a side table near the main bar, bobbing my head along to Neil Diamond's classic *Cracklin' Rosie* while nibbling on crispy spiral potato chips and freshly caught, lightly fried mahi-mahi. All served up with coleslaw, lemon wedges, and a local brew. In that moment, I felt utterly at peace.

Yet even the calm of a perfect evening can be punctuated by life's unpredictability. After getting back on the road, Argo carried me along Florida's rugged west coast until I decided to make camp for the night at a charming state park on Tampa Bay's northern shore. The setting sun painted the sky in shades of orange and pink as I set up camp, the promise of a new day stirring quietly on the horizon.

◄ ▲ ▼ ►

With some time to spare before dinner, I took a leisurely walk along the bay. The waters shimmered under fading light, and everything felt serenely idyllic—until the quiet was shattered by raised voices. After I entered the campground's small shower building, a heated confrontation unfolded outside. Reluctant to become entangled in the conflict, I stayed inside the shelter, peering through the louvers at the scene.

A burly man, his muscles tense with anger, shouted at a woman whose small stature belied the force of her words.

"Then you just get your shit and get out of here!" she screamed, her tone raw with frustration.

"I ain't goin' nowhere!" he bellowed back.

It was clear this wasn't their first quarrel—an all-too-familiar storm of emotions. Their words turned sharp. Tempers flared dangerously. Tension was thick in the air. The man lunged forward toward the woman, brandishing a metal cooking spatula as if it were a weapon. For a singular moment, time seemed to hold its breath. The man raised his muscular right arm with the spatula ready to strike; his eyes wild with anger, as she taunted him with obscenities. "You son of a bitch! You pile of shit! Go ahead and hit me!"

She leaned toward him, in a pose to provoke. Then, as if struck by an unseen force, he hesitated, his swing faltering mid-air.

"But he called you, didn't he!" The man took another step back, keeping the spatula firm in his hand as he yelled at her. "He wouldn't have called you unless you had given him your number!"

She slumped and began to cry, exhausted from the rage. "I didn't! I didn't! I just …"

The man lowered his head and, finally, his hand. She sat down at the picnic table with her back toward him. He began walking in a circle, and after a moment of pause, he walked away from her.

I made my way back to my campsite, half-expecting a stray sound of gunfire or of a hand slapping a face. I couldn't shake the thought: in a place meant for peace, conflict still finds a way to intrude, reminding me that safety is often just an illusion. There were lessons hidden in their discord—how emotions can spiral out of control when communication fails, and how, in every argument, both sides lose more than they gain.

As darkness fell into the gentle hush of the night, fatigue descended over me. I retreated into Argo's comforting embrace, its silver skin offering refuge. Lying down, my thoughts drifted to a pristine white sandy beach, saltwater lapping gently at the shore, and my toes sinking into wet sand—a peaceful vision to soothe the day's rollercoaster of events. My good angel whispered that perhaps I should spend Memorial Day weekend on the beach, recouping and regrouping, far from the clamor of human discord.

In that quiet moment, I understood: every journey, no matter how idyllic, carries its share of turbulence—and every day is a lesson in embracing both the beauty and chaos of life.

Note to Self

Life's way too short to waste arguing with people who thrive on drama, negativity, or that weird, toxic energy that drains your soul faster than a Florida sunburn. Honestly, some folks walk into a room and suck the joy out of it like a vacuum in flip-flops.

The truth is, even the dreamiest journey comes with occasional turbulence. So, keep your peace close, your circle tight, and your beach chair ready. My good angel (probably wearing aviators and holding a margarita) is whispering, "Maybe spend Memorial Day weekend where the ocean laps at your feet—recharging, not reacting." Amen, beach angel. Amen.

23

MOONLIGHT MADNESS

Never was so much owed by so many to so few.
WINSTON CHURCHILL

AS ARGO AND I ROLLED into Seaside, a charming enclave nestled along the Florida Panhandle, I couldn't help but be enchanted by the picture-perfect scene unfolding before me. This town—small, upscale, and seemingly custom-built for Instagram—felt like a movie set. I half-expected someone to shout, "Action!" as I cruised down the streets, the landscape almost too idyllic to be real.

Teenagers dotted the streets like extras in a film. They wore effortlessly stylish beach attire—flip-flops, shorts, and the occasional Hawaiian shirt—and talked amongst themselves, their conversation punctuated by the constant swipe of a phone screen. They were debating dinner plans, deliberating between pizza and—this one cracked me up—grilled cheese sandwiches.

One thing was certain: they didn't see me. At my age, you could be invisible. The only way you'd catch their attention was if you were a parent or worthy of their mockery. And I wasn't the former.

Bicycles lined the town square like sentries, leaning against light poles, evidence of the youth-driven energy here. I guessed the parents were either tied up with something—or worse— tucked away somewhere. I decided I'd figure it out later. Right now, I have a much more pressing concern: hunger.

With grilled cheese on the mind, I strolled into the Melt Down Cafe and ordered the classic. What arrived was nothing short of magical: warm American cheese oozing between crispy toasted bread. It was the quintessential comfort food—cheese, bread, butter—the holy trinity of simplicity. Satisfied, I returned to Argo, full and content, only to be knocked out by the sleep bat. I barely made it back to my van before I nodded off.

The following morning, the rhythmic patter of rain on Argo's metal roof nudged me awake. The sound of thunder rumbled in the distance, setting the stage for what looked like a stormy Memorial Day. I could still hear the distant sound of waves gently lapping at the shore, almost serenading me as I lay there, enveloped in the warmth of the covers. Outside, 30-A, the road running parallel to the dunes, moved at a crawl, barely reaching the 15-mile-per-hour speed limit. It was as if even time slowed down in Seaside.

If you've seen *The Truman Show*—the 1998 movie with Jim Carrey—you've experienced Seaside in cinematic form. It's not only a town; it's a meticulously designed community, and it feels that way from every angle. This isn't just a place to live; it's an experience. The town was crafted by Robert Davis, whose grandfather purchased the land in the early 20th century, a stretch of "worthless" eighty acres. Little did they know, decades later, this very stretch would become one of the world's most acclaimed beaches.

Once named "World's Best Beach for Families" by *Travel & Leisure*, Seaside is a model of careful planning. The streets are narrow, designed to slow traffic and encourage human connection. With only about 350 homes, the community is small enough to remain intimate yet large enough to be an attraction. If you want to stay here, don't even think about booking lastminute. Reservations are made a year in advance.

My biggest question, however, was about the parents. Where were they? All I saw were teenagers. As I watched them, I realized how rare it was to see such a large group of teens hanging out without the chaos of today's world. Quiet, polite, hanging out without phones glued to their faces—imagine that! For a moment, I felt a twinge of nostalgia. Seaside was a place that felt familiar, almost like stepping back into my childhood.

It reminded me of simpler days when you could trust your kids to walk or bike to the store without worrying about them. Back when families knew each other, and your parents weren't fretting over every detail. The town had brought that feeling back—a place where kids roamed free, with the safety of their parents' proximity.

It's no surprise that Seaside is a model for creating a neighborhood that feels secure. The well-crafted plan allows children the freedom to roam while keeping parents close by. It's not just a design choice but a deliberate attempt to recreate the best of small-town America. With the beach closed to minors after dark unless accompanied by a parent, it's the kind of place where families can relax without fear.

As I sat there, reflecting on the nature of neighborhoods, I couldn't help but think about how life in cities had changed. The modern world, with its emphasis on disconnection, has largely destroyed the tight-knit communities I grew up in. But in places like Seaside, that feeling of connection still thrives. I guess there's hope for the classic neighborhood yet.

By the time I had my coffee, the beach outside was calling to me. It was a beach day through and through—sun, sand, and sea, all awaiting my undivided attention. And with temperatures topping out at only eighty-two degrees, it promised to be a perfect day. No agenda, no rush—just a long, leisurely walk along the shoreline, a nap in the sun, a good book, and plenty of time to do absolutely nothing. The day stretched out before me, and for once, I didn't feel the need to pack it with tasks. As the Beach Boys would say, "We'll get there fast, then we'll take it slow."

It was Memorial Day weekend—time to relax, grill, and enjoy family. But I didn't want to forget the purpose of the day: honoring the men and women who have given so much for our freedom. These sacrifices are easy to take for granted, but I couldn't help but feel an overwhelming sense of gratitude.

The road ahead beckoned. Tomorrow, I'd be back on the move, heading towards New Orleans—toward a destination that couldn't be more different than Seaside, but then again, that's the beauty of life on the road.

Later that afternoon, I made a pit stop at a state park campground near Spanish Fort, Alabama. The setting was tranquil, the sky a perfect blue, the breeze gentle, and the water shimmering nearby. I parked under a tree, made myself a sandwich, and settled in at a picnic table that had seen better days. A small spider, no bigger than my thumb, sat quietly in its web, patiently waiting. It reminded me of the nursery rhyme: "The itsy-bitsy spider went up the water spout …"

I couldn't help but smile. The little creature, so small, so determined, was living its quiet life in this vast world, much like me—another traveler, passing through, finding moments of peace along the way.

As the day wound down, I began to make notes about my travels so far, my thoughts punctuated by the peaceful setting and the fading light. Just as I was about to close my eyes for the night, I was jolted awake by a strange sensation—Argo rocking as though someone was trying to push it over. It was a sensation I couldn't ignore, and my pulse quickened as I readied myself to confront whatever it was.

I grabbed my flashlight, heart racing, and cautiously peered outside, only to find no one there. To my relief, the noise had been the result of falling pine cones, large ones, making an unexpected racket as they dropped from the trees above. I chuckled at my overreaction. Just another reminder that sometimes, the things that rattle us aren't always as they seem.

As the wind calmed and the storm passed, I settled back in, grateful for the stillness. Life on the road, with its unpredictable twists, was never dull. And for tonight, at least, the adventure could wait.

Note to Self

Take time to recharge. Seriously. We're not machines—even smart ones. We're human beings with limits, emotions, and a nervous system that occasionally needs to sit down and shut the world out. So, remember to take a break when the body cries out, before life gives it to you the hard way.

It's not lazy to rest; it's survival. You can't pour from an empty cup, and you definitely can't conquer the world running on cold coffee and fumes. Because when you're full, focused, and rested? You're unstoppable. And maybe even pleasant to be around.

24

JAZZ AND JAMBALAYA

There are a lot of places I like, but I like New Orleans better.

BOB DYLAN

AS I EASED INTO THE heart of New Orleans' bewitching French Quarter on a rainy afternoon, I could already feel the city's rhythm calling to me. First stop? Café Du Monde. It's a tradition that goes back years, ever since my first visit, to swing by for a few beignets, those glorious, pillowy creations dusted with powdered sugar like a snowfall in the tropics. Well, that, and a mug of steaming Cajun coffee.

How I need my daily java fix. It's the spark to my ignition, the firecracker that wakes me from slumber and propels me into the day's adventures. I've tried to lay off it before—tried, but never succeeded. For a time, I went cold turkey, dragging my body around like a limp rag doll, my personality nowhere to be found. I'd nod off mid-conversation, and my friends—bless their hearts—begged me to bring back the old, lively version of myself, the one that greeted mornings with a coffee cup and a smile.

It's a scientific thing. You see, in the ninth century, Ethiopian monks noticed their goats had more pep after munching on coffee berries. And so, the monks brewed up a little concoction, infused it with water, and—well, the rest, as they say, is history.

As I approached Café Du Monde, the rain began to fall with increasing intensity, but it did nothing to dampen my spirits. If anything, it lent the scene a little extra mystery, turning the city streets into slick mirrors that caught the glow of neon signs. My heart quickened as I neared the iconic open-air café, where history and sugar-coated bliss were waiting for me just beyond the threshold.

Café Du Monde, tucked at the edge of the French Quarter near the river, is like stepping into a living postcard of New Orleans. It's steeped in history—and chicory. Coffee first arrived in North America through New Orleans in the mid-1700s, carried here by the French, who had cultivated it in Martinique before settling along the Mississippi. The drink didn't become widespread across the U.S. until the Boston Tea Party, when revolutionaries decided tea was unpatriotic and began drinking coffee as a symbol of independence. "No more tea, thanks—I'll take a cup of freedom!"

The French, of course, developed a taste for coffee and chicory during their civil war, when coffee was hard to come by. They discovered that adding roasted chicory root to the brew softened the bitterness, and, naturally, this flavor found its way to Louisiana. The Acadians from Nova Scotia (the original "Cajuns") brought their love for chicory and many other French traditions with them, turning it into the coffee we enjoy today—dark, rich, and with a touch of chocolate flavor. And so, I make my way to Café Du Monde, a name so French it probably smokes unfiltered cigarettes and looks disdainfully at non-French things.

I park a few blocks away when the rain starts falling in sheets. I soon realized the "waterresistant" label on my jacket was just a cruel joke. By the time I get to the café, I'm soaked through. But nothing's going to stop me now.

A young waiter, all crisp white shirt and black bow tie, leads me to a table beneath the canopy. The city's rhythm dances in the background as I sit, noting the sound of raindrops on the canvas above, blending with the hum of conversation around me. I sip my coffee, warm and comforting, and sink into the pleasure of the moment. The beignets arrive in all their glorious sweetness, and within moments, I've entered into a blissful haze of caffeine and sugar, a momentary escape from the storm outside.

A man sits down at the table next to me. He nods in my direction, clearly wanting to strike up a conversation. He was middle-aged, rough, but with a certain charm like someone who'd lived hard but hadn't quite given up. I could tell he had seen more than one round of drinks and late nights. Didn't take himself too seriously.

"So, you left your wife at home, and you're out here on your own, eh?" he asks.

I glance up. "Well, no wife. Just out here alone, escaping the rain."

He chuckles. "I'm escaping the rain… and all three of my wives."

"Three wives?"

"Yeah. All exes. Been married three times."

"Wow. Three times, huh? Must've learned a lot along the way." I laugh.

"Oh, yeah," he says, flashing a big grin. "First lesson: I tell anyone I date that straight up. I warn 'em, just in case. I'm not marriage material. Women have even testified in court to that effect."

"Ha! Legally documented, not marriage material. You're upfront about it. Guess that saves a lot of time, doesn't it?"

"Time, money, heartache. Sometimes, I think the whole world would be better off if we were all just honest from the start. No promises. No expectations."

He continues to talk, sharing more nuggets of wisdom from his well-worn experiences.

The rain lets up, and I decide it's time to stretch my legs.

I wander through the French Quarter, popping into curio shops that seem to have no purpose other than to lure you in. You don't mean to buy anything, but then you spot something —a plastic alligator pen, perhaps, or a voodoo pendant—and before you know it, you're handing over your cash for a trinket to remember the rainy day you spent in New Orleans. For me, it's a white coffee mug, emblazoned with the Café Du Monde logo. Yes, I know—there will be a halfprice sale at my garage someday, and this mug will be among the first to go. For now, it's my most prized thing.

The rain has stopped, and the streets are quieter now. I stroll down famous French Quarter streets—St. Anne, Royal, Bourbon, St. Louis—some of them beautiful, some downright gritty. At dawn, the place is still recovering from the revelry of the night before, the streets littered with cigarette butts, empty bottles, and other detritus. But there's a certain truth to it all— New Orleans, in its messy, lived-in way, isn't quite the picture-perfect tourist destination. It's real, and it's unapologetically itself.

Beyond the Quarter, New Orleans is like any other city, with its universities, its economy, and its businesses. But what sets it apart is its older neighborhoods—those with the trolleys that rumble down streets draped in moss and oaks. If you look up into the trees, you'll see Mardi Gras beads hanging from every branch, remnants of last year's celebrations. The city, always on the edge, teeters between decay and vibrance.

New Orleans has always been a city at risk—flooded regularly, forever scarred by Hurricane Katrina's aftermath—but still, its people remain fiercely loyal. No one ever wants to leave. It's a place where all kinds of people—black, white, Hispanic, Asian, immigrant—have lived side by side for centuries, and the spirit of community runs deep.

As night falls, I return to the Quarter, curious to see how the place transforms after dark. The energy shifts; many of the street people have been moved along by the police, and the streets have been swept clean. Couples and groups of revelers spill from one bar to the next, their laughter and music spilling into the night. It's a scene straight out of a postcard, the kind that makes you want to stay forever.

But I'm alone in the crowd, and a strange sense of loneliness settles in. It's time to leave.

I walk back to Argo, my faithful ride, parked in a public lot that charges like a small mortgage. One more hour in this lot and I'd have to take out a loan. Soon, I'll be driving over the Lake Pontchartrain Causeway, the longest straight bridge over water in the world. Nearly twentyfour miles long, it's a narrow stretch of road that can feel like a dicey drive, especially if the wind picks up.

The party in the Quarter will rage on long after I leave. But for now, it's time to roll out of New Orleans. *Laissez les bon temps rouler.*

Note to Self

Funny how fast the energy shifts. One minute it's fun and wild characters—couples laughing, music thumping, and bars spilling out life like it's going out of style. It's the kind of scene that makes you think, yeah, maybe I could stay here forever. But then reality taps on the shoulder, because in the middle of all that noise and neon, I'm still alone. No hand to hold, no one looking for me in the crowd. Just me, standing still while the night dances away. And that's when it hits—maybe it's not your scene anymore. Maybe it never was.

So, I leave. Not out of sadness, but self-awareness. Because sometimes the bravest thing you can do is recognize when it's time to go—and trust that wherever you're headed next? It's got a heartbeat that matches your own.

25

Pilots, Pine Trees, and the Panhandle

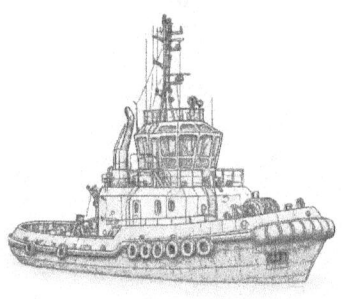

Sometimes the most scenic roads in life are the detours you didn't mean to take.

ANGELA N. BLOUNT

AFTER WALKING THE SULTRY STREETS of New Orleans, Argo and I drove north, across the Lake Pontchartrain Causeway. It is one of the longest continuous bridges over water in the world, stretching for about twenty-four miles. I continued to Covington, Louisiana, heading to the Maritime Pilots Institute. My love for the ocean and boating kept me there for several days, captivated by the training of ship pilots brushing up on their skills for docking towering container ships.

The tireless individuals behind our global supply chain are easy to overlook, but they are the lifeblood of modern life, ensuring our shelves are stocked and needs met. The Maritime Pilots Institute is a vital cog in the machine, training pilots who take control of massive ships upon arrival at port and guide them safely to dock.

Docking a ship is like a ballet—if the dancers were much larger and the stage a shifting, unpredictable sea. Docking a cruise ship is like trying to parallel park a whale in a goldfish pond — awkward and amusing.

George Burkley, the institute's founder, invited me to observe some training. I asked him how he found his way to this point. "I grew up in a military family. My father taught me to sail, and I fell in love with the ocean," he said. "I joined the Navy, then the Merchant Marines, and later taught radar to new sailors. At the time, satellite navigation was a new frontier."

After his naval service, George helped start the Maritime Pilots Institute, which has since trained hundreds of pilots and ship officers from thirteen countries.

The romantic notion of piloting waterways caught my imagination after reading about Mark Twain. As a riverboat pilot on the Mississippi, Twain's firsthand knowledge of the river shaped his vivid storytelling, most famously in *The Adventures of Huckleberry Finn*. His piloting may have been on a river, but navigating the mighty Mississippi was just as challenging as steering a tanker into New York Harbor.

As a boy, I was enchanted by the sight of ships gliding into Galveston Bay, the air thick with salt, the cries of seagulls trailing behind. It sparked the spirit of adventure in me, as it does for all who love the sea.

My first "ship" was a yellow canoe bought with lawn-mowing money. My "sea" was a Texas lake and the Bosque River.

Water's primal allure runs deep in me. Perhaps it's because we, like the oceans, are made of water, drawn to the source of our being. The rhythm of the tides mirrors the steady beat of our hearts, connecting us to something vast and mysterious just beyond the horizon.

At the Maritime Pilots Institute, I felt as if I had entered a temple devoted to the maritime gods. Simulators for pilots resemble those used to train airline pilots—allowing students to make mistakes safely before navigating real ships through bustling harbors.

The students also practice in miniature harbors, models scaled 1/25 to simulate real-world conditions. Watching the miniature ships navigate through narrow channels felt like observing a ballet in a tiny, undulating world.

From my own experience on the water, I know how quickly things can go awry. A case in point: the freighter *Bright Field* lost power in the New Orleans waterway and narrowly missed the Crescent City Connection bridge. Captain Ted Davisson steered the freighter away from disaster, missing a shopping mall and a cruise ship, before grounding it in a parking garage. "What could have been one of the worst tragedies in the city's history turned out to be one of the greatest miracles," said Harbor Police Chief Robert Hecker.

George explained that docking a boat involves many variables: crosswinds, currents, tides, and weather. Each factor must be carefully considered by the boat operator, whose calm communication with the crew is crucial.

"Want to try your hand at it?" George asked.

"Absolutely," I said.

The next morning, I spent the day learning to dock a model cargo ship. Let me tell you, it's harder than it looks, but I did manage to dock without causing a major catastrophe.

◄ ▲ ▼ ►

Next, Argo and I drove to Thomasville, Georgia—a town enveloped in Southern charm, where magnolias bloom in defiance of the heat, and history lingers in the air.

In this genteel enclave, I visited Pebble Hill Plantation, an estate founded in the 1820s by Thomas Jefferson Johnson. The mansion now serves as a museum, showcasing the grandeur of the antebellum South.

While there, a gentleman approached me, curious about my travels. "I've always dreamed of exploring America," he said, "driving the back roads, stopping at small cafés. What's it like?"

"I love it," I told him. "I'm making my way around America, talking to people, discovering the country."

He invited me to meet his wife and friends, eager for me to share my experience. When I did, his admiration for my journey became clear.

As I spoke about my travels, his wife smiled politely, but her body language said something else—this dream of his would never come to fruition. I finished the conversation with a light-hearted remark about the difficulties of chasing dreams, and after some banter, I politely declined an invitation to dinner. I left them with their dreams and their reality, wondering if they would ever find common ground.

Mark Twain once wrote, "Twenty years from now, you will be more disappointed by the things you didn't do than by the ones you did. So throw off the bowlines. Sail away from the safe harbor. Catch the trade winds in your sails. Explore. Dream. Discover."

Argo seemed emboldened by the attention, lifting her fenders high as we headed back to Florida. I found a place to camp in Lake Talquin State Forest, ready to relax in the Panhandle for Memorial Day weekend.

Note to Self

Hey genius, next time you're whining about your Amazon package being a day late, remember there are tireless, probably caffeine-fueled legends out there moving heaven, earth, and about twelve million shipping containers to make sure you never run out of oat milk or phone chargers. These supply-chain superheroes keep the world spinning — and your pantry from turning into a sad snack desert.

Respect the grind, even if you can't see it from your comfy couch.

At the end of the Mother Road, Route 66, Santa Monica Pier, California.

ARGO

Hanging out with Larry Gator Rivers Former Harlem Globetrotter. Savanna, Georgia

Forced back due to weather.

Stopping at the Continental Divide.

Miles and miles of billboards. Road trip entertainment

Fishing along the way.

Top of the USA. Hwy 83 - Canadian Border

Lobster in Maine. On a snowy night

45th Parallel - Halfway between Equator & North Pole

A gator in Florida's Everglades.

Spending time with the Hopi Tribe.

Bottom of the USA. Key West

After talking to Cubans in Miami's Little Havana, I took a detour to Hemingway's Havana in Cuba.

Me, Rick Christian, Capt. Vinnie, & Craig Clemmer in the lobby of Hotel Nacional de Cuba.

Sailing to Cuba in a 47' sailboat.

Cigar time after dinner with Franco Nocero.

Owner of Little Italy Restaurant in Nassawadox, Virginia

An immigrant who arrived with nothing and became a big success in America.

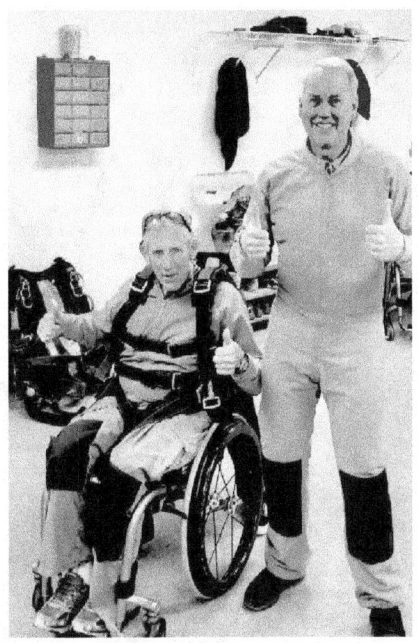

Mike Fick & John Butler. Fulfilling Mike's bucket list

Flashback to an earlier long-distance track, over 500 miles. Racing fellow radio DJs across Texas. sky diving wish.

Nowhere Cafe New London, Connecticut

Historic Texas Oil Fields

Louis Jason, Harvey Jason, & John Butler

Mystery Pier Books. Sunset Strip, West Hollywood

26

TEXAS

Texas is a state of mind. Texas is an obsession. Above all, Texas is a nation in every sense of the word.

JOHN STEINBECK

RAIN, RAIN, RAIN. THE DRIVE from New Orleans to Houston was a soggy blur, a world smeared by water. Argo's windshield wipers protested each pass, their rubbery shrieks dragging across the glass like the nails of some discontented cat—bitter, unwilling, and clearly, quite feral. The sound should have driven me mad, but the Grateful Dead on the radio offered me a patch of distraction—though it wasn't quite enough to drown out the relentless wiper wails. Lemon-sized raindrops thudded against the windshield, as though the sky itself were throwing a tantrum. It was like trying to look through a shower door, thick with steam and frost, only to catch shadowy glimpses of the cars ahead.

Then, as if the sky had finally given in, the rain lightened. The thick veil lifted just in time for me to cross into Texas—what a land this is, what a whole new world. The moment you hit the border, you feel it. Maybe it's that famous Texas saying, "Everything is bigger." Maybe it's the way everyone here greets you like a long-lost relative. You move to California, and you'll always be a transplant; you move to Texas, and in a heartbeat, you're a Texan.

To reach Dallas-Fort Worth, I head north through the heart of Texas, leaving Houston's sprawling concrete behind. As the flatlands stretch out, my tension starts to melt into the horizon. The land opens up—an ocean of farmland that seems to go on forever, before giving way to the Hill Country's rugged beauty. The hills roll like the back of an old, wise giant, their green folds dotted with lone oaks. There's something about this land, a kind of slow magic to it.

San Antonio isn't far now, and as I pass the Alamo, I can't help but reflect on the battle that turned the tide of the Texas Revolution. The forces of Bowie and Travis, small but fierce, held out against Santa Anna's overwhelming Mexican army. Thirteen days of fighting, and the cry, "Remember the Alamo," was etched into the very fabric of Texas pride.

I also remember the Great Texas Bike Race, that silly, glorious radio stunt, where I joined two other disc jockeys—Scotty from Houston and Woody from San Antonio—and we set off in a race across this massive state. I was the voice of KLIF in Dallas, and we were supposed to ride from San Antonio to Houston, no shortcuts, no gimmicks. Just pedal.

I'll never forget that March day in 1972, when we lined up in front of the Alamo. The mayor gave us the kind of pep talk that could only come from someone who has a flair for public speaking, and then the starting gun fired, and we were off, flying into the wind like a gust of rebellion. We were accompanied by a motorhome and a police escort, none other than Officer Sal Gambino, the motorcycle cop from Houston, who kept intersections clear and our spirits high.

The Texas heat blasted us like a furnace, but we couldn't be stopped. Up one hill, down another, legs burning like I'd set fire to my muscles. The sweat stung my eyes, but the crowds kept us going. People at the roadside, in little towns, in suburban neighborhoods, cheering us on as if we were heroes. They didn't care about our race times; they cared that we were out there—pushing, striving, fighting.

Scotty was the first to hit Austin, then I led the charge into Dallas. The streets of downtown were packed with KLIF fans, all of them eager to see us cross the finish line. From there, we continued towards Houston, the miles stretching out, each one longer than the last.

But the thing about those long rides, those long days on the road, was the stillness. In between the pushes and the pedal strokes, I'd close my eyes for a split second and whisper the Lord's Prayer.

It became a kind of rhythm, one I repeated with every breath, with every push.

And somehow, despite the exhaustion, I found a quiet strength. The road never stops calling. And then, we reached Houston, and I crossed the finish line, legs barely holding me up, but with a sense of victory that felt deeper than the ride itself. The crowd cheered, and for a moment, it wasn't just about the race—it was about pushing yourself past what you thought you could do. But time doesn't stop, and neither does the road. As I continued to drive, the memory of that race faded into the rearview mirror, replaced by a ringing phone. It was Mike Fick, an old friend from high school.

◀ ▲ ▼ ▶

Mike Fick, the drummer in our local garage band, the Malibu's, was always cool, always ahead of the curve. A talented guy, an athlete, and a heart as big as Texas itself. But life has a funny way of changing things, doesn't it? A freak accident left Mike a paraplegic, and the news hit me like a punch to the gut. A reminder, sharp and sudden, that we are all fragile. One minute, invincible. The next, vulnerable.

Mike's accident changed everything. But Mike didn't. He took it, took the blows, and rolled with it. He adapted in a way that was pure Mike. He took the bad and turned it into something good, finding joy in the smallest moments. He found strength in what he could do, not what he couldn't.

His tradition? Christmas lights. Every year, his home becomes a beacon in the neighborhood—bigger, brighter, more electric. Like something straight out of *Christmas Vacation*, the Fick house glows with cheer, a testament to Mike's joy in the season. One year, though, the tradition almost took a turn for the worse.

Mike, eager to get the lights up, was up on the ladder before the sun had even cracked the horizon. He was determined to get the lights perfect, as always, but something went wrong. A slip. A fall. A spine crushed beneath the weight of his own body.

In that moment, Mike's life changed. His mind raced, his body crumpled, but his spirit remained unbroken. The pain was immense, but his resolve was stronger. When Angie rushed to him, he said, "I think you're married to a paraplegic now."

Mike's journey after that was long and difficult, but there's a quiet power in his story. The power of resilience. The power of living each day as it comes. He's never seen his disability as a burden but as an opportunity—a challenge to grow stronger, to adapt, to be present.

As I thought about Mike, I felt a swell of admiration. He was teaching all of us something about life. It's not the weight we carry but how we carry it. And he carried it with grace, with humor, and with a kind of quiet power that made him stronger than anyone I knew.

When I finally made it back to Dallas, I sank into the comfort of my bed, my body weary from the miles traveled. The road had called, and I had answered. But there was something about being home, about the simple peace of being still, that felt right.

The next day, the rain began to fall. Just as I had planned to head out again, the weather conspired against me. But the rain was soothing, like a lullaby for my restless soul. There would be other roads, other adventures. For now, I could rest. And dream.

I stayed longer than I had planned, taking the time to catch up on everything that had piled up while I was away. There's always that settling-in moment, when you return to familiar faces, familiar places, and let the stories flow—stories of the road, of home, of all the things that make up the texture of life.

A rainy day in Dallas arrived just when it was needed. After weeks of suffocating heat, the downpour felt like a blessing, a reminder of how the world takes its time and gives you what you need when you least expect it. The rain came down hard, the kind that makes you want to stay inside with a cup of coffee and a good book. But I had work to do—Argo needed attention.

I thought of the repairs as I looked out at the wet world. A bit of water might delay me, but it couldn't stop me. Argo leaked her belly, a reminder that even the road-weary need care and attention. The rain came down in sheets, but as it fell, it soothed something restless in me. It had been a long stretch of travel, and the stillness of the storm felt like the pause I needed.

When the rain stopped, I was out the door and under the vehicle. I'd packed lighter this time—no need for excess. A few shirts, a pair of jeans, some shorts, and the camera gear are already waiting. The essentials. What else do you need when the road is calling?

But first, I had to deal with the leak. It wasn't a big deal, but it had to be fixed before I went any further. I'd been on the road too long not to take care of her—Argo was my companion through all of this, a constant and loyal one.

I called Roger. He's from the Philippines, and while his English is a bit broken, we've always understood each other just fine. It takes a little more patience, sure, but there's something about the rhythm of our conversations that feels more genuine for it. It's the kind of friendship that doesn't need perfect words, just understanding.

"Hey, Roger, I've got a leaking hose on Argo. Do you think you can help?" I asked.

"Oh, yes, yes, leaking hose! Very bad! I fix it!" Roger replied, his voice crackling with that eager optimism.

"You sure?"

"Yes! Yes, yes. Fix it good. Good hose!"

It wasn't a tough job, just a matter of getting underneath, finding the leak, and deciding if the hose could be patched or needed replacing. Roger had worked on ships, so he knew the drill.

We'd been through this before.

When Roger arrived, he wasted no time. "Turn off the water! Turn off!" he called, hands flying as he grabbed tools from his truck.

I watched him, an expert in the way only someone who's done this a thousand times can be. He was quick but never rushed. Every motion was purposeful. A man who had worked with his hands, his entire life marked by the quiet labor of fixing things.

"Good hose, good fix," Roger said, tightening the last bolt. "You drive now, no leak. No more leak. It's good for you."

I nodded, grateful for his help. I'd need to be back on the road soon. The horizon was calling. The Texas plains stretch out under an endless sky, always wide and open, like the promise of something just beyond the next hill.

As we worked, my mind drifted back to the place where I had grown up. It's a curious thing, how the places of our childhood stay with us, tucked into corners of our memory. The old farm, just north of here, where my dad supported the family off the land with a mule team and an iron plow.

My dad was a teenager when he moved with his family to Texas to farm north of Fort Worth. Shortly thereafter, his dad, my grandfather, died and left him the responsibility of the farm and caring for his mother, two younger brothers, and two sisters. He never complained about it—not to us. But I think about it now, how a seventeen-year-old boy was suddenly tasked with keeping a farm running, keeping a family fed. That weight had to have been heavy.

I remember him telling me stories of that time—how, when my grandfather passed, he didn't have the money to pay for anything extra. They were poor, just getting by. But my dad had something else. He had a drive—a true grit.

During the night, the neighbor took the mules my grandfather had purchased from him on a monthly payout. The neighbor said he didn't think a teenager, my dad, would be able to finish paying for them. My dad stood his ground.

The neighbor didn't think much of a teenager standing up to him, but my dad wasn't afraid. With the shotgun in hand, he walked to the neighbor's barn and made it clear—those mules were his, and he was taking them back.

"You stole 'em," he'd said, voice steady.

The neighbor shrugged, but he didn't argue. In that moment, my dad stood tall—strong.

He wasn't just fighting for mules. He was fighting for his family, for the land, for survival.

I never saw my dad cry, not in the way you'd expect. But when he talked about that time, about the loss and the fight and the weight of it all, his eyes would get a little glassy. There was something in that moment—a quiet strength in the way he carried it, a look in his eyes I will never forget.

I turned the wheel, watching the road wind ahead, thinking about how much of who I am today was shaped by that farm, by those years my dad spent under the Texas sun, working the land. He never said much, but in the stories he told, the lessons he taught, it was clear. The road ahead may not always be easy, but you keep walking it. You keep planting trees.

I was born in Cowtown, which isn't as much a place as it is an attitude. Fort Worth, Texas, where the hum of cattle ranches and the smell of oil are in the air. Western lore abounds. The infamous outlaws Butch Cassidy and the Sundance Kid once posed for photographs standing proudly and unyieldingly at a hotel in the Stockyards, just north of downtown Fort Worth. Men drove herds there once, long before the highways and the noise of cars, when the rail lines clattered and steam engines hissed. They drank whiskey in the saloons and bet on the weight of steers. Cowboys leaned on fences and told lies they half-believed. Now the crowds come to watch the ghosts of it all—longhorns, old brick streets, the rattle of spurs on wood.

My dad, after farming for his entire young life and serving in the Navy during WWII, got a job in the Stockyards, pushing sides of beef around in the cold storage lockers of Swift Packing Company. It launched his career on the business side of that industry, helping feed a growing nation.

Cowtown! Fort Worth wears that bovine moniker as a badge of honor. The place bears the marks of cattle ranchers and oil tycoons who made their fortunes from the land. Back in the day, guys in big hats made insane amounts of money pulling black gooey stuff out of the ground and convincing large, stubborn cows to stand around until they became steaks.

Note to Self

A native Texas old timer told me, "It turns out we've been guarding the wrong borders," he said. "The real invaders aren't coming from the Southern border and from overseas. Nope! The real threat to Texas is the Northern border. Yankee's rolling in from the East and West Coast with gluten-free snacks and opinions about how to barbecue. Like putting ketchup on brisket. That ain't right."

Another old timer said, "Come on down, just don't mess with the brisket, 'cause that's where Texans draw the line. You can bring your fancy lattes, your yoga mats, even your unsolicited advice about cowboy hats, but don't you dare try to put ketchup on the brisket. It's not just meat—it's state pride, smoked glory, and a spiritual experience wrapped in butcher paper. Otherwise, welcome y'all."

Most Texans are standing tall with open arms and open hearts to everyone. But beware: just in case you're not one of the good guys ... it's open-carry, and Texans know how to shoot.

27

FIELDS OF OIL

The secret of success: Get up early, work late ... and strike oil.

JOHN D. ROCKEFELLER

ONCE YOU DRIVE THROUGH THE Grand Prairie and Western Cross Timbers regions west of the Dallas–Fort Worth metroplex, you're into the West Texas Rolling Plains—an expanse of sandy soil dotted with scrub oak, juniper, live oak, and pinyon pine. The landscape doesn't change much in the High Plains of the Texas Panhandle, where you find the same desert terrain, with a few additions—cottonwood, mesquite, and prairie crabapple scattered along the way. It feels like West Texas could go on forever, a stretch of land that seems endless as Argo and I continue along its vast, often monotonous roads. I'm fortunate, though, to be traveling in an airconditioned motor coach, not on horseback or in a covered wagon like the pioneers once did. Columnist Michael Barr once shared a quote from a *New Yorker* journalist who said, "I know all about West Texas. It's the place with the most cows and the least milk, the most rivers and the least water, where you can look the farthest and see the least."

Or, in the words of the iconic film *Thelma and Louise:* "Well, we're not in the middle of nowhere, but we can see it from here."

Texas spans 880 miles from east to west (excluding the Panhandle) and covers nearly 270,000 square miles. It's the second-largest state in the U.S., behind Alaska—about 10 percent larger than France, almost twice the size of Germany or Japan, and more than twice the size of the United Kingdom. If Texas were its own country, it would rank as the fortieth-largest nation in the world. It is, in a word, *vast.*

The drive ahead is long, stretching across unbending roads that seem to go on forever. It's a perfect time to think—about Texas, about life, about where I am.

The Native American tribes that originally inhabited the area now known as Texas included the Alabama, Apache, Atakapan, Bidai, Caddo, Aranama, Comanche, Choctaw, Hasinai, Jumano, Karankawa, Kickapoo, Kiowa, Tonkawa, and Wichita. The name "Texas" comes from the word *táysha'*—meaning "friend"—in the Caddoan language of the Hasinai, which the Spanish often spelled "Tejas."

The first Europeans to claim Texas were the Spanish, who controlled the region for the next couple of centuries, up until the Texas Revolution. The Spanish were notoriously cruel toward the

Native American populations. The United States got involved in the Texas Revolution, fighting the Spanish for more land to fuel westward expansion. After winning the war, the U.S. inherited the land and continued to mistreat the Native Americans, passing the Indian Removal Act and forcing the relocation of tribes to what would become Indian Territory (now Oklahoma). I won't dive deeper into this here, but Texas history—its expulsion of Native Americans, its history of slavery, and its wars with Mexico—is both fascinating and disheartening.

The Republic of Texas officially became a U.S. state on December 29, 1845. Perhaps what Texas is best known for is its oil boom, which began in the early twentieth century. In 1901, the discovery of a vast petroleum reserve near Beaumont, Texas, ushered in an era of rapid industrialization and growth unlike any before it. By 1940, Texas was the dominant force in U.S. oil production. The state we know today owes much to that boom.

I'm driving northwest from Fort Worth, taking the smaller highways past Wichita Falls and heading a bit further north to Burkburnett, Texas. Burkburnett has a rich history tied to Texas oil, though beyond that, there's not much to write home about.

Ranchers settled here around 1856, and the population barely broke 100 until 1912, when someone drilled a hole in the earth that would change everything. A hole much deeper than any of the surrounding wheat fields ever grew.

I pass a small roadside monument and pull over to check it out. The plaque honors Burkburnett's role in Texas oil history, commemorating it as one of the more famous boomtowns of the era. Nearby, on the S.L. Fowler farm, a 2,200-barrel oil gusher was struck, igniting an oil boom that would bring thousands to this corner of Texas.

Oil poured up from the earth, money poured down from the sky, and people rushed in. At its peak, about 20,000 people descended upon Burkburnett, setting up makeshift camps near the oil fields. Behind the plaque, a few rusted remnants of the old oil rig still stand as silent witnesses to the prosperity, the labor, and the conflicts that came with it.

As I drive past the empty fields where the boomtown once stood, I spot a few oil pumps still working, pumping the same black gold that once fueled the town's meteoric rise.

One of the more notable conflicts that followed the discovery of oil in Burkburnett was a dispute over state lines. The Red River had long been the natural boundary between Texas and Oklahoma. That was fine until oil was found near the river. The U.S. Supreme Court settled the matter in the early 1920s, determining that the Texas border would be the south bank of the Red River. The decision added a little fuel to a rivalry—one that plays out each year in the college football game between the Texas Longhorns and the Oklahoma Sooners.

The wildcatters' bold history made Burkburnett famous, and the town earned international recognition when the book *Lady Comes to Burkburnett* was adapted into the movie *Boomtown*, starring Spencer Tracy and Clark Gable. The film romanticized the Texas oil boom years and Burkburnett's role in it.

Texas has a long, storied history, but to complete my loop around the United States, I need to keep moving west. I stop at a gas station, and while filling up, I strike up a conversation with a guy standing at the pump. His skin is darkened by the relentless Texas sun, and his worn steel-toed boots carry the marks of hard work. A mix of faded denim covers him, stained with oil smudges. His baseball cap, bearing an oil company logo, is caked with grime.

"So, you used to work in an oil field, huh?" I ask, motioning toward his hat.

"Yep, sure did ... for about five years. It was like being in a cross between a cowboy movie and a heavy metal concert—only with more dirt and less music."

"Ha! I can imagine it's a lot of hard work."

"Picture this," he said. "There's a giant metal beast—called a 'derrick'—standing 200 feet tall. When it starts swaying in the wind, you realize that if it ever decides to fall, you're dead. But hey, at least there's coffee. Lots of coffee."

"Were you ever afraid of, you know, blowing up?"

"Only every day. You're standing next to a 10,000-pound pipe of raw chaos, and it's one spark away from turning into something out of *Die Hard*. It's like playing dodgeball with dynamite. But eventually, you stop worrying about it."

"Were there ever any big screw-ups?" I ask, unsure why that question slipped out.

"Oh, buddy, they happen. One time, we had a spill so big it looked like a lake of crude oil. You could've water-skied across it. Spent the next two days cleaning it up. And let me tell you—nothing says 'good times' like shoveling oil in 110-degree heat. But we got it done."

"Dang, that sounds like hard work," I said, "but I bet the pay's good."

"Yep, the pay's great, but if you're not sweating, you've probably already died. And I learned that coffee can replace sleep. Thinking about giving it a try?"

"Nope, just curious."

After all that, I figured if you can survive a job like that, you can survive anything. As for me? I'll take my chances on the open road, a bit safer, a bit quieter. But West Texas? It doesn't change. And neither, I think, do the people who live here. They're built for it.

Note to Self

Cruising across Texas, I spot two things working harder than a caffeinated squirrel — oil wells bobbing like they're doing squats to keep our lights and AC running, and massive wind turbines spinning like they're trying to cool off the whole state. One pumps up and down for crude, the other spins round, and together they prove that Texans don't choose sides — they just want to dominate all forms of energy. Because why settle for one kind of power when you can run the whole dang country?

Sure, L.A. was built on rock 'n roll, Botox, and bad parking. But Texas? Texas was built on grit, determination, pride, and the sweet, slick nectar of the Lone Star economy: oil, y'all.

28

CADILLAC RANCH

All things are engaged in writing their history ... Not footsteps in the snow, or along the ground, but prints in characters more or less lasting, a map of its march. The ground is all memoranda and signatures, and every object covered over with hints. In nature, this self-registration is incessant, and the narrative is the print of the seal.

RALPH WALDO EMERSON

I HAD BEEN ON the lonely stretch of Highway 287 northwest of Wichita Falls for what felt like a lifetime. Somewhere past Electra, near Oklaunion, Texas, with Vernon by my side, I was feeling the full wrath of the Texas sun, which beat down mercilessly on Argo's hood. It wasn't just heat; it was an assault, pushing relentlessly into my eyes, like some kind of personal vendetta from the sky.

The desert stretched endlessly in all directions, an ocean of emptiness that made me wonder if I had lost my mind. Just as the sun seemed to swallow the horizon whole, I caught sight of something in the distance, a shimmering illusion—perhaps a break from the monotony, or maybe a mirage, borne from the heat.

I squinted. Up ahead, two figures lounged on what looked like a Cadillac convertible. Were they real? Was I finally losing it? It seemed impossible, but as I closed the gap, the truth became undeniable—two girls in bikinis, posed as if waiting for a photographer to snap a shot. One blonde. One brunette. Too perfect. Too still. Were they mannequins? Maybe. But at that moment, who was to say?

As I drew nearer, I could see the details. The girls were as flawless as they were surreal— smooth faces like something plucked from an artist's dream. Maybe they were sculpted by a skilled hand, or maybe their beauty was preserved by some secret cosmetic elixir. Whatever the case, they sat there—perfect in their strange stillness on the plush white leather back seat of a 1972 green Cadillac convertible, which, as it turned out, was more than just an idle tourist attraction.

No, these two "girls" were part of a twisted tribute—art, or eccentricity, depending on how you looked at it. I later learned that the man who lived in the house behind the car had placed the mannequins there, a quirky homage to his lost daughter and her friend. The whole thing was a surreal spectacle, a bizarre break in the dull, desert landscape.

It made me chuckle. Only in America could you find such a strange and oddly beautiful roadside feature—part art, part heartache, all strange. I felt the stories of this country pressing in on me, stories of laughter, loss, and the odd beauty that comes from both.

As I pulled away from the Cadillac, I couldn't help but smile, knowing that the road had more surprises in store. I left behind Highway 287 for the quieter, lonelier Highway 20, only to find more oddities waiting.

This time, I saw people parking their cars and walking into a field, not aimlessly but with purpose. A pilgrimage of sorts. The cars were abandoned on the side of the road, and what lay beyond the gate was more of the same: Cadillacs. But not just any Cadillacs. These were partially buried, nose down, tail fins boldly pointed skyward. Dozens of them, covered in layers of graffiti. A makeshift graveyard of luxury, reborn as public art.

Each car seemed to stand like an eternal monument to wanderlust, a middle finger to the conventional, and a testament to the people who passed through. I watched as folks eagerly painted over old messages, leaving their own words and images behind—graffiti as communication, the ultimate mark of public art. Some painted declarations of love, some wrote messages of peace, others just left their name or added a splash of color. It was a community of strangers, uniting over something as simple as spray paint and metal.

But this wasn't just random vandalism. It was art in the making, a public collaboration with a rich history behind it. This surreal roadside spectacle was the brainchild of a group of San Francisco artists, Chip Lord, Doug Michels, and Hudson Marquez, who, back in 1974, had the strange idea to plant Cadillacs in the

Texas soil. They'd convinced millionaire Stanley Marsh III of Amarillo to fund the project—and perhaps more impressively, they had secured a plot of land from Marsh, who had a knack for supporting bizarre projects. The Cadillac Ranch was born.

It was a tribute to the evolution of the Cadillac tail fin, yes, but more than that, it was a statement of rebelliousness—a monument to the creative spirit that refuses to be contained. I smiled to myself as I watched people interacting with the cars, adding their personal expressions to this ever-evolving canvas.

I'd expected nothing less from the open road. It had given me strange beauty, humor, and history all in one. And I realized, in that moment, that the road wasn't just about getting from one place to the next. It was about the stories along the way, and the odd, quirky marks left by the travelers who came before you.

That's West Texas for you—where the bizarre feels normal and every mile holds a new surprise, reminding you that sometimes, the most unexpected detours lead to the most unforgettable sights.

I hit the gas, leaving the Cadillacs in my rearview, headed for New Mexico—the Land of Enchantment. The road never ends, and neither does the story.

Note to Self

A bunch of old Cadillacs nose-first in the dirt and call it art — and you know what? It totally works. Fun stop. It's a spray-painted, chrome-covered reminder that art doesn't have to hang in a museum — sometimes it sticks out of the ground off the highway and dares you to bring a can of paint and a little imagination. You're *encouraged* to graffiti them. So, I did.

29

Mother Road

Well, if you ever plan to motor west, Just take my way that's the highway that's the best; get your kicks on Route 66.

BOBBY TROUP

AS IT TURNS OUT, YOU can still drive on pieces of the original pavement of America's "Mother Road." The remaining fragments of Route 66 are mostly dusty and desolate, but they remain a thrilling draw for travelers seeking to connect with a bygone era. Road signs from the forties, fifties, and sixties linger, and a handful of refurbished motor courts, lovingly restored by mom-and-pop owners, greet anyone who stops to soak in the historical charm.

Today, I'm getting my kicks on Route 66, first cruising along what's now the expressway, I-40, just west of Albuquerque. When the opportunity arises, I veer off the modern highway, returning to the old road. Route 66 is a path well-worn by dreamers and schemers heading west.

Spanning 2,448 miles from Chicago to Santa Monica, this legendary route was one of the first public highways designated in 1926, during America's shift toward the automobile. It became the primary east-west road for the western two-thirds of the country and served as a vital military supply route during wartime.

That old song about Route 66 started playing in my head—the one Bobby Troup wrote in the '40s. I grew up hearing it, and later my friend Tim Hauser sang it with The Manhattan Transfer, giving it that smooth jazz polish. Nelson Riddle's version made it famous all over again when it kicked off the TV show back in the '60s. It's one of those songs that plants itself in your brain, all swagger and swing, inviting you to follow the highway west like it's the road to freedom. And honestly, today it feels like it is.

With that tune looping through my mind, I imagine the ghosts of Route 66 still lingering at every curve, their stories haunting the road. I see young couples and desperate families, driving west, searching for something better—anything better. Old jalopies broke down, their owners at the mercy of unscrupulous mechanics. Canvas water bags hung from grills, ready to quench overheated engines as they labored through the desert sun.

The characters of Steinbeck's *Grapes of Wrath* float among those ghosts—the Joads and the Wilsons, the "Okies" fleeing the Dust Bowl of the 1930s and 1940s. The Dust Bowl, an environmental catastrophe, was a savage combination of drought and dry-land farming that turned fertile soil into dust. When high winds swept across the plains, they churned up vast clouds of dust, darkening the day and choking the life out of everything in their path.

Families, their livelihoods destroyed, piled their belongings onto rusty vehicles and headed west, hoping to find fertile soil in California. They rolled into the unknown, filled with hope and dreams of new beginnings in the land of opportunity. But California's farming communities were soon overwhelmed by the flood of migrants, forcing officials to set up roadblocks and turn people away. The Dust Bowl devastated lives, and the Great Depression worsened as a result.

Argo and I are driving west from the Laguna Pueblo, with the Acoma Pueblo to the south and Mount Taylor to the north, on our way to Gallup, New Mexico. We turn off onto the Cubero Loop, heading toward Cubero in Cibola County, a town once used as a Spanish garrison dating back to 1776.

It's here, at the Villa De Cubero Trading Post, that I'm confronted by the ghost of Ernest Hemingway. I've crossed paths with the writer before. In the Bahamas, I visited his hotel room in Bimini, where he penned his work overlooking the marina. I've been to his haunts in Spain, where faded black-and-white photos capture his visits to local bars. I even visited his home in Key West and his home in Cuba, just outside Havana.

And now, his shadow falls again in the dusty desert of New Mexico. The Villa De Cubero Trading Post, built in 1937 after Route 66 was realigned, once served as a stop for travelers refueling and resting. I park Argo near the brown stucco store, its traditional mud-red tile roof standing out against the tan desert.

Around back, I find a collection of dilapidated motor court rooms, each with a barn-door garage and a small overhang leading to a single red door. Once, these would have been a safe haven for weary travelers. Now, they stand silent, ghosts of the road.

I step inside the convenience store and make a beeline for the restroom, only to find it occupied. As I wait, I kill time reading a laminated magazine article about the trading post, mounted on a mahogany board on the wall. The piece chronicles the Hemingway connection, how the famous writer stayed here, writing in a ten-by-twelve-foot room and frequenting the cafe across the street.

While the trading post remains, the cafe where Hemingway frequented has long since been demolished. Mary Gunn, who ran the cafe from 1941 to 1972, was known for serving good home-cooked meals and becoming a beloved figure to the regulars. But she didn't care much for Hemingway. She said he never changed his clothes, and his room was always a mess, with empty liquor bottles tossed out his bathroom window. She called him the "Dirty Devil," though not to his face—she spoke it in Spanish, unaware that Hemingway was fluent in the language. As a response, Hemingway sent Mary a copy of his novel *Old Man and the Sea*, signed, "The Dirty Old Devil."

Continuing westward to Grants, New Mexico, I stop for a photo-op with Argo at a neon Route 66 sign, designed to fit the classic highway shield. The sign stands out during the day, but it truly comes alive at night, with the words "Grants, New Mexico" lit up in bold letters. Flames shoot up from the pavement, making for a dramatic scene.

After snapping a picture with Argo, I press on toward Gallup, passing through Bluewater, Prewitt, and Thoreau, just north of the Cibola National Forest.

When I finally reach Gallup, I spot the iconic El Rancho Hotel sign—a neon gem that looks like something straight out of the movies. "Home of the Movie Stars, the Restaurant 49er Bar," it boasts, along with "Amand Ortega's World Famous Indian Store." Beneath it, a sign advertises a salad with chicken for lunch and grilled salmon for dinner. And, of course, 40 percent off jewelry—an irresistible draw for collectors.

The El Rancho looks like it belongs in a film set, with its fluted-column entryway and neon-lit trim. It's a place where the charm of yesterday meets the convenience of tomorrow. Inside, the lobby is a step back in time. Navajo rugs and Hopi artifacts line the walls, with carved wood furniture and a massive stone fireplace. The place feels like a refuge for mythological heroes, the kind who once tamed the wild lands of the West. And it's precisely where Hollywood stars—like John Wayne, Katherine Hepburn, and Kirk Douglas—came to unwind after long days of filming Westerns.

The hotel was built with the movies in mind. D. W. Griffith's brother was behind its construction in 1936, providing a luxury retreat for film stars who graced the area. It's a far cry from the days when Lopez de Cardenas passed through Gallup in 1540, or when the Hopi lived here long before the first films were shot.

Curious about the history, I decided to drive through the Native American reservation lands, heading north on Highway 491. But before I leave Gallup, I have a minor run-in with a local. A man in a dirty white shirt pulls up alongside me in heavy traffic, giving me the finger and shouting something I can't hear. I catch a glimpse of his lips: the message is clear, though I can't make out the exact words. He's cursing at me, a real show of class.

I glance at him, hoping the message I send back will be clear enough: "You're not worth the fight." I turn the wheel and drift into the next lane, keeping my eyes on the road, but my mind starts racing. This can go one of two ways, I figure. I could rev it up, chase him down, get tangled up in something ugly—though I'd be an idiot if I did that—or I could just breathe, let it go, and keep rolling along the old highway. So, I do what any sane person would do in a moment like this: I hit the gas, pulling Argo ahead, and leave the encounter in my rearview mirror.

Gallup fades behind me, and with it, the tension, the irritation, and all the other distractions that didn't belong. Out here, it's just the open road and me. Something is soothing about that. After all, this is Route 66, the place where the road doesn't just connect towns and cities; it connects you to a different way of thinking, a different mindset.

The further west I go, the more I sense it—the past. It's all over the place, hanging in the air like the scent of sagebrush after a summer rain, whispering the stories of all the people who've passed this way before me. They came in search of something—an answer, a place, a future—and they found it—or they didn't.

As I press on, I can't help but think of the people who've made this journey before me: the Okies, the dreamers, the drifters. I think of Steinbeck's Joads, driving west in search of hope, of a better life, of redemption. Their struggles. Those terrible, overwhelming struggles are etched into the very pavement of Route 66. And I wonder: what drives a person to make such a journey, to leave behind everything known for something unknown, something uncertain?

The wind picks up, tugging at the edges of my mind, and soon, I'm crossing over the New Mexico border, leaving the past behind and venturing deeper into the unknown. The land here is open, wild, and raw, with the occasional cactus or rocky outcropping dotting the landscape, casting long, crooked shadows in the bright sunlight. The kind of place where anything can happen, and everything seems possible.

Somewhere in the distance, the silhouette of a lone coyote cuts across the horizon. It's like a living reminder that life here is still wild and untamed. And maybe that's the way it's supposed to be, after all. No matter how many roads are paved, no matter how many towns are built, there will always be that ragged edge, that spirit of the land, that calls out to the dreamers, the wanderers, the ones who still believe in the magic of the road.

Note to Self

Route 66 — the original American express lane with the taxidermy-decorated gas station with gas, donuts, Dr. Pepper, jerky, and questionable hot dogs. Before Google Maps and Yelp, people just got in their cars and hoped they didn't end up in a ditch or abducted by UFO aliens.

I loved cruising through Texas on the Mother Road.

It's not just a black-top jaunt as much as a crosscountry fever dream with visions of the ghost of the dreamers and Dust Bowl farmers heading West. Well, and that one guy dressed like Elvis riding a unicycle.

30

Pueblos of the Southwest

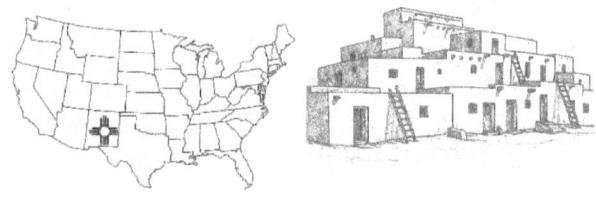

All dreams spin out from the same web.
HOPI PROVERB

PERHAPS I HAD BEEN STARING toward the sun too long, driving west. I felt a foreshadowing—a spiritual overhang—as I passed through the various Native American tribal territories in New Mexico and Arizona. As unlikely as it may seem, these landscapes felt vividly familiar. Strange, since I had never been here.

The rugged terrain unfolded before me, a canvas painted with earthy red, orange, and brown hues. The soil held stories of generations. The high mesas and buttes stood proudly against the azure sky, seeming to guard the secrets of the Hopi people, whispering tales of resilience and connection to the land.

The mesas created a dramatic backdrop against the horizon with their flat tabletops. Clusters of ancient dwellings perched on cliffs like sentinels of time, speaking of a civilization that has endured for centuries. The architecture blended seamlessly with the natural contours of the landscape.

As I ventured deeper, the desert flora revealed itself in bursts of color. Hardy sagebrush and resilient desert flowers dotted the arid land, offering a stark yet vibrant contrast to the sunbaked earth. The scent of desert plants lingered in the air, a fragrant reminder of the resilience of life in this seemingly harsh environment.

The familiarity of the desert scenery and the déjà vu feelings were likely from all those childhood Western movies and TV shows I watched growing up.

The kids in the neighborhood and I would play "Cowboys and Indians" in our reenactments, switching parts willy-nilly. On television, the Lone Ranger rode his horse, Silver, with his trusty sidekick, Tonto, who rode Scout, fighting for justice against the lawless Cavendish Gang. With a "Hi-yo Silver! Away!" the Lone Ranger set out while Tonto shouted, "Git-um up, Scout!" And off they went, chasing down the bad guys.

Of course, the Lone Ranger was a Texas Ranger in the show, filmed most likely on a California sound stage, but the settings I remember were more like what I was driving through now in Arizona. The desert scenery, with rolling yellow dunes reflecting the harsh sun, is beautiful and foreboding. How could anyone survive out here?

Initially, I had planned to stay on the Hopi reservation near one of the mesas, at a place I found labeled on a map as an RV park. When I arrived near sunset, a narrow winding road took me past a smashed trailer—windows broken, sides beaten in. The next trailer had been set on fire. Another one had been violently smashed by something or someone.

Spooky. I felt like bad voodoo spirits surrounded me, evidenced by the hair standing up on my arms and neck. Was I in a haunted RV park, one that could easily have been a setting for a Stephen King book? I was creeped out.

I couldn't get out of there and back on the main road quickly enough. Later, when I inquired, no one wanted to talk about what had happened in that place. I never solved the mystery.

As the sun dropped further down the horizon, my energy faded. I needed to find a place to camp for the night. Down the road, I parked Argo between the pinyons and junipers. The quiet of the desert shifted from eerie to calming as I put my fears to rest, and my body gave way to exhaustion from the long drive.

The next day, after waking, I drove a bit further, discovering I wasn't too far from a small Hopi hotel on what is called Mesa 2. It's the only hotel in this part of Arizona on Hopi land. It also serves as their cultural center, museum, craft shop, and restaurant.

I sampled traditional Hopi *talavaynova* (breakfast food), *wuu'taqa* (blue corn mush), and blue pancakes, and I also tried the *noqkwivi* (tortillas dipped in lamb stew). Blue corn is their iconic survival food, sustaining generations in these desolate sands.

That was on Mesa 2. I drove down the road to the Old Oraibi village, which maintains a more traditional Hopi way of life. While visitors can go to the front road to the pueblo, the residents tend to be private. They do not allow photographs to be taken in the town. There are few ground-level photographs of the settlement today, though public satellite imagery is readily available to the curious.

A young Hopi, maybe in his late teens or early twenties, steps out of one of the mud huts to see why I am there. He is cautious. As am I.

After we talk for a few minutes, he allows me to walk with him into the village of Oraibi —a series of mud structures. He shares some history as we walk over the sandy soil mixed with tiny shards of broken pottery left behind over thousands of years. I sense generations of spirits lingering in this place, one of America's oldest continually inhabited villages.

Life moves slower than a turtle on the Hopi Reservation, especially compared to where I started the road trip six months ago in frantic New York City—on the peculiar, manic-paced election night of November 2016.

"The white man's world moves too fast," the young Hopi says, looking out across the Arizona desert. As a fair-skinned reporter from the city, I have to agree as I stand with him outside the storied village of Old Oraibi, a Hopi village in Navajo County, Arizona. Founded sometime before AD 1100, Oraibi is one of the oldest inhabited settlements within the United States.

The young Hopi calls for his uncle to join us. My two new friends are real-life, flesh-and-blood descendants of the Pueblo peoples who thrived here when the Spaniards explored the area in the sixteenth century.

Both were born on the Hopi reservation. The older one is Brad. Clinton is the Americanized name of the younger one. As a teenager, Clinton rebelled against his roots, moving to the city to experience a more exciting lifestyle. It was stimulating for a moment, then became disturbing—it was nothing like he had imagined. Finally, he had had enough of the constant hustle and bustle of the world and returned to his more meaningful life on the reservation, close to the earth, a place considered sacred by his tribe.

I want to be sensitive to my new Hopi friends, and I'm confused by conflicting terms used to refer to their tribe. Different names are widely used: Indian? Native American? First People? First Nations?

So, I take the direct approach (which I am known to do). "How do you prefer to be called?"

"Hopi ... call us by our tribe name, Hopi. I am a Hopi."

None of the other names are offensive, except for "First People" and "First Nations," which they tell me are used only by the Canadians. "Calling us Native Americans and Indians is not offensive to us, but we prefer our tribe names."

With that cleared up, we started talking about the water. There is still no running water in Oraibi.

"It was told to us, do not rip Mother Earth open to lay your pipeline," Brad says. "And do not put these wires across your yard [referring to the phone and high-voltage electricity wires on poles running along the highway] because they bring something down on you, which is radiation.

All these things have been foretold to us."

They constantly refer to both the land and their ancestors with reverence and respect.

"They say ... live the simple good life, and you will go a long way. If you turn from this, your life will be cut short." Brad sums it up: "Don't mess anything up. Respect Mother Earth.

That's who we call our Mother. She provides for us. We should take care of her."

Oddly, of all the places I've been on this road trip, I want to stay longer here. The little boy side of me tugs at me to roam these desert lands and learn more about the surviving caretakers of Mother Earth in this seemingly forsaken, remote part of America. Maybe this is where you find God—in the seemingly forsaken parts.

I'm taken by the Hopi's spiritual approach to all things in life—a deep respect for all forms of life on Earth, from rocks to animals. "We are all one—the Earth, the animals, the rocks, the people," they tell me. "We are to respect all."

If every human could live by and practice the simple creed, "Respect all," there would be no need for 99 percent of our laws.

I leave Old Oraibi with great reluctance. Driving toward the Grand Canyon, I visualize the ghosts of many Hopi who traveled this same trail, walking and on horseback, over the past centuries. Now, Argo and I travel the path.

And then, as night fell, the sky transformed into a celestial masterpiece. The absence of city lights revealed a blanket of stars stretching from horizon to horizon, a cosmic spectacle that connected me to the ancient stargazing traditions of the Hopi people. The silence of the desert night seemed to echo with the wisdom of ages, inviting contemplation under the vast celestial dome.

In every crevice of the Hopi Reservation, there was a palpable sense of connection to the land—an interwoven tapestry of nature and culture that told a story written not just in the rocks and canyons but also in the hearts of the Hopi people.

Note to Self

My more "enlightened" friends told me not to say, "Indians" like from the old Westerns and never say "tribesmen" unless you're narrating a 1950s National Geographic special ... from a time machine. Wanting to be respectful of my new Hopi friends, I asked what they thought on the matter, and guess what they reported? They have no trouble with either name. Actually, they prefer to be called by their tribe's name—Navajo, Hopi, Zuni, Apache, and the Pueblo peoples. They said, "indigenous people" is what they call people who live in Canada.

Got it? Good. Now pass the fry bread, and let's move on.

31

Canyon Rim

Landscape can enlarge the impinged range for self to move in.

GEORGE ELIOT

CAMPING IN THE U.S. NATIONAL PARKS is a humbling experience. As I made my way through America's vast and diverse landscapes, I found solace in knowing that most of these parks welcome weary travelers like me to spend the night amidst their natural wonders.

And that's a gift, because it takes more than a day to truly appreciate the unique features of each park. Camping is typically arranged through reservations, and it's affordable, whether you're tent camping or staying in an RV.

So, despite not having advanced reservations and it being a busy time, I lucked out finding a campsite for the night on the rim of the Grand Canyon. As the sun hung low on the horizon, casting a warm, golden hue over the rugged terrain, I marveled at the sheer magnitude of the universe. The Grand Canyon demanded time to be truly appreciated, where the layers of history and nature told stories spanning millions of years.

It was a place where you could feel the weight of time itself. And for a moment, I realized that in the heart of nature's grandeur, even without a reservation, I had found a home for the soul.

The next morning, I brewed my coffee as usual, savoring the quiet. Remembering the camp host volunteer's warning that the few "walk-up" campsites fill up early each day, I dressed and moseyed over to the machine near the shower building that dispenses paid reservation receipts. I made sure to secure my spot for another night.

Returning to Argo, I poured another cup of coffee and grabbed a protein bar from the overhead cabinet for breakfast. As the clock inched closer to nine, I reclined in my seat, read a few pages of my notes, and began writing. My muse whispered in my ear. I was aware of nothing else.

The words flowed effortlessly until nearly three o'clock. That's what happens when I focus—time ceases to exist. I'd forgotten to eat. I was transported to a different place, a different world.

That's what it's like when the creative muse visits. She's assertive, a force that sweeps me into a creative flow when I let her. Too many times I've swished her away, ignoring her. But I've learned—if I do that, she vanishes. She becomes elusive, and when I call, she ignores me. She is a jealous and vengeful muse. But I know I need her, so when she whispers my name, I heed the call and give her my time.

The pain in my lung returned. I didn't want to panic, but it grabbed my attention. My muse had to wait. I drove to the hospital in Flagstaff, where I spent three hours in the waiting room, followed by an even longer stretch in an exam room. I was never questioned, touched, or examined for eight hours. No blood work. No urine samples. No MRI scan.

The distant thudding of helicopter blades filled the air, an unexpected and unsettling soundtrack to my night at the Grand Canyon. I watched as they descended, one after another, like giant birds alighting on the earth. A calm nurse explained that the helicopters were bringing fall victims from the canyon's treacherous trails.

"It's an unfortunate part of life around the canyon," she said, her voice steady, as though she had witnessed this many times before. "Most falls are minor, from hiking the trails—broken bones and such."

As I waited, my sense of urgency about my situation began to fade. I realized how fortunate I was. My discomfort and pain were nothing compared to the ordeal of those souls who had fallen, bouncing off the canyon's rock walls into the abyss. It was a sobering reminder of the fragility of life in the face of nature's grandeur.

Finally, it was my turn to be examined. The doctor's diagnosis brought both relief and a tinge of embarrassment. My condition wasn't life-threatening; there was no blood clot, no dire emergency. In the grand scheme of things, my discomfort seemed trivial.

I couldn't help but feel a mix of emotions—gratitude that my condition wasn't worse, and a sense of foolishness for taking up valuable medical resources for what now seemed like a minor ailment. But ultimately, it was a lesson in perspective, a reminder that even in the shadow of dramatic events, our worries can sometimes pale compared to the challenges others face.

Note to Self

Camping on the rim of the Grand Canyon — because nothing says "living on the edge" like sleeping near the edge of a million-year-old hole in the ground that could swallow both Argo and me whole. You're in a national park, baby! Which means no Wi-Fi, no Uber Eats, and no Starbucks for another time zone or two.

But hey, where else can you wake up to a sunrise so epic it looks like God painted it with a blowtorch? The views are unreal, the air is pure, and my cell phone's just a paperweight with Internet withdrawal. It's characterbuilding with a side of "Did you hear that noise?" every five minutes.

32

Night Cometh

When man ignores the supernatural, he does not become natural, but unnatural.

G. K. CHESTERTON

THIS MORNING, I HEAD BACK to the old Route 66 that cuts through Arizona, picking up the road where I left off to continue my westward journey. But before I do, I feel a pull toward Sedona, that spiritual enclave hidden among the high desert. There's something about the way the light dances on the red sandstone formations that calls to me. In the early morning or late evening, when the sun spills its last golden rays over the rocks, those formations ignite, glowing in brilliant oranges and reds, as if they're alive. It's a place where the earth seems to hum with something ancient, something sacred. And yet, for all its quiet beauty, Sedona also pulses with the energy of outdoor enthusiasts—hikers, bikers, and seekers all drawn to its mystic promise. Sedona's human history dates back between 11,500 and 9,000 years ago, with Native American tribes calling this place home long before the first tourists arrived during the 1950s. The town's been immortalized in Hollywood too, with films like *Angel and the Badman* and the original *3:10 to Yuma* putting it on the map as a cinematic backdrop.

I point Argo south toward Sedona, the open road unfurling ahead of me. The highway is a narrow strip of blacktop, bordered by tall pine trees that stand like sentinels on either side. As I draw closer to Sedona, the landscape shifts, and the red rocks begin to emerge from the earth, their colors more vivid the nearer I get. Around each bend, the rocks loom larger, bold and proud, their deep oranges and reds glowing as though the light itself is rising from within. Every curve in the road offers another breathtaking view, as if the earth itself were putting on a show, revealing formations shaped like something from an old fairy tale—tall, proud, and impossibly grand. This is a place where the myths of the land seem to take form before your eyes.

Wandering through the town a little, I take in its spas, health-conscious stores, and the quiet hum of people searching for something. Time, however, is slipping away. I need to find a place for Argo and me to sleep, but in Sedona, that's no easy task. Even hotels are few and far between, and those that exist tend to cater to last-minute travelers like me—small inns full of New Agers on pilgrimages of self-discovery.

Finding a campsite for an RV is even rarer. But somehow, I've always managed to land on my feet. At least that's what I tell myself when luck seems to favor me.

I pull out my map of the Coconino National Forest, a green-and-brown patchwork of shaded woodlands and rocky outcrops surrounding Sedona, and find a few spots labeled "primitive" or "dispersed." Primitive camping means no fancy bathrooms or paved roads. Dispersed camping is as old-school as it gets—you find a patch of earth, pitch your tent, and call it home for the night.

That suits me fine. I trust my instincts, and they tell me there's something out there waiting. I find a spot where the signs of previous campers are scattered about—an old campfire ring, some charred remnants of wood—and decide this is where I'll settle. The land around me is wild and untamed, desert grass swaying gently in the breeze, with hills rising like ancient sentinels all around. Cedar trees climb the slopes, standing tall and proud in the fading light.

The sunset comes like a painter's final flourish, splashing the western sky with hues of orange, yellow, and blue that could've been pulled from the most vivid of dreams. There's not a soul around, just me and the land. I stand outside Argo for a moment, breathing in the stillness, my ears playing tricks on me—banjo music from somewhere deep in the hills. It's a strange thought. Perhaps I'm imagining it, or maybe it's something else. But for a second, I think I hear the eerie, off-kilter twang of banjos from the movie *Deliverance* playing in the distance.

Suddenly, the idea of being all alone in this wild stretch of desert hits me. No cell service, no one around for miles. What if something happens? What if I need help and there's no one to call?

But my adventurous side pushes the fear aside. Silence. How often do I get to experience this kind of silence? The silence of the desert, the silence of nature—deep and unbroken. The silence of the real world, unfiltered by the noise of modern life. I stood there for a long while, watching the clouds stretch lazily across the sky. Slowly, the peace of the place seeps into me, quieting my restless thoughts. The sunset wraps around me like a blanket, and I let it in, soaking up every minute of it.

The desert heat begins to fade as night approaches. It's a familiar transformation—the sweltering daytime heat gives way to a coolness that never ceases to amaze me. How can a place so hot in the day become so cool at night? It's as though the earth itself inhales and exhales differently when the sun sets.

The sky darkens behind the hills. "Night cometh," I whisper to myself, feeling the stillness settle in.

As the desert air cools, I lie down, the silence wrapping me like a soft cocoon. I drift into sleep, the desert night filling my dreams, only to be interrupted by the startling, absolute quiet of the place. I wake briefly, my senses alert.

Then, it happens—a noise. Tires crunching along the rocky road near my campsite. No way. I jerk upright in bed, straining to hear. The sun's just beginning to rise, and there's enough light now to see—yes, there's something out there. Not far from the campsite, behind the scrub brush, I catch a glimpse of a tattered, fading blue pickup truck, creeping past the campsite. Its tires grind against the rock.

My heart leaps. I fumble for my binoculars, digging them out of the front passenger seat of Argo. I slide over to the rear window, peering through the nightshades as I try to make sense of what's going on.

The truck's gone. Just like that. My heart's still racing, my mind spinning with possibilities. There's always something unnerving about the early morning hours—times when strange, unexpected things happen.

But there's no sign of anyone, no movement, just the eerie quiet that had greeted me earlier. I grab my nightstick "defender," crack open Argo's sliding door, and scan the area. Ready to defend or make a quick escape if need be.

And then—an enormous sound shatters the calm. A roar from the sky, a sound like nothing I've ever heard before. *Ba-rahrrrrrrrrmmmm!*

What in the world?

Again—*ba-rahrrrrrrrr… ba-rahrrrrrr…*

I cock my head upward, squinting into the morning light. A balloon. A giant, colorful hotair balloon drifts overhead, the burner firing off bursts of sound, pushing the balloon higher into the sky. The roar of the flame is deafening, like a beast bellowing from above.

Out of the corner of my eye, I spot a blur of motion—something scurrying across the brush. I turn, focus, and see it more clearly this time: a lizard, racing after breakfast.

Then, another sound, this one different—a high-pitched whine, like the scream of a jet cutting through the air. I look to my left, and there it is—a scale model airplane zooming through the sky, performing loops and rolls, piloted by a man standing next to the old truck. He's gripping a controller, his brightly painted blue-

and-yellow model soaring through the air like it's got a mind of its own.

I can't help it. The laughter spills out, sudden and uncontrollable. Here I am, in the middle of nowhere, in the desert, thinking I'm all alone—and yet, the place is alive with people chasing balloons, flying model airplanes, and carrying on with life like it's any other day. I laugh even harder as I make my coffee, sipping it slowly, watching the people in the balloon's basket wave at me. I wave back, grinning at the absurdity of it all—the quiet desert morning shattered by the sound of laughter, engines, and adventure, a new day unfolding in the most unexpected of ways.

Note to Self

The quiet in the Arizona desert isn't just "peaceful" — it's so quiet I start hearing weird stuff: my heartbeat, my eyelids blinking, my stomach questioning why I thought beef jerky was a sufficient meal. It's so still, even the tumbleweeds roll by like, "Sorry, didn't mean to interrupt" while I'm having a full-blown existential crisis. But hey — sometimes you gotta get lost in the desert to find yourself. Or at least to find a rock that looks like Nicolas Cage.

Either way, worth it—as long as I have water. Lots of water.

33

WALL OF SAND

If you sing of beauty though alone in the heart of the desert you will have an audience.

KHALIL GIBRAN

THE SKY ERUPTS IN A riot of orange, pink, and violet, as if the heavens themselves have caught fire. The Arizona desert, sprawling and relentless, stretches in all directions, its dunes rolling like waves frozen in time, its scrub brush clinging stubbornly to life. One thing never changes out here—the heat.

One hundred five degrees is oppressive, like standing too close to an open oven. But one hundred fourteen? That's when the air itself turns predatory, a flamethrower licking at everything in sight. At that temperature, you're not just hot—you're being slow-roasted, the desert's latest offering to the sun.

Argo's gauge confirms the cruelty of the day, and the night isn't much kinder. Even after sundown, the heat lingers, as if the desert and the sun have sworn an oath never to part ways. I chuckle at the old "dry heat" excuse, the favorite line of anyone who hasn't felt this kind of inferno firsthand.

"Yeah," I always say, "so is the inside of an oven."

Out here, you don't just sweat—you desiccate. The air drinks you dry. It's a place that demands respect, a landscape beautiful in its brutality. From Phoenix to Sedona, through Yuma, and along the U.S.-Mexico border toward California, I drive, my appreciation growing with every mile. Something is mesmerizing about how life clings to this place, how it refuses to be beaten.

Then the border appears, an invisible yet indelible line dividing two worlds. On the lonely road ahead, two U.S. Border Patrol agents work with an almost eerie calm, dragging a chain of old tires behind a pickup, smoothing a twenty-foot stretch of sand. Their job is simple: erase the past, then wait for new footprints to tell the next story.

The desert does not give up its secrets easily, but human movement leaves marks. And so the agents watch, scan, and wait. They know the tricks—the ones who carry each other across, the branches dragged to obscure steps, the constant game of evasion and pursuit.

It's a battle of wits, fought under an unforgiving sun.

Yet, despite the struggle, there's an odd understanding here—a silent agreement between survival and enforcement. The border is a place of contradictions, where the law is clear but humanity still flickers through the cracks. I think about the people who attempt this crossing.

How many never make it? How many fall, unseen, into the belly of this vast, indifferent land? The vultures know the answer.

For decades, the U.S. has tried to deter crossings by forcing migrants into the deadliest parts of the desert. The theory: hardship will stop them. The reality: it doesn't. They still come, chasing hope, fleeing something worse. And many don't survive.

In 2000, John Hunter, a scientist and brother of Congressman Duncan Hunter, decided survival shouldn't be a gamble. He founded Water Station, a nonprofit placing high-flagged water jugs in the Imperial Valley Desert. Today, the group maintains more than 125 stations— simple, life-saving gestures in a brutal land.

There's an understanding here, too. The Border Patrol doesn't interfere with these water sites. A gentleman's agreement, they call it. Out here, politics takes a back seat to survival.

Still, the desert remains a lawless place. At night, smugglers and traffickers slip through, their promises often as dry and empty as the land itself. They tell desperate migrants that cars will be waiting, ready to carry them to safety, to jobs, to new lives. Sometimes, the cars are there.

More often, it's a lie.

I pull over on the dusty roadside, answering nature's call in the middle of nowhere.

Before I finish, a Border Patrol SUV eases up behind Argo. I wasn't alone after all.

The officer steps out, uniform crisp, demeanor unreadable. His arm rests near his holstered gun, not threatening, but ready. The desert has its own rules.

"What are you doing?" His voice is firm but not unkind.

"Just taking a break," I say, hoping my tone strikes the right balance between casual and cooperative. "On my way to San Diego. This road leads there, right?"

"Eventually," he says, nodding. "This can be a dangerous stretch. A lot of people stop here ... sometimes to pick up crossers. Not safe."

"I get it." I nod, then pause. I shouldn't say more, but curiosity wins out. "This might sound dumb, but ... I expected to see a wall."

He smiles slightly. "No wall. Some fence. Mostly markers."

I follow his gaze and spot them—small, unassuming posts, barely noticeable. Each one in sight of the next, just enough to remind the world of the invisible line they represent.

As the conversation continues, the desert looms around us, stretching endlessly, swallowing voices, holding stories in its sun-scorched silence. The borderlands are a strange place, where laws are firm, yet mercy finds a foothold. Where the land is harsh, but survival, somehow, persists.

Out here, everything is a contradiction. Even the heat.

NOTE TO SELF

Everyone's talkin' about the border wall, but from what I'm seeing here in the desert, Mother Nature already built her version — made entirely of sand, sun, and regret. Yeah... It's not steel, not concrete, not even barbed wire. It's sand. Just miles and miles of sun-blasted, ankle-deep, soul-sifting sand — nature's original "Do Not Enter" sign. You don't climb this wall... you trudge through it. Slowly. It's hot, it's dry, and it'll test your soul.

Forget politics — the real border patrol is the desert itself. The air carries the heat, but the sand carries judgment. The real barrier's a sunburned wasteland that smells like hot tires and lost dreams. Welcome to the border wall Mother Nature built.

34

La Jolla Sunset

*We are scattered, as well as affirmed, by
the places through which we move. ….
paths connected real places, but they also
led outwards to metaphysics, backwards
to history, and inwards to the self.*

ROBERT MACFARLANE, *THE OLD WAYS*

REACHING SAN DIEGO ALONG THE peaceful shores of the Pacific Ocean, I find a camping spot right on Silver Strand State Beach, a calm and sparkling sliver of seashore between the beach towns of Imperial Beach and Coronado.

The sun hangs low in the sky, casting long shadows across the golden sand. It's one of those moments that makes a man feel small, but not in a bad way.

I park Argo by the dunes alongside other campers. As I walk along the beach, the warm tropical breeze whispers secrets in my ear. The sand crunches beneath my feet, and I can taste the salt in the air. The Pacific Ocean stretches out like an endless expanse of blue, its waves crashing against the shore in a rhythmic dance.

Seagulls, those feathered scavengers, wheel overhead, calling out like old friends who've seen it all. They don't care about my journey; they have their affairs to attend to.

Silver Strand is no fancy resort. No, it's the kind of beach where people come to kick off their shoes, toss a frisbee, and let the water tickle their toes. Families set up picnics on the shore, kids build sandcastles, and couples stroll hand in hand.

I walk along the waterline, the cool waves lapping at my feet, and I can't help but chuckle. There's a sort of magic in the simplicity of it all, a reminder that life doesn't always have to be complicated. The beach has a way of making you forget your troubles, even if just for a while.

After my wife died, I took the kids for grief counseling. I thought it was essential to help my two children deal with the flood of emotions and adjust to our "new normal." Of course, I needed help too.

"What are you doing for fun?" the counselor asked me in a private session.

"Fun? I don't know what that is anymore. I'm so busy trying to keep everything afloat— being Master Mom and Mister Dad, taking them to school, soccer, music, and juggling my business on top of it all."

"Well, you need to carve out some time for yourself," she said. "What's something fun you used to do? What's the first thing that comes to mind?"

"Ah, geez, the first thing that comes to mind is walking on the beach. I'd like to feel sand between my toes."

"So, go walk on the beach! Take a weekend and walk on the beach."

"I'm not sure it will be fun now like it used to be," I said, obviously depressed.

"It probably won't be the first time," she said, "but keep walking. Do it a second time and a third, and it will be again after a while. Reconnect to what you love about the ocean and the beach."

As I walk, feeling the grains of sand between my toes, I can't help but think about that advice. "Live in the moment," she'd said. It sounded like some cliché you'd find on a motivational poster, but it makes perfect sense here, on the shores of Silver Strand Beach.

◄ ▲ ▼ ►

The sun, a fiery orb, sinks below the horizon, casting its last warm embrace on the world. The sky turns into a masterpiece of red and orange, as if some divine artist had taken a brush and painted the heavens. I watch in awe, feeling like a speck in the grand tapestry of the universe.

It's a moment to savor—to forget about the miles behind me, the roads as of now undriven, and the destinations yet to be reached. The road trip across America can wait; for here and now,

I am in the right place. The sound of the waves crashing on the shore is a soothing lullaby, and the cool breeze kisses my face like an old friend.

At that moment, I knew I had stumbled upon something extraordinary that would remain etched in my memory forever. It's a reminder that sometimes, the greatest treasures are found in the simplest of moments. I close my eyes, take a deep breath, and let the serenity of Silver Strand Beach wash over me.

After my quiet respite of sand and sun, the following day, I drive through San Diego, heading north toward the metropolis of Angels—Los Angeles. Or, as the rock-n-roll deejays back in the day called it, Boss-Angeles.

◀ ▲ ▼ ▶

Before leaving San Diego, I detour, meandering up to the stately veterans memorial atop Mt. Soledad. The road twists and turns, much like my journey across America. At the peak of an 822-foot suburban hill stands a twenty-two-foot white cross, a sentinel reaching into the heavens.

It's a sight to behold, a symbol of sacrifice and remembrance.

From that monument, the world lies at my feet. To the south, the sprawling city of San Diego stretches out. To the west and north, La Jolla, that gem of a town, perches on the cliffs, and the vast Pacific Ocean meets the horizon.

The view makes a Texas boy like me feel like a lone cowboy gazing at a wide-open range. But it isn't just the panorama that leaves me in awe; it's the history and the stories that echo through the air.

La Jolla, the jewel of the coast, clings to the cliffs like a precious gem. Gregory Peck, the old Hollywood legend, was born in these quiet streets when La Jolla was just a small town, a far cry from what it has become today. It evolved into a playground for the rich and famous, where mansions hug the sea, and luxury lives in every corner.

And then, there was Ted Geisel—Dr. Seuss himself. This was his final home, where he penned whimsical tales that generations of children adored. The hilltop and the sea breeze carry whispers of his rhymes, reminding me that great stories are born even in the most unexpected places.

A Dr. Seuss book was once left for me on a cold December morning by Santa (and hey, don't try to tell me otherwise about who left it under the tree) on Christmas morning. Holding the book was magical, with its colorful, quirky characters and artwork.

"You're off to great places! Today is your day! Your mountain is waiting, so … get on your way!"

I guess I took that to heart after all.

Dr. Seuss's characters resonated with me because of their whimsy—especially the mischievous Cat in the Hat, the kind-hearted Horton the Elephant, and the stubborn Grinch. However, as a kid, I didn't truly understand the poignant life lessons. The stories just made me laugh.

Looking back, Dr. Seuss's characters had an emotional impact, igniting hope and inspiring change—focusing on kindness and perseverance. They encouraged me to believe in my capacity to make a difference—like the Lorax's compelling assertion: "Unless someone like you cares a whole awful lot, nothing is going to get better. It's not."

As I pulled away from the coastline, the last light of the sunset lingered in my rearview mirror. I felt something stir within me—a quiet assurance that the road ahead, with all its twists and turns, would bring more moments like this. More reminders that life is meant to be lived, not just endured. With Argo rumbling beneath me and the scent of the ocean still clinging to my skin, I pressed forward. Toward tomorrow, and the tomorrow after that.

NOTE TO SELF

So there I was, pulling away from the coastline like a movie character who forgot to return their beach chair rental. And I gotta say, I felt something big stir inside me. Either it was inspiration or the fish tacos from lunch. TBD. There's this weird, quiet confidence hitting me. Like, "hey dummy, this road ahead? It's gonna throw some curveballs, sure, just like it has in the past. But it's also gonna give you more of this—more moments where life doesn't feel like a to-do list, but like an actual story worth telling."

So, to future me: When you're knee-deep in nonsense, stuck in traffic horns honking, doing ten in a sixtyfive, remember this sunset. This feeling. And for the love of all things holy, never underestimate the healing power of salt air and a little forward motion.

The ocean smell still stuck to my skin like it paid rent. And as I pressed forward—no GPS, just vibes—I wasn't just heading somewhere. I was becoming someone.

Keep drivin'.

35

La La Land

*Wildflower, pick up your pretty little head,
It will get easier, your dreams are not
dead.*

NIKKI ROWE

AS ARGO AND I ARRIVE in Los Angeles, cruising down the infamous Hollywood Boulevard, the palm trees sway in the breeze as the glitzy signs scream for attention. It is a setting of a strange beauty, a world of glamour and excitement just out of reach. A city of dreams and broken promises, where drivers will cut you off with a flick of the wrist—turn signals, it seems, are for amateurs.

Memories flood back from when I lived in California with Beverly in the seventies, when we were newlyweds. It was a time when Southern California still had orange groves—before developers replaced them with stucco houses to accommodate the endless stream of new arrivals. Beverly and I spent much of our time in Hollywood, where I had an office for voice-over work and she was at EMI Screen Gems, a music publishing giant just off the Strip. We mingled with the creative crowd, relishing the city's energy with our Texas friend, JD Hinton, a budding actor, songwriter, and singer. Those were magical days, like catching lightning in a bottle. All around us, hopefuls were conjuring dreams, and some managed to spin them into reality.

Hollywood still glimmers, but not as it once did. Driving through its streets today, I see a different city. The Walk of Fame, once pristine, is lined with X-rated stores, its stars lost beneath the shuffle of the homeless, amid the scent of urine and the scattered debris of forgotten ambitions. It wasn't always this way. In the seventies, eighties, and nineties, Hollywood Boulevard and the Sunset Strip were relatively clean, a haven for wide-eyed tourists.

Despite what the song says, Hollywood wasn't built on rock and roll—that came later. It was built on radio, then movies, then television. Westerns once ruled the screen, both silver and small. One of the longest-running TV Westerns was *The Rifleman*, starring Chuck Connors and a young Johnny Crawford. I met Johnny through Barb Hauser, widow of my old friend Tim Hauser, the founder of Manhattan Transfer. Johnny invited me to park Argo at his place, and I gladly took him up on it.

Johnny had been in the industry since childhood, one of the original Mouseketeers personally selected by Walt Disney himself. But after the first season, Disney cut down the cast, and Johnny was out. It didn't slow him down. At age twelve, he landed *The Rifleman*, which made him a household name. For five years, he played Mark McCain, a motherless boy raised by his father, Lucas—played by Chuck Connors—on the untamed frontier of a young, developing nation. The show was built on themes of morality, justice, and integrity, all wrapped up in a Winchester 1892 with a rapid-fire lever action.

Johnny worked alongside legends, including John Wayne, Dennis Hopper, Claude Akins, and Sammy Davis Jr. He even made guest appearances with baseball greats such as Don Drysdale and Duke Snider. But when I asked him what he remembered most about being on set, he grinned and said, "The donuts."

"That makes sense," I said. "Five a.m. call times? You had to have something to get you through. Did you drink coffee with the crew?"

"Nah. Never liked coffee," he said. "But I do like coffee ice cream."

In his backyard, Johnny tried to teach me some trick roping. He made it look easy. It wasn't. But watching him work a rope, I saw what had driven him all these years: he just wanted to make people smile. And he did.

Hollywood is still a place where dreams are made—sometimes in the most unexpected ways. I met Angela Parrish, a singer-songwriter with a golden voice who, for a time, lived in her car while chasing her break. That break came when her voice was chosen to open the movie *La La Land*, singing "Another Day of Sun."

Angela had a regular gig playing piano at Vitello's, a restaurant known in Hollywood lore as the place where Robert Blake's wife was murdered just outside.

I visited Vitello's the night my singer and songwriter friend, J.D. Hinton, was performing upstairs to a sold-out room. Afterward, we lingered to hear Angela play, and I was captivated by her talent.

"I've been lucky," she told me. "This place has given me a steady gig, a way to make a living doing what I love."

I asked her what it was like hearing herself on the opening of an Oscar-winning film. Her face lit up.

"It was the best feeling of my life! It was roses the whole time."

The pull of Hollywood is undeniable. Some chase fame; others stumble into it.

Hollywood has never been just one thing. It is light and shadow. Grit and gold. Promise and dust. Smoke and mirrors. Bright teeth. Bad roads. Some come poor and leave rich. Others come whole and leave empty. You can sell your soul here for a drink and a smile. Some folks do. Some folks find gold in the gutter. Most just go back home.

I park Argo beneath the hazy California sky, high above Hollywood. The Hollywood lights twinkle below. I think of the old ones who tried and failed here, and the few who did not.

One thing I know for sure: there are songs to be written, songs to be sung, and this town has a million stories still to be told. Weird ones. Wild ones. Ones that start in backseats and end on billboards, and some in rehab with an emotional support llama.

Some make it. Most don't. But every one of 'em starts with someone brave enough to show up.

NOTE TO SELF

Hollywood! Smoke and mirrors. Grand illusions. Basically a Criss Angel illusionist show, but with better teeth and worse traffic. It's a cocktail of light and shadow ... shaken, not stirred, and always overpriced.

Some friends of mine have shown up with nothing but a dream and a headshot. Next thing you know, they're starring in a Hollywood hit and dodging TMZ like it's dodgeball in gym class. When they left, they said it felt like leaving an old lover you don't talk about. You feel lighter and ashamed. You tell yourself you learned something. You tell yourself it was worth it. You do not say how much you gave away for nothing. You keep that to yourself. And when you dream at night, sometimes the hills come back to you, bright and cruel, and you wake up angry that you ever believed.

Okay, this script ain't finished yet. So buckle up. Lights, camera, action, let's freaking keep moving forward.

36

GRAPES OF WRATH, THEN AND NOW

*And the little screaming fact that sounds
through all history: repression works only
to strengthen and knit the repressed.*

JOHN STEINBECK, THE GRAPES OF WRATH

THE HIGHWAY UNFURLED BEFORE ME like a ribbon, carrying me away from Hollywood's glitz and into the quieter, more intimate towns along the California coast. The radio crackled with Canned Heat's "On the Road Again," and I sang along, gravel-voiced and grinning: "I'm going up the country, babe, don't you wanna go?" I did. And the road obliged.

Santa Barbara, for all its postcard perfection, wasn't immune to the times. Behind the palm trees and Spanish-tiled roofs, vacant storefronts stood like missing teeth. Maybe I'd been tricked by the glossy illusions of TV shows set here, imagining a prosperity that was only ever set dressing. The charm was real, but the cracks showed.

I wondered about those shuttered businesses. A dream, once nursed, now nothing but dust and a "For Lease" sign. Maybe it was just the churn of commerce. Or maybe it was something deeper, the slow turning of history's wheel. Either way, I couldn't just pass through as a mere spectator. The road has a way of making you a witness.

By the time I reached Salinas, it was midafternoon, and the story remained the same. Empty windows. Hollowed-out storefronts. The quiet echoes of a once-bustling downtown. It wasn't just Santa Barbara. It wasn't just here. It was everywhere.

Monterey, though, had something waiting for me: Clark Roberson. My old friend from the Brazos River, where we once turned my yellow canoe into an accidental surfboard, riding a wall of water miles downstream. His parents never quite forgave either of us for that one. Clark and his wife, Nancy, had invited me to dinner, and there are few better places to swap stories than around a table in Steinbeck Country.

Steinbeck Country. The name sticks to this stretch of California, from Carmel Valley to Santa Cruz, though its people haven't always worn it with pride. When *The Grapes of Wrath* was first published, locals bristled at the way their towns and farms were portrayed. Now, they embrace their prodigal son, happy to welcome tourists eager to trace his footsteps.

At the Steinbeck Museum, I wandered through his old haunts, even stopping at his boyhood home—now a restaurant and gift shop—to have lunch in his living room. Hard to say what he would've thought of that.

Steinbeck painted the Dust Bowl with words, turning the wind-blown exodus of sharecroppers into something immortal. He chronicled the Joads and the thousands like them who packed everything they owned into rusted-out jalopies and headed west, chasing California's promise. Most found something better than dust and hunger, but not by much. The land they hoped would save them had its own brand of cruelty.

It's an old story, one that never really ends.

Driving through Salinas, I put on Springsteen's "The Ghost of Tom Joad," his voice raw as he sang: "Families sleeping in their cars in the Southwest; no home, no job, no peace, no rest." Different faces, different accents, but the struggle remains the same.

Past the fields of blackberries, I spotted the modern-day Joads—migrant farm workers bent low, picking fruit. Their cars were lined up along the roadside, newer than the dust-choked Fords of the 1930s. That was one difference.

Blue portable toilets stood between the cars, bolted onto a frame that kept them a foot off the ground. A man in a wide-brim straw hat stepped out of one, adjusting the long-sleeved purple shirt tucked loosely into his baggy jeans. The hat shadowed his face as he disappeared back into the fields.

I pulled over, watching them work. The scene wasn't so different from Steinbeck's time, though the "Okies" were gone, replaced by mostly Hispanic laborers, with a few Filipinos, Chinese, and Japanese mixed in.

Two women, dressed in oversized yellow overalls and red blouses, rolled up their sleeves as they worked. Their straw hats hid their faces, but when they glanced up, I saw smiles. They spoke in bursts, laughing between the rows. Each wore a dust mask over her nose and mouth. I wanted to talk to them, to ask: What brought you here? Was it freedom? A steady job? Did your family see you as a hero, escaping the shantytowns on the other side of the border? Did you leave children behind, watching them grow up through phone calls and grainy pictures?

But I didn't interrupt.

Steinbeck's *Grapes of Wrath* made it easy to see these workers as shadows in a long, weary story of hardship. But the truth is always messier. Today, there are no Hoovervilles along the roadside, no work camps straight out of a Depression-era nightmare. The exploitation hasn't vanished, but the world has shifted in ways Steinbeck himself might have struggled to put into words.

Later, I found myself in Salinas, trying to settle in for the night. The state park was full, so I made do with a parking lot.

◀ ▲ ▼ ▶

In the morning, I headed downtown to the John Steinbeck Center. The museum is a shrine to the town's once-disowned son, a boy who made good by telling the stories others wanted buried.

The highlight? *Travels with Charley.* On display was Rocinante, his green GMC pickup with the custom Wolverine camper fitted on its bed.

That truck carried him across America, looking for what had changed and what hadn't. Standing there, I wondered what Steinbeck would see if he retraced his route today. Would he find the country he feared was vanishing? Or would he recognize it, bruised but enduring?

Hard to say.

But the road still unspools ahead, and I keep on keeping on.

NOTE TO SELF

Steinbeck didn't invent struggle. He just wrote it down. And the story hasn't ended.

The faces have changed. The accents, the clothes, the pickup trucks. But the weight they carry? Still heavy. Still holy.

Remember this: When you see someone bent low over a field or standing tired behind a counter, don't look away. Don't make them a backdrop to your journey. They are the journey.

Bearing witness matters. Not for applause, but for clarity. For compassion. For the slow shaping of your own soul.

So look longer. Ask the questions, even if only in your heart. Let the road teach you what comfort never will.

37

A Rare Total Eclipse

Science does not know its debt to imagination.

RALPH WALDO EMERSON

DRAWN BY THE PROMISE OF a celestial spectacle, I made my way to Oregon's picturesque Willamette Valley and on to Salem on that August day in 2017. I had been told it was one of the prime locations to witness a total solar eclipse—one of those rare moments when the moon completely cloaks the sun, casting an eerie, otherworldly spell over the land.

Salem, a city steeped in history and quirks, offered more than just a front-row seat to cosmic grandeur. It was a haven for eclectic personalities, a rich tableau of humanity. On this particular day, in addition to eager sky-watchers, it was a showcase of free-spirited thinkers, artistic eccentrics, and some who seemed to be floating on a slightly different plane of reality. I found a spot to park Argo—my trusty home on wheels—on a downtown street that didn't require me to move overnight. So, I didn't. I camped right there in the heart of Salem, and the city put on a show even before the eclipse began.

The streets were alive with an energy that was part festival, part fever dream. A loose congregation of new-age enthusiasts paraded in tie-dye shirts and beaded necklaces, their heads adorned with all manner of headgear. One young man wore an oversized replica of the Cat in the Hat's iconic striped top hat, a fitting symbol of the mischievous and whimsical spirit of the day. At least, until he lost his balance, tumbled against a lamppost, and his hat took a swan dive into the gutter.

Salem also has a reputation for passionate activism, but on this day, the only fervor was directed skyward. I had heard tales of a dedicated protest community, always ready to rally for a cause—any cause. But there were no marches or picket signs in sight, just an odd but endearing camaraderie among those gathered to witness the celestial event.

As I wandered the streets, taking in the characters and the anticipation in the air, a young entrepreneur caught my eye. He stood confidently on the sidewalk, a cardboard box of eclipse glasses at his feet, his sales pitch smooth and sure.

"Hey, sir, you're gonna need these special glasses to view the eclipse." He waved a pair at me, his conviction unshakable.

"Why can't I just wear my sunglasses?" I asked, just to see what he'd say.

"Ah, these are more than just dark lenses," he said. "These will save your eyes!" "How can I tell?"

"They're certified."

Well, that settled it. I bought a pair—and gave the kid a tip for his persistence and salesmanship. He had spotted an opportunity, seized it, and was making things happen. He wasn't waiting for luck; he was creating his own. That spirit—the hustle, the ingenuity—was the same spirit that built the country, and as long as kids like him existed, I figured America would be just fine.

With my newly acquired protective spectacles, I made my way to the grounds of the state capitol, where a congregation of eclipse chasers had assembled. The sky was a brilliant blue, the sun unchallenged—until, slowly, the moon began its advance.

Shortly after nine a.m., a hush settled over the crowd. The light softened, the temperature dipped, and an almost reverent stillness took hold. The sun, that unyielding force of life, began to yield to the moon's encroaching shadow. The world dimmed as though some cosmic hand were gently turning down a celestial dimmer switch.

By 10:17 a.m., totality had arrived. The sun was gone, replaced by a perfect black void encircled by a ghostly halo of light—the corona, luminous and otherworldly. The city fell into an eerie twilight, and for two breathtaking minutes, time seemed to hold its breath.

In that moment, we were all just humans—strangers turned silent companions, bound together by a shared sense of awe. The universe had orchestrated a spectacle beyond anything man could construct, and for once, no one was distracted. No one was arguing. No one was checking their phones. We were simply present, witnesses to the grandeur of creation.

And then, just as quickly as it had come, the darkness retreated. The first sliver of sun reemerged, and with it, the spell was broken. The world exhaled, the hum of life returned, and we all went back to our separate stories, forever connected by that fleeting moment of wonder. As I walked back to Argo, I couldn't help but think about how rare it is, in our fast-moving world, to experience something together—something pure, something bigger than ourselves. Maybe that's what we need more of. Maybe that's what we're missing—those moments that remind us we're all part of the same story.

The eclipse in Salem was more than a celestial event—it was a quiet invitation to pause, to see differently, to stand together. And in that brief silence, something shifted.

Note to Self

Wonder is underrated. It doesn't make headlines or trend on your feed, but it still has the power to hush a crowd, soften cynicism, and remind you that you belong to something vast and beautiful. That morning in Salem— when the sun bowed behind the moon and a thousand strangers looked up in collective silence—I remembered what awe feels like. For two quiet minutes, no one argued, no one scrolled, no one looked away. The world stood still, and we stood together beneath a sky that made us feel small in all the right ways.

In a world addicted to speed and noise, moments like that are rare—sacred, even. So chase them. Chase what pulls your gaze upward, not to escape, but to remember why life is worth engaging in the first place.

And when the shadows fall—and they always do—don't panic. Light always returns. It just takes a little silence to see it.

38

SLEEPLESS IN SEATTLE

God gives us sleep to remind us we are not him.

CHARLES SPURGEON

WITH THE INTENTION OF HEADING north from Salem, I drifted through Oregon's countryside, taking my time, savoring the wide-open spaces. A twist in the road revealed a slice of heaven: a peach orchard, open to the public. A hand-painted sign beckoned, inviting me to pick my own. The sun hung in a cloudless sky, and the sweet fragrance of ripe peaches drifted on the breeze. How could I resist?

I was stepping into a world far removed from the urban pulse of Salem. At the edge of the field, a small wooden shed marked the entrance; inside, the farmer's daughter handed me a basket and wished me "happy hunting" as I wandered toward the orchard. The trees were heavy with fruit, their branches bending under the weight of plump, sun-kissed peaches. There's something almost magical about the search: the anticipation of finding the juiciest, ripest fruit, and the moment you reach out and pluck it from the tree. A childlike thrill washed over me, a grin spreading across my face as I snapped a selfie with my prize.

It was one of those serendipitous moments, lost in the simple joy of an unexpected pleasure—an all-American experience, up close and personal with nature. I could've stayed forever, but the road was calling me onward, and with peaches in tow, I continued north.

Eventually, I crossed the river into Washington State, where a new chapter awaited. And what better place to start than Cape Disappointment? The name alone promised a particular kind of grim history, and boy, did it live down to it.

I camped nearby, in the shadow of another ominously named place—Dismal Nitch.

Nestled in the heart of Chinook Indian Nation territory, this spot nearly claimed the lives of Lewis and Clark in 1805. The expedition had been battered by a relentless storm, battling through a suffocating, soggy hellscape. For days, they fought exhaustion, hunger, and the harsh elements, all while struggling to hold onto hope. The storm nearly stopped them from seeing the

Pacific Ocean, just a few miles away. The thought of it sent a shiver down my spine.

If they could endure the misery of Dismal Nitch, I reasoned, I could survive a night in my trusty Argo. As I settled into the comfort of my van, the river quietly flowing below me, I reflected on how different my experience was. The setting may have been the same, but the circumstances couldn't have been more different.

The next three nights promised less peace and quiet, starting with Seattle.

When Seattle's skyline finally rose into view, my brain hit play on the most random track imaginable—the theme song from Frasier. That bizarre little jazz jingle about eggs and salad, and emotional instability, came crawling out of the archives like a raccoon in a bathrobe. I hadn't heard it in decades, but there it was, clanging around my skull like a saxophone-powered fever dream. I laughed because I knew I was doomed. That thing was going to loop in my head forever, like some cursed chant summoned by the sight of the Space Needle.

My GPS led me through the steep streets, and before I knew it, I was parked beside Safeco Field—the locals call it The Safe. As I waited for the light to change, two guys approached, white envelopes in hand. They waved them at me like a pair of hustlers peddling their wares.

"Wanna buy tickets?" one shouted.

"Need tickets? I got tickets," the other chimed in, leaning over his buddy's shoulder.

Within seconds, I was being offered tickets to a Mariner's game—an all-American experience, a brew, a dog, a seat in the bleachers. I almost took the offer, picturing myself sitting in the stands, relishing the simplicity of it all. But then the light turned green, and with the line of cars behind me, I eased forward.

"Nice rig, buddy!" one of them shouted as I drove away.

I continued into downtown, circling until I found parking, right next to Pike Place Market. There, I performed what I can only describe as a bit of "good parking karma." I'd like to think it's a gift, though I've never quite figured out how it works. I don't take it for granted, though. A friend of mine's mother swears by her version of it. "Mother Mary, full of grace, help me find a parking space," she says with devotion. And sure enough, it works every time.

With my parking fate sealed, I strolled down to Starbucks for a venti caramel macchiato, then spent a leisurely afternoon meandering through the vast market. I watched the fishmongers tossing fresh catches, a skill that started as a practical means to speed up the process but evolved into an outright show. A must-see, and an essential part of Seattle's charm.

The sun hung low over Puget Sound, casting a breathtaking glow as it sank into the water, and I stood at the edge, momentarily lost in the view. The city buzzed with its usual energy, but for a moment, all was calm.

As I stood by Argo, deciding where to spend the night, I noticed a sign near a parking meter: payment was required from 8 a.m. to 8 p.m. It was well past 8, and I realized I didn't have to move the van at all. I could stay right where I was, sleep soundly, and be on my way in the morning before the parking attendant arrived.

The block was quiet, save for a few homeless souls talking on the street corner. I pulled up my seat, cracked open *Infinite Jest*, and lost myself in David Foster Wallace's labyrinthine sentences. Some of his paragraphs are longer than entire novels. Once you get swept into his rhythm, though, you can't help but go along for the ride, even if it sometimes takes you to places you didn't expect. It's a meandering, offbeat style that fits the mood of my journey.

By the time midnight came, exhaustion overtook me, and I fell into a restless sleep. But at two a.m., a voice jolted me awake.

"Stop … stop, I didn't do anything," the voice cried, high-pitched with pain or fear.

"I'm not letting you manage my money anymore!" another voice snapped back, firm and threatening.

The sounds of fists pounding into flesh followed, the distressing thuds punctuated by muffled yelps. A fight, or worse, broke out just outside my window. My heart raced, and for a moment, the possibility of gunshots crossed my mind. I lay low, straining to hear. The voices ebbed and flowed, chasing each other up and down the street, until finally, they faded into the distance.

The next night, I found another parking spot, this time near the ferry terminal. Free overnight parking until eight a.m., I thought. Perfect. Except for the two sets of train tracks right across the sidewalk.

What was supposed to be a peaceful night turned into an endless series of trains passing by, one after another. Each time, I thought, *That's the last one.* But it never was. I missed the ferry that morning, too tired to do anything but stay put, hoping for some sleep. But the trains kept coming, their wheels clacking loudly, never giving me the peace I needed.

I gave up on sleep and decided to catch the ferry the next day, after another sleepless night.

By the fourth day, I made my way over to Bainbridge Island. There, I found a peaceful county park, nestled in a world far removed from the constant noise of the city. I set up camp, ready for a good night's sleep, watching the lights of Seattle twinkle across the water. It felt like an end to the madness of the past few days—a promise of quiet, at last.

Note to Self

Even in the most postcard-perfect places, peace isn't guaranteed. Sometimes, it's fish flying through the air at Pike Place and caramel macchiatos by the Sound. Other times, it's fists pounding pavement outside your window at two a.m. And still other times, it's you—just trying to sleep—while the night train barrels by like it's on a personal mission to keep you humble. Welcome to the paradox of travel: the sublime and the stressful, the scenic and the sleepless, all wrapped into one gritty, unpredictable reel.

But this is how you learn what it means to be present. Not just for sunsets over Puget Sound, but for the tension, the discomfort, the surprise of it all. It's easy to appreciate beauty when it's served up neat and quiet. Harder —and holier—is learning to find grace when the city won't shut up. Next time you can't sleep, don't curse it too fast. Some truths only arrive when everything else is wide awake.

39

Unsheltered

We think sometimes that poverty is only being hungry, naked, and homeless. The poverty of being unwanted, unloved, and uncared for is the greatest poverty. We must start in our own homes to remedy this kind of poverty.

MOTHER TERESA

MODERN-DAY NOMADIC TRIBES haunt nearly every American city, stretching from the cool, rocky shores of Maine to the misty streets of Seattle. They stand at intersections, holding cardboard signs scrawled with desperate messages, their edges curling from the wind. They sleep in the doorways of old brick buildings or huddle beneath bridges, their bodies pressed against the cold, hard pavement. The smell of whiskey and smoke hangs heavy in the air as they linger near stores, asking for spare change, their faces worn and tired, their eyes haunted. The homeless.

Lost. Forgotten. Left to drift, untethered, on a concrete sea.

In Seattle, I find myself walking through a historic district, taking in the remnants of old architecture. The city feels like a place that's seen both prosperity and decline. As I turn a corner, I find myself standing amid a ragtag assembly of street people. They stand together like an uninvited crowd, waiting for something, for anything. Their eyes follow me as I take in the scene. Above them, the sign on the brown brick building reads: Union Gospel Mission.

I don't feel quite right. Uneasy. But I muster a smile and say hello to one, then another. By the front door of the mission, I see a young woman with bright eyes and fiery red hair. She's perched on a box—her only possessions—watching the world with a wary expression. I greet her, learn that her name is Nicole, and ask what things have been like for her.

"I've seen Hell," she says without hesitation. It's almost dinner time, and she's waiting for the free meal that's about to be served inside. "I've seen violence. I've seen shootings. I've seen ..."

She trails off, her gaze far away, lost in the memory of something too terrible to speak of.

I watch her, sensing the weight she carries, and ask her to tell me more.

"I was raped," she says quietly, almost as if admitting it for the first time, "almost killed." A nervous smile flickers across her face as if she's trying to shake off the worst of it. "It's been hard."

Her eyes, pale and clear, hold a strange dignity that doesn't match the ragged edges of her life. She's been on the streets for years, from New York to Seattle. "Nine years," she tells me.

"Nine years of running."

And yet, there's something about her, some unspoken strength in the way she carries herself, the way her hair is brushed back, her hoodie neat and clean, a gift from the churches and shelters that still try to catch the broken ones.

I start to notice the others around me. Most of them wear laminated badges, hanging from cords around their necks—proof they've been approved for entry to the hot meal that's soon to be served inside. The smell of whiskey and cigarette smoke drifts past me as several men stand nearby, their faces hard as stone.

A thin, scrappy African American man stands next to a tall, pale woman with deep pockmarks on her face. Her eyes burn with a strange, frantic energy, like a wounded animal caught in a cage. She spins in circles, grinning at me with a wild look in her eyes, muttering to herself, "I'm a badass ... I'm a badass." Her voice is shrill, her words sharp, and yet the man beside her remains statue-stiff, staring with unblinking eyes as empty as an abandoned house.

His silence is louder than her laughs.

My heart picks up pace, but I try to look calm, try to act like I belong in this fray. I don't.

Not really.

Down the sidewalk, I spot a young man—a young African-American with a wool cap pulled low over his brow and a hoodie pulled tight against the chill. He's slumped against the brick wall near the door to the mission, staring at me, though I'm not sure if he's really looking at me or just lost in some other place.

His name is Troy. I walk over and ask him about his story.

"I've been on the streets five, seven years," he says, the words heavy in his mouth as he takes a drag from a cigarette stub. He's quiet for a moment, drawing in smoke, and then he drops a word on me like a rock dropped in a lake. It sinks fast.

"There's one word that explains it all," he says, his eyes burning into mine. He mutters the word several times, the syllables coming in a rhythm I almost can't follow. I lean in closer, trying to understand.

"It's in the ten-million-word dictionary," he says, "the one that has the word. And it costs a lot to get it."

I try to decipher it, asking him to spell it out. His words stumble, but he's persistent.

"J... S... K... M-I-A... ah... O-M-R-Y."

I don't quite get it, but the word *Jakari* comes to mind, and I ask him about it.

"Jakari," he nods. "It's about what happens out here. What life is. It's what it is."

Jakari. In the *Urban Dictionary*, it's described as someone who's always dropping trouble on others, a constant source of chaos. It fits.

"What's the worst thing that's happened to you on the streets?" I ask him, trying to grasp what this life has done to him.

"I've been robbed," he says. "Shot at. Stabbed. I've been murdered." His voice is flat, almost disinterested.

"I ain't gonna say I'm not scared of stuff," he adds after a beat, "but I won't let it stop me. I'll do what I want, when I want."

His resignation is strange—an odd sort of peace in the chaos of his life.

Nearby, a wiry man with a ball cap and a mustache walks up to me. He's smiling, but the smile flickers like a faulty light bulb. His name is Trevor.

"I've been on the streets since I was sixteen," Trevor says, the words coming out in a dull, matter-of-fact way. "Lost four family members, my mom ..." His eyes wander, not really seeing me.

He tells me he used meth for years, started at twenty-four, and always knew it was a problem. But here, on these streets, the drug feels like it's as much a part of him as the dirt that coats his skin.

Nicole, Troy, and Trevor are just a few of the thousands living on Seattle's streets. There are over five thousand homeless people in the area alone. And beyond them, another twelve thousand sleep in shelters. But the numbers don't capture the human cost—the broken families, the lost souls.

Nicole laughs darkly when I ask her about the violence here.

"New York's not half as bad as here," she says. "That's 'cause we get everybody from New York."

Her story's typical—she came to Seattle from New York, hoping for a fresh start, but ended up on the streets instead. She tried to work on a fishing boat, but it was a scam. Now, she lives under a bridge, in a tent. The mission gave her a new sleeping bag. She hopes to someday get into the program that offers tiny houses for the homeless.

The rumor mill among the homeless says Seattle is the place to be. "Free-attle," they call it. Everything is free here—food, shelter, help. Or so they say.

But the reality is different. The city declared a homelessness emergency years ago, but not much has changed. Still, the people come. And more stay until they die. Overdose, suicide, or murder—there's no guarantee.

The homeless Remembrance Project holds memorial services for those who pass, a grim reminder of the lives lost on the streets.

"The resources are here," says one of the workers at the mission. "But the people have to want to leave this life. Most of them don't. They'd rather live on their terms."

And that's the sad truth. Giving spare change seems like an act of kindness, but it often only fuels the addiction, the spiral deeper into the abyss.

In Salt Lake City, they've put up signs saying, "Give a hand-up, not a handout." The idea is to give to agencies that can offer real help—hot meals, medical assistance, substance abuse support. I get it. But as I walk past a man sitting by the curb, my heart aches. He's wrapped in a blanket, staring down at the ground.

"Bread pudding?" I ask a ridiculous question, but one I can't take back.

His eyes light up, and he thanks me. I walk away, feeling like I've done something good.

But maybe I haven't.

This Christmas season, I count my blessings and remember those less fortunate, those who sleep on the streets. I remember the words of Matthew 25:40: "…whatever you did for the least of these, you did for me."

The homeless are a growing slice of America. The problem is complex, tangled in drugs, mental illness, and broken systems. It feels cruel to leave them out here, to let them fend for themselves in a world that's long forgotten them. But somehow, they survive. And we, in turn, must ask ourselves how long we can keep turning away.

Note to Self

When you walk past someone sleeping in a doorway, don't just lower your eyes and keep moving. Don't pretend they aren't there. Their name might be Nicole. Or Troy. Or Trevor. And they might've once stood where you now stand—clean clothes, warm bed, a dream still intact.

You don't have to fix it all. You can't. But don't let your heart harden. Let it break. Let it ache. Let it stay tender enough to recognize the sacred in every single face.

Because what we do for the least is what we do for Christ.

And in this upside-down kingdom, compassion isn't weakness. It's the beginning of justice.

40

BORDER-BUSTING

> *Many Canadian nationalists harbor the bizarre fear that should we ever reject royalty, we would instantly mutate into Americans, as though the Canadian sense of self is so frail and delicate a bud that the only thing stopping it from being swallowed whole by the U.S. is an English lady in a funny hat.*
>
> WILL FERGUSON

IT WAS A DECISION MADE on a whim—a spontaneous summons by that strange, mischievous cosmic hand that keeps guiding me here and there, never quite explaining itself. I am driving north with no real reason except the feeling that I was supposed to be. Not told, not instructed — pulled. That hand, it never shows its face. Just nudged at the wheel, tugging gently, heading me north, into Canada, without a clear plan or intention.

The catch? I didn't have my passport. Yes. Ridiculous. But in my defense, I hadn't exactly been planning on going to Canada. That unseen hand guiding me, as it often does, has a way of turning the ordinary into the extraordinary detour. So I'm heading to America's neighbor, Canada—land of maple syrup, hockey, and endless apologies.

I wasn't about to let something as trivial as a lack of proper documentation stop me. What was the worst that could happen? A stern word from a border agent? Maybe some polite Canadian reprimand? Or, worst-case scenario, a dramatic confrontation with the Canadian Mounties' elite Emergency Response Team? In my mind, this was all an amusing thought, the stuff of travel anecdotes. After all, this was Canada—the home of kindness and politeness. What could go wrong?

I joined the long line of cars at the border checkpoint between the United States and Canada, feeling surprisingly confident despite my passport-less predicament. As I inched my way forward, I steeled myself for the inevitable moment of truth. Then, as I rolled up to the uniformed border guard, he flashed that trademark Canadian smile—the kind of smile that doesn't just acknowledge your existence but actively welcomes it. A smile that, at that moment, made me feel like I was already halfway to my destination.

"Passport, please."

I took a deep breath, squinting in mock concern, and tried to put on my best "Oops, I made a little mistake" face. "Well, uh, I got here and realized my passport is at home, but I do have my driver's license," I said, widening my eyes and flashing the friendliest smile I could find.

The guard nodded, his polite smile unwavering. "Nice, but you have to have a valid passport. You can't just waltz into Canada without proper identification, eh?"

"Oh, I understand," I said, feigning disappointment as dramatically as I could manage.

"Guess I'm just a little loonie!"

"Loonie, eh?" The guard's face flickered for a moment, then transformed into a mild, almost imperceptible grimace. One eyebrow arched as he squinted with the other. At first, I thought it was just an expression of mild confusion, but as I replayed the moment, I realized what had just happened. I had unintentionally ventured into an area of Canadian slang that was far more nuanced than I could have imagined.

You see, "loonie" isn't just a whimsical word for "crazy" in Canadian parlance. No, it refers to their one-dollar coin, which features the image of a loon, the iconic bird of Canada. And I, in my forgetfulness and ignorance, had dropped that term like a clumsy tourist, not knowing it carried connotations that went beyond the literal. To a Canadian, "loonie" wasn't just a playful jab; it could imply something entirely different—perhaps even a subtle suggestion of bribery. Realizing my blunder in real-time, I quickly recovered, though not without a bit of nervous laughter. "Oh, not *loonie*, I guess," I stammered. "I'm just forgetful, that's all. But, in addition to my Texas driver's license, I've got a photo of my passport on my phone, if you want to check me out."

I could feel the line of cars behind me inching forward, the impatient stares of the other travelers growing more pronounced by the second. Now, in America, I might have been dismissed with a sharp "next!" and sent on my way. But this was Canada, where politeness is an art form, a national pastime, and possibly even a way of life. The border guard, not missing a beat, softened his tone even more.

"Well, eh, pull over under the cover next to the guard house," he said, with a reassuring nod. "I'll see if my supervisor wants to help you out, eh?"

I nodded, thankful for his patience, and steered my car into the small waiting area as directed. There, I sat—feeling a bit like a child who had just been sent to the principal's office, but in a very Canadian way. While I waited, I reflected on my lack of preparation and the unexpected kindness of this man who, despite my mistake, never once made me feel like a fool. And then, of course, there was the "eh"—that little verbal signature that punctuates everything Canadians say. It was at once endearing and universally charming, like a friendly nudge inviting you to join in, a way of softening the impact of the moment. It reminded me of how, in the U.S., we might add "right?" or "huh?" to the end of a sentence, a subtle prompt to invite agreement or affirmation. But in Canada, it was more than that. It was a linguistic hug, a quiet way to make sure no one felt left out. A little maple syrup on a pancake.

As I sat there, waiting to see whether my passport photo would suffice as a proper substitute, I couldn't help but appreciate the absurdity of the situation. Here I was, in a country where the border guard was, quite literally, the embodiment of politeness, trying to cross into a land famous for its warmth and courtesy—without the right paperwork. But at the same time, I had to admit, it was a small reminder of life's unpredictable detours. Sometimes, the path you think you'll take isn't the one you end up on, but it can still be full of surprises, full of moments that will make you laugh, cringe, and perhaps even teach you something.

And just like that, my brief foray into the land of maple syrup, apologies, and Mounties' emergency response teams became a quiet lesson in patience and humility. As the border guard returned, my situation resolved with a level of calm efficiency that only added to my admiration for the nation I had briefly trespassed into.

"Everything checks out," he said with a smile. "Welcome to Canada, eh?"

And in that moment, I understood what made Canada, well, Canada. It wasn't just the politeness or the sweet linguistic lilt. It was the willingness to let people make mistakes, to offer kindness even when things go awry.

So, I passed through the border, officially on my way into Canada—passport, or not. And as I drove farther into this strange land, I couldn't help but think that sometimes, the most memorable experiences are the ones that aren't planned at all.

Note to Self

Every now and then, the road tests more than your tires—it checks your posture, your patience, and whether you can grin your way through a good old-fashioned bureaucratic hoop. Sometimes, the ID you're missing gets outweighed by the grace you're given. Turns out a warm smile, a humble spirit, and the ability to laugh at your forgetfulness can get you further than anything stamped and laminated. Especially in places where kindness is standard issue and even red tape is wrapped in maple syrup.

So go ahead—take the wrong turn, forget the right papers, wander into the unexpected. The best parts of the journey are rarely the ones you plan. And in the end, what matters isn't always what you remembered to pack, but who you became when the detour found you.

41

Forced Back

*Winter is the time for comfort, for good
food and warmth, for the touch of a
friendly hand and a talk beside the fire: it
is the time for home.*

EDITH SITWELL

AS ARGO AND I MADE our way back into the United States from Canada, the cold Pacific air settled in my bones like the warning bells of winter. We had crossed from Vancouver to Seattle aboard the ferry, a perfect reflection of our journey thus far: unpredictable, but always with the sense of movement—of heading somewhere, even if I wasn't entirely sure where that was. The ferry had glided across the water like a great whale, cutting through the fog and mist that clung to the bay. In a way, it had been a perfect metaphor for my travel companion, Argo, a faithful home on wheels, carrying me from one chapter to the next without fail.

And yet, as we disembarked and the familiar streets of Seattle began to unfold before me, a new challenge loomed—a challenge that had been creeping closer with each passing mile, like an old friend you don't quite recognize until you've shared a few more stories. The weather forecast, with its ominous warnings of freezing temperatures, felt less like a prediction and more like a threat. I had planned to make the loopback journey to New York, completing a crosscountry route that would wrap up our travels, but nature had other ideas. The thought of facing icy roads with Argo—my trusty, albeit ungraceful, travel partner—wasn't an inviting one.

Argo, despite her unflagging reliability, was no machine of grace on ice. She had the mobility of a hippo attempting ballet. Though she had carried me without question from state to state, city to city, her resilience had its limits. The idea of winterizing her for the bitter cold made my stomach churn. The thought of abandoning the convenience of running water inside, of freezing pipes and burst water lines, was not a trivial matter. And the worst part? It wasn't a simple decision to turn around and retreat to warmer climates.

But then again, maybe it was. The warmth of Texas beckoned, a soft, sunlit promise compared to the sharp, biting reality of snowdrifts and frost-covered windows. As I sat in the quiet of the van, watching the rain fall in sheets outside, it seemed the world was divided into two realms: the road ahead, glistening and dangerous with winter's bite, and the road behind, warm with the comfort of familiarity. Was I ready to pause our adventure? To abandon the grand loop for the safety of the South?

In the end, I knew what had to be done. The decision wasn't made lightly, but it was made with the weight of experience. I had come to know that sometimes the unexpected detours weren't just interruptions to the journey—they were the journey. And so, with a quiet nod to the weather and to reason, I resolved to head south to Texas, postponing the loopback until spring's thaw had kissed the earth and removed winter's grasp. There was no shame in retreating; in fact, it felt strangely freeing. The road would still be there when the weather turned, waiting, patient, as always.

Seattle made it difficult for me to leave. I don't know if it's the energy of the place or the contrast between the fog-bound city and its pulsing heart of innovation. Perhaps it's the rain that does something to the soul, urging you to slow down, to let go of the rush. Seattle is a city of contrasts, of young, quick-paced techies walking with an urgency that belongs to them alone, their eyes fixed on some distant horizon that they are surely rushing toward. And then there's the older man in the suit, his tie a relic of another era. He moves among the tech-forward youth like a ghost, but his presence is unmistakable, a vestige of a time when the business world was more formal, more structured, a time when men wore suits and carried briefcases, and progress was measured not in bytes and data but in deals and handshakes.

The man in the suit caught my eye as he moved through the crowd, a reminder of how the world has evolved, yet in many ways remained the same. The tech dreamers of Seattle, their backpacks full of ambition and gadgets, were a world away from this man. They rushed toward the future while he held onto a piece of the past, quietly watching over the digits and numbers that moved the world now. I liked to imagine that he was still here, performing a kind of quiet surveillance over the machine, keeping the balance between the new world and the old. I nodded to him in my mind, though he never saw me.

But the city, bustling with innovation and new ideas, carried on without pause. The rain drizzled down, the kind of drizzle that's almost a whisper, and the energy in the air was palpable. I felt it, too. That current of creation that runs through places like Seattle, where the fog isn't a hindrance but a muse. People here don't wait for the sun to shine; they just create in the rain. And as they did, the machines hummed, the apps were built, and the world was made a little bit easier, a little more efficient, one tiny tech advancement at a time.

It was time to leave Seattle, though the city's pull felt like an anchor I wasn't quite ready to cast off. I pointed Argo's nose eastward, taking I-90 through the mountain passes of Washington. The road wound through the hills, mountains rearing up on either side like silent sentinels. It was beautiful, in that way that only nature can be when you're alone with it—quiet, immense, and sure. I passed military convoys along the way, the soldiers inside looking out at me, their eyes steady and calm. We exchanged a simple gesture: a thumbs-up, a wave. No words needed. We were fellow travelers, bound to the road in different ways.

As I continued south, I found myself drawn to the odd, the quirky, the American roadside attractions that seem to appear when you least expect them. A sign for the historic Teapot Dome Gas Station caught my eye, and I couldn't resist pulling over. The station, built in 1922 to commemorate the infamous Teapot Dome Scandal, is one of those strange, delightful curiosities that embody the spirit of American adventure. Shaped like a giant teapot, complete with a spout and handle, it now serves as a visitor's center in Zillah, Washington. It felt like a small victory in a country of often overblown landmarks—simple, amusing, yet strangely significant.

Pendleton, Oregon, was next on my list. I wandered into the town, finding its heartbeat in the old Western store, Hamler's, which has been operating for more years than I could count. Pendleton has a story to tell, too. Beneath its surface, it holds the ghosts of an old Chinatown, with its hidden opium dens and jails where Chinese workers were disciplined by their own. The town's history is both gritty and grand, as all towns' histories are.

Lunch at the Rainbow Café in Pendleton was a treat, especially as the drizzle began to fall again, turning the day a deeper shade of gray. The locals seemed at home in the small, bustling space. The café, with its walls covered in animal heads and old photographs, felt like a snapshot of another era, yet alive with the chatter of the present. Over coffee, the town's pride swelled as the locals shared their stories—the Pendleton Roundup, a rodeo event that's been drawing crowds since 1910, and the school buses that turned into mass transit during the festivities. They spoke of their history with a sense of ownership, a shared love for their community and its traditions.

Listening to their stories, I couldn't help but feel the strong, sure pulse of Pendleton— alive with community, history, and a pride that radiated through every word, every smile. It wasn't just a town; it was a living testament to the spirit of the West, and I was honored to be a part of it, even if just for a moment.

JOHN W. BUTLER

NOTE TO SELF

There's no shame in changing course.

Sometimes wisdom isn't found at the next overlook or inside the next roadside diner—it's found in the quiet decision to turn around. To admit the road ahead might not be yours to travel today. To let winter win—for now.

The old you might've seen retreat as failure, but the real traveler knows: weather isn't the enemy. Pride is. The detour isn't a pause in the journey; it's part of it. Heading south when the frost sets in? That's not giving up.

That's living to roam another day.

Keep an eye on the horizon, sure. But don't forget to check the forecast.

42

ROGER TO THE RESCUE

> "Well," said Pooh, "what I like best," and then he had to stop and think. Because although Eating Honey was a very good thing to do, there was a moment just before you began to eat it which was better than when you were, but he didn't know what it was called.
>
> A. A. MILNE, WINNIE THE POOH

My body senses it before my mind does. My heart begins to race, and a familiar adrenaline surge courses through me as I make my way toward Argo. It's an instinctive reaction, not something I've planned for or even thought about beforehand. It's as if I'm a dog eagerly anticipating a walk, or more aptly, it's the feeling Don

Quixote must have had when he prepared to mount his faithful steed, Rocinante, and set off on yet another quest for chivalry and justice.

And here I am, preparing to hit the road again, to continue my journey across America.

Argo, I think, is a more trusted transport than Don Quixote's wobbly, scrawny horse. Though, in all honesty, Argo has her moments of mischief. Take Miami, for instance, when she shed a few engine parts right onto the roadway, forcing me to drag her, tail between her legs, to the repair shop. Or that time the sliding side door started leaking rainwater like a sieve, right onto the floorboards, forcing me to reevaluate my idea of waterproofing. Then there was the infamous moment when I neglected to turn on the black water tank heater on a freezing winter night, and —well, let's just say things got unruly from there.

Still, I trust Argo—maybe not always in the traditional sense, but in the sense that she gets me where I need to go. I've had some strange adventures with her, to be sure. But that's the way it is with these journeys, right? Half the battle isn't just about getting there—it's about surviving the road itself. I suppose it was the same for Don Quixote, though he probably never expected to be chasing windmills across the plains of Spain. Much like me, awkward, perhaps a bit past my prime, and certainly engaged in a task that might seem beyond my capacity.

And yet, the mission must be completed. The journey, as bizarre as it might be, must continue. I have to circle back to Maine, back to New York, across the middle of America. It's something I have to do. The thought of failing is simply unthinkable. It's not so much about the destination but about seeing the mission through to its completion—no matter how silly it may seem to anyone else. It's necessary to me, and that makes it all the more significant.

At least today, I don't have to worry about Argo's heater failing me. No, today it's Texas —mid-summer heat pressing down from above, thick and oppressive. Today, air-conditioning is my lifeline.

I reach for the door handle, and as my fingers make contact with the metal, I jerk back with a yelp. "Ouch!" I wince, as if I've just touched the edge of a frying pan left too long on the stove. It's hot enough to roast marshmallows—if you don't mind them being slightly charred.

I dig into the pocket of my jeans, and there it is—my trusty handkerchief. It's a habit I picked up years ago, a gift from my grandmother. She always said, "A handkerchief is washable. Tissues are expensive." It was back in the day when paper tissues weren't a dime a dozen. Back then, places like Walmart and Costco didn't exist to make bulk buying the norm.

With a quick flick of my wrist, I wrap the handkerchief around the scalding door handle. The fabric creates a barrier, a protective shield that saves my skin. Thanks, Grandma. Her practical wisdom has stuck with me over the years in more ways than one. I can't help but smile, a small victory over the blistering Texas sun. You can't beat Mother Nature, but I've learned how to sidestep a few of her more fiery moments.

Settling into the driver's seat, I glance over the mental checklist for my trip. Am I fully prepared? Not quite. But then again, I never seem to be. There's always something I forget, always some little detail I push to the back of my mind. Maybe it's the fear. Maybe it's the procrastination. Or perhaps I just think the trip won't happen until it's already underway. Either way, I'm here. I'm in Argo. And though I'm not fully organized, most of what I need is packed away in her many compartments, though I'm aware there are still a few things I should've thought through more thoroughly.

But this is the United States, right? Even in the middle of nowhere, there's always a store just a stone's throw away. God bless capitalism and the convenience of a well-stocked country.

Argo has been parked in the parking garage next to my apartment in Dallas. She's plugged into electricity, keeping her batteries charged and ready for the next leg of the journey. I learned the hard way about battery maintenance after replacing the house batteries last year. Those batteries power everything from the lights to the microwave to the flush on the toilet. It's not just about comfort; it's about survival.

And speaking of survival, it's Roger to the rescue again. Roger is the skilled service technician who installed the new house batteries. He's from the Philippines, with a thick accent and broken English, but we get by just fine, thanks to patience and a little repetition. He spent years working at the US Navy harbor in Guam, fixing ships and picking up all sorts of mechanical skills along the way. If something breaks, Roger's your guy. I've even seen some of the gorgeous carvings he's made from rosewood—work that's simply stunning.

I like Roger. There's something about him that I connect with. Maybe it's because of his connection to Guam—an island that holds a piece of my heart, too. My dad was stationed there during WWII, though he didn't talk about it much. He used to say, "Guys who talk about war haven't been in one." But now and then, when I was a kid, I'd get to rummage through an old green Navy chest he kept in the garage, full of relics from his time in the Pacific:

photos, a peculiar knife with a leather handle, and the letters he and Mom wrote to each other during his service.

When I was a teenager, my dad finally opened up about those days. He'd sit me next to the chest and pull out item after item, each with a story attached. I never knew it at the time, but those stories would be all I had left of him when he passed, followed soon after by my mom. I never read those letters until after they were gone, but when I did, I understood—those letters were filled with the kind of love and longing that transcends time.

But now, it's time to finish getting Argo stocked and ready for the road.

◄ ▲ ▼ ►

It's a rainy day in Dallas, a welcome break from the oppressive heat of the past week.

The temperatures had climbed into the nineties, creeping toward the hundred-degree mark, but today the rain cools the air, and there's a little relief. Of course, it's also the perfect day to finish loading Argo and make the repairs she needs. Isn't that how it always goes?

I'm taking less with me this time—fewer clothes, fewer gadgets. A few pairs of jeans, some fishing shirts, and even a dress shirt, just in case. A couple of T-shirts for the warmer days, and a few pairs of shorts for when the temperature cranks up again. My camera and photo gear have been waiting patiently for me to pack them, and today I'll finally get them into Argo's overhead compartments and rear storage area.

I could technically leave right now, but there's a problem. Argo's midsection is leaking. Roger's on his way to help finish the repairs, and we've got some parts waiting for us. We both know the drill by now. His broken English and our constant back-and-forth to ensure understanding have become a kind of ritual. We respect each other in a way that's hard to put into words, though it's exhausting at times.

Roger's small enough to crawl under Argo and get to the heart of the problem. The leak is coming from a hose connected to the macerator pump. It's a bigger problem than we thought— one that needs to be fixed before I hit the road. The damage occurred when I pulled Argo over a driveway hump without remembering the low clearance. The scraping noise still makes me cringe just thinking about it.

But Roger's got it handled. We'll fix it, get Argo packed, and then ... then, the open road awaits.

With the repairs done, Argo loaded, and anticipation high, I'm ready. The mission is on.

Note to Self

Every hero's journey needs a Rocinante—and every Rocinante needs a Roger.

So, if the hose leaks, the batteries die, or your black tank betrays you in the dead of winter, remember this: the road is rarely glamorous. It's patched together with duct tape, diesel, handkerchiefs, and hope.

But the real magic?

That's in the helpers—the ones who crawl underneath, who speak with their hands when language fails, who fix what you can't, and teach you how to carry your people with you, even when they're gone.

The road is long, but you're not alone. Not really.

43

Crease on a Paper Map

"The greatest adventure is what lies ahead. Today and tomorrow are yet to be said. The chances, the changes, are all waiting for you. And you may not know it yet, but the adventure is calling."

J . R . R . T O L K E I N

THE NEXT MORNING, quick math tells me it's around day 655 of this wild journey, and my steady steed Argo and I are tearing up Highway 83, heading north into the great, coveted unknown. Glancing down, I see why at every stop along this stretch, locals have slipped me a yur-not-from-here side-eye: untucked light-blue

Columbia fly-fishing shirt, khaki cargo shorts, loafers without socks. Yeah. No denying I kind of stand out.

To find the road I'm traveling on a paper map, should you happen to know what a paper map even is, you'll need to hold the unfolded map of the U.S.A in front of you, west side in your left hand, east side in your right, meaning the direction North is at the top. You'll then fold the sheet in half from left to right or right to left, and then crease it in the middle before opening it back up. Highway 83 should be there in the crease, or perhaps a smidge to the left.

Some folks have been calling this road the "Last American Highway," quite a heavy title, something like this stretch of asphalt's swan song. Then there's the published guidebook that straight-up slapped it with the label "The Road to Nowhere," which I read as a cosmic insult.

I'm no geographic savant, but even I can see that this road indeed goes somewhere, specifically from the fiery Mexican border all the way to the ice-hockey-loving land of Canada— spicy tacos, sweet maple syrup, and everything in between. To me, this road is simply the Heartland Highway, the thread that stitches together the tapestry of this land, border to border.

The Heartland Highway—yes, a more fitting moniker, indeed.

◀ ▲ ▼ ▶

This mostly two-lane road unfolds for more than 1,885 miles, stretching throughout Texas, the panhandle of Oklahoma, western Kansas and Nebraska, South Dakota, North Dakota, and into Manitoba, Canada, with narrow shoulders most of the way and occasional trucks hauling everything from mammoth round bales of hay to cattle to large farm equipment, all whizzing toward their targets, way too close in the opposing lane. And all along the way, Heartland Highway is sparsely dotted with small classic American towns—the kind of towns that whisper of simpler times, where Main Street still matters and the soul of a nation lingers in every weathered storefront and waving hand.

People in these towns—and on the farms scattered around them—are hardy. They live in the heart of the nation's breadbasket, surrounded by endless fields of corn, wheat, and grain. And if feeding the country and the world isn't enough, oil gets pulled from beneath the surface while tall wind turbines spin overhead, harvesting energy from the sky.

Argo's fuel gauge was getting low. I pulled off Heartland Highway into a little gas station that looked like it had been there forever. The old pumps were sun-faded and chipped, standing like relics from another era. The wind was dry and dusty as I hooked the hose to Argo's tank and wandered into the wooden station building to grab a snack.

The man behind the counter looked weathered—creased face, gray stubble, the kind of man who'd seen decades roll by from that same window.

"So, looking at my map, this is the road that runs through the center of the heart of America, huh?" I said.

"Center of the heart is a good way to put it," he said, taking a long drag off his cigarette.

"If you ain't seen it, you don't know it. Where ya headed?"

"Making a trek from Texas to Canada. Wanted to see the breadbasket—the corn, the wheat, the soy, the sunflowers." The wind rattled the door, dust hissing against the glass.

"Doesn't look easy out here."

He pulled his hat lower to block the sun cutting through the window. "You get used to it." "You ever think it's too much?"

He shrugged, easy and slow. "Can't think about it. Born here. I'm here. It's about the land. It's what it does."

The wind gusted again, swirling the dust like it was part of the conversation. I understood what the old man and the wind, and the dust were telling me. At least, I think I did. From the natives who first walked this land to the settlers who followed, the heart of America—its pulse and its grit—was something bigger than anything I could see down that long stretch of road.

"I'll keep that in mind as I head north," I said, wishing him well. His wrinkled face held stories I wanted to hear, but I was just a stranger passing through. Best to let them stay with him.

Out on the highway, it's the same story over and over—hardworking people fixing what's broken, filling a need, making a life. The old man at the station, like the young kid selling sunglasses down the road, carried that spirit—the one that built farms and railroads and factories, the one that made this country rise from nothing. As long as that spirit passes from one generation to the next, America will never die.

As I drive north through the Texas panhandle, nearing the Oklahoma border, I pull off at a small rest area just west of the Heartland Highway. I'm about seven miles north of Wellington, Texas—the birthplace of composer Jimmy Webb.

I'm standing near the spot where, on June 10, 1933, Bonnie and Clyde's wild ride almost came to an abrupt end. Their final reckoning would come later, but this patch of earth at the top of Texas, near the Salt Fork of the Red River, changed Bonnie's life and added another chapter to the layered history of this stretch of road.

Bonnie Elizabeth Parker and Clyde Chestnut Barrow were Depression-era desperados— folk legends and outlaws in equal measure. Maybe Clyde's parents giving him the middle name "Chestnut" explains some of the fire in his blood. Okay, I'm playing armchair psychologist here, but it's a thought worth considering.

Bonnie and Clyde, along with Clyde's brother and a rotating cast of gang members, tore through Texas, Oklahoma, Kansas, Louisiana, Arkansas, Missouri, and Illinois on a crime spree that left behind a trail of robbed banks and dead bodies.

Side note: As a teenager, I interviewed one of their former colleagues, Frank Hardy, for my high school paper. He had retired to Waco, Texas, after a life of crime and a long stretch in prison. He died of a heart attack not long after our interview. But that's a story for another time. In June 1933, Bonnie and Clyde were driving this same route—though with a little more urgency. They were fleeing Texas law, racing toward the Oklahoma state line where local jurisdiction would end and give them a brief reprieve. In a time before cell phones or instant communication, state lines were more than political boundaries—they were lifelines for outlaws. But desperation breeds carelessness. They missed the detour sign warning that the bridge was out. Their Ford coupe plunged into a dry creek bed off the Salt Fork of the Red River.

A local farmer, John Pritchard, and his family saw the wreck from their house. Not knowing they were dealing with criminals, Pritchard, his father, and his brother-in-law rushed to help. They pulled Bonnie and Clyde from the burning wreck. Bonnie's leg was badly burned by fire and battery acid, leaving her with a limp for the rest of her life. Clyde was bruised but mobile.

The Pritchard family took them into their home. Pritchard's son-in-law even drove into town to find a doctor. But before the doctor arrived, the sheriff and his deputy showed up. Clyde reacted fast. Bonnie, despite her injuries, sprang into action. They overpowered the sheriff, took their guns, handcuffed them, and shot up the Pritchards' car so they couldn't be followed. During the chaos, the farmer's daughter was shot in the hand while holding her baby.

Before leaving, Clyde offered Pritchard money.

"No," said Pritchard. "If a man can't help another man, things are in pretty bad shape."

Bonnie and Clyde crossed into Oklahoma, tied the sheriff and deputy to a tree with barbed wire near Sayre, and disappeared into the night. They'd live for another year before meeting their violent end at the hands of Texas Rangers.

Bonnie left behind a leather glove in the wrecked Ford. Clyde left an ammo clip, still loaded with twenty rounds. Both artifacts remain at the Collingsworth County Museum in Wellington—a quiet reminder of the day history rolled through town.

But Bonnie and Clyde's story isn't the only one buried in this stretch of dirt and dust. Along these 1,885 miles, there are a million stories—some lost to the wind, others passed down around kitchen tables. Stories of settlers and railroaders, outlaws and lawmen, ranchers and dreamers, all trying to carve out a life from the stubborn earth.

And that's why this region has me rapt. It's not just the land— it's the people. The quiet resilience of farmers, the grit of small-town mechanics, the neighborly nods from strangers at the gas pump. The spirit of America isn't in monuments or museums; it's in the hands that till the soil, fix the fences, and wave at you from the front porch.

This road through the middle of America is more than a stretch of asphalt; it's a thread that stitches together the soul of a nation. And if you listen closely, you can still hear the hum of it under your tires.

Note to Self

The middle of nowhere is often the middle of everything.

A dusty highway. A farmer's shrug. A gas station that hasn't changed since Reagan. This isn't flyover country—it's the pulse point. The heartbeat. The quiet reminder that strength isn't always loud, and history doesn't always leave a plaque.

So, fold the map. Crease it right through the middle. There's something sacred there.

44

LAND OF OZ

The ache for home lives in all of us, the safe place we can go as we are and not be questioned.

MAYA ANGELOU

SOMETIMES, YOU HAVE TO LEAVE a place to learn how special it is. Dorothy Gale learned this truth the hard way. Not that she had much choice in the matter, what with the whole tornado thing. But in her whirlwind journey to Oz, Dorothy found a lesson that resonates with anyone who's ever set out to leave their home, only to discover just how deeply it's etched in their heart.

Today, I'm heading toward Dorothy's house—the one that didn't get swept away by a tornado to a land of technicolor wonder, but the one that stayed behind, grounded in the flat, wide-open heartland of Kansas.

Ah, the old story—leave a place, and suddenly, you see it for what it is. It's a classic tale, the kind with roots deep in the soil of human experience. And if anyone could back me up, it would be Dorothy. But her adventure? That one took a distinctly more twister-filled turn. Right now, I'm northbound on Highway 83, slicing my way through the very center of America. I've crossed the Texas Panhandle, rolled through the Oklahoma Panhandle, and now, I'm here— deep in the frying pan of Kansas.

This land is as storied as it is vast. The original inhabitants, like the Kickapoo, the Kaw, the Cheyenne, and the Potawatomi, were the first to call it home. European explorers came later, like Don Francisco Vasquez de Coronado, searching for those elusive Seven Cities of Gold. And here I am now, cruising through this history in my trusty Airstream, *Argo*—a vehicle they never could've imagined in Dorothy's day.

The landscape stretches endlessly, painted in the rich greens and golds of corn, soybeans, wheat, hay, and sunflowers. But there's also the quirky broomcorn, the waving switchgrass, and the majestic bluestem, each of them part of the subtle poetry of this land.

I've swapped my blue shirt for a simple brown khaki one— sort of a tribute to the hardworking souls I meet in local diners. My cargo shorts and sock-less loafers might catch a few curious glances from the locals, but comfort is king on this long, winding journey. After all, in the grand expanse of America, it's the quirks that make us who we are.

Kansas is famous for a lot of things—its wheat, its tornadoes, and, of course, the beginning and end of *The Wizard of Oz*. The movie, based on L. Frank Baum's 1900 novel was brought to life on the big screen in 1939 and has become a true cinematic classic. If you haven't seen it, then it's time to drop whatever else you had planned, get a bag of popcorn, and make an evening of it. Judy Garland's portrayal of Dorothy is nothing short of endearing, and the special effects, while primitive by today's standards, were cutting-edge at the time.

But today, my adventure brings me to Liberty, Kansas, where Dorothy's house—the *real* one, not the magical one from Oz—sits, beckoning travelers like me. The town may have once resisted the Oz association, but today, it's fully embraced its ties to Dorothy, Toto, and all the other unforgettable characters of Baum's tale.

And tornadoes? Well, let's just say they're a part of Kansas, too. The National Weather Service reports that each Kansas county has experienced anywhere from thirty to fifty tornadoes since 1950. So, the tornado part of Dorothy's story isn't just fiction—it's a slice of reality here. So, I find myself in Liberty, touring Dorothy's farmhouse and strolling through a delightful little diorama recreating the Land of Oz. It's campy, it's charming, and it's utterly whimsical. My guide? A teenager in a gingham dress and ruby slippers who, with a twinkle in her eye, leads me through the whole show. I'm not supposed to know her real name—mums the word—but she's part of the Dorothy Program, an educational initiative where girls memorize lines from the movie, gain confidence, and learn the art of storytelling. Once they pass the test, they don the gingham and the famous slippers, stepping into the shoes of one of pop culture's most iconic characters.

The tour is charmingly low-budget, with rooms staged to simulate Dorothy's journey. The first stop? Inside Dorothy's house, a typical Kansas farmhouse living room, where the walls rattle, curtains whip in the wind, and lights flicker as the tornado nears. The storm builds to a crescendo, and just like that, I'm six years old again.

At the start of elementary school, my family lived for a few years in Durant, Oklahoma, and one spring evening, while the smell of fried chicken and apple pie filled the air, I was standing by the back door of our house when a cloud in the sky, peculiar and ominous, caught my eye. "Hey, Mom, look at that funny-looking cloud," I said, pointing it out.

Mom rushed to the door, saw it too, and in an instant, panic set in. "That's a funnel cloud! A tornado!" she cried. She pulled me inside and extinguished the flames on the stove. We huddled in the center of the house, my little sister Cathy clinging to her side, as Mom urged us to get down and cover our heads. Her voice, usually calm, trembled with urgency as she led us in The Lord's Prayer, her words rushing out in a desperate plea for protection.

The noise outside was deafening, like a freight train passing over us. And then, just as quickly, it stopped. Silence.

We'd been in the tornado's path, but it veered off course at the last second, sparing us, though a tree fell nearby and a neighbor's roof was damaged. My dad rushed home, and I'll never forget his tight embrace.

Afterward, we learned that others hadn't been as lucky. My mom kept saying, "This meal could have been our last." And I think back on that moment whenever I feel the stirrings of nostalgia, even as I stand here in Dorothy's house, reflecting on her fictional tornado ride. In the movie, Dorothy's whirlwind adventure flips her world from a dull, black-and-white Kansas to a vibrant, technicolor dreamscape. She meets strange new friends, faces dangerous foes, and experiences a world far beyond her imagination. But in the end, the wisdom she gains is the same we all learn eventually: there's no place like home.

Unlike Dorothy, I wasn't whisked away to a magical land. But the lesson is the same. Home is where we are most truly ourselves. It's not about the house, the walls, or the roof over our heads—it's the love and connection we find there. That's the place that becomes our anchor in the storm, our refuge from the world's chaos.

And in the end, the only place that matters is the one where you feel most seen, most loved, and most at peace.

Walking through Dorothy's house got me thinking about home. Not Oz. Not Kansas. But the place I call home today, the one I was hundreds of miles away from just then. There's something about being in a place that isn't yours that makes you appreciate the one you left behind.

Note to Self

Funny how it takes standing in someone else's story to see your own more clearly.

It isn't the painted farmhouse or the simulated windstorm that gets you—it's the memory that stirs when you weren't even looking.

Turns out, home isn't a place you arrive at. It's a thread that tugs at you in quiet moments, somewhere between make-believe and memory, reminding you who you've always been.

45

Coffee Talk

Four horses cannot overtake the tongue.
CHINESE PROVERB

CONTINUING MY ROAD TRIP NORTH on Highway 83—the beloved Heartland Highway—I cross the Kansas state line into Nebraska, named after its "flat water" by the Otoe people, referring to the Platte River.

As I cruise into this prairie wonderland, the landscape shifts ever so subtly, yet remains profoundly familiar. More of that charming tapestry of farmlands, each plot painted like an artist's brush across the canvas. Corn here, soybeans there, wheat waving like a sea, and the sunflowers—oh, those sunflowers—stand tall, nodding as if to say, "Welcome, traveler." Mile after mile, the land stays mostly flat to gently rolling, peppered with acres of crops — corn, soybeans, wheat, and sunflowers.

And bugs.

I am accompanied by countless tiny-winged creatures on this stretch—bugs upon bugs upon bugs, all of which have taken a real liking to Argo. Each time one meets its untimely demise against my windshield, it sounds almost celebratory—like Mother Nature throwing a going-away party for them. Soon enough, a warning on the dashboard blinks at me: "Washer Fluid."

Up ahead, a town emerges, in this case comprising a lone gas station that stands like an oasis on this stretch of highway. It's funny. These rural stations are a bit like mini malls. You can get anything from a wrench to wrench-shaped candy. And, on a hot day, this one offers soft-serve ice cream. A sweet promise of reward on this road less traveled.

I pull in, and, lo and behold, stacks of window washer fluid, standing like soldiers awaiting my arrival. A dollar a gallon? In the city, that wouldn't even buy you a snack-size bag of M&Ms. I grin, grateful that the universe has my back.

As Argo's gas tank fills, I scrub the windshield clean with the station's long-handle squeegee. After a thorough cleaning, I raise the hood to its locked position and happily fill the washer fluid tank with that bargain gallon. Had this been a cartoon, I'd have been whistling a tune, fingers snapping to the beat, while watching that fluid fill up. Too bad I can't whistle worth a darn.

Anyway, feeling good about the whole thing, I close the hood and head back to the station for a celebratory ice cream cone. A little "roadie," as we say in Texas. Roadies can be anything for the journey—a drink, an ice cream cone, even a beer. Whatever fuels you for the miles ahead.

All is good. That is, until I walk back outside. An old farmer stops me. His face is weathered, like it's been carved from an old barn door. He's got worn boots, overalls, and a battered brown farmer's hat that probably should've been retired a decade ago.

"Hey," he says, pointing at my car. "You got a leak." I glance down. Sure enough, there's a little puddle forming under Argo's engine. "Fluid," he adds, just in case I didn't catch that part. "Looks like it's from your engine."

I stare at the leak, trying to make sense of it. "Ugh, okay. What kind of fluid are we talking about here?" He gives me a look like I've asked if cows are mammals. "Well," he says, "it's not soda pop, if that's what you mean."

I bend down, trying to take a closer look. "I hope it's not serious."

He scratches his chin thoughtfully. "Nah, not yet. But if it keeps leaking, you're gonna have a problem. Could be oil, coolant, or ... you know ... 'mystery fluid.'" He grins like he's cracked the funniest joke in the world.

"Mystery fluid?" I ask, raising an eyebrow. "Is that a thing?"

"Oh, sure," he says, tapping his temple like he's imparting ancient wisdom. "Every car's got some. You'd be surprised what's hiding in there. It could be the transmission fluid or power steering fluid. Could be something that shouldn't even be in there at all."

I stare at the growing puddle beneath Argo, a dark liquid steadily dripping onto the concrete. Oil? Diesel? I touch it with my index finger and sniff. Dang, it's the vinegar smell of washer fluid.

I hold the cone in my left hand, still licking the cold, sweet vanilla, while raising the hood with my right hand. The fluid tank I just filled is now draining rapidly, almost empty before my very eyes. And there it is—a loose hose clamp allowing my dollars' worth of washer fluid to drip onto the ground.

Maybe it's the bugs getting revenge. One of them must've lived long enough to pull this stunt.

I spent the next twenty minutes wrestling with the hose under the tank, using only my sense of touch to feel my way through the cramped space. After some struggle, I managed to reattach the hose securely enough to keep the fluid inside where it belongs. I buy another gallon of washer fluid, fill the tank, and shut the hood. This time, nothing leaks.

Now, I'm back in Argo's captain's chair, the road ahead looking clearer with a clean windshield, Argo topped off with diesel and washer fluid, and me wishing I had another vanilla ice cream cone heading to the next small town in Nebraska. Forgive me for withholding its name; it's for a good reason. I'm about to overhear some gossip about a guy named Walter—and Walter's wife.

Like many small towns, this one's got its share of empty storefronts, windows that once housed thriving businesses now shuttered by big-box stores and the internet. You can almost hear the echo of what once was. But this town feels a little more alive than most. A few people are walking along Main Street, chatting as they go. There's more activity than the usual ghost towns I've passed.

One storefront catches my eye—a bakery. It's mid-morning, and I haven't eaten yet. The sign outside says: "We have a coffee shop now, too." Bakery plus coffee? I'm sold.

I park Argo and head toward the door, my "schnozzola" leading the way. Let me pause here and say—I just like saying *schnozzola*. It's a word that reminds me of the old comedian Jimmy Durante, a favorite of my grandmother's. We'd laugh together at his jokes. Who doesn't love a funny guy with a big schnozzola?

Anyway, my schnozzola guides me inside the bakery, where the aromas of dark coffee and cinnamon apples swirl together, drawing me in. But as I approach the display case, I'm disappointed to see that most of the baked goods are gone. Only a few remaining treats linger— like a lonely Danish with cinnamon. I point to it.

The menu looks like it was copied from that green-logo empire—lattes, macchiatos, espressos. When my turn comes, I order a latte with half a shot of caramel, and I wonder when coffee turned into algebra. Really, I just want jet fuel in a cup: "My coffee should be strong enough to walk across itself," I say. The barista chuckles, probably because he's heard worse.

Six men are having coffee and jawing at a table. They stopped talking when I walked by. I put my backpack down in a quiet space in one of the rear booths. I'll be able to write. Maybe read. Sip my coffee in peace. But the room's acoustics carry the men's voices my way. Four of them are slim men with disappearing butts. One is on the heavy side; another has a beach ball tummy that hangs well over his belt buckle. Of course, I am assuming he has a belt buckle. A new guy walks in, joining the group.

"Where you been?" one of the guys says to the new arrival, "We missed ya the last few days."

"Had to get my medicines adjusted," he answers.

"Oh," says another man sporting a camouflage ball cap with the logo of a bridge on it, "you okay now?"

"Yep, had to go to the hospital for a day … just to do it."

"You go here?" another asks, "or the new one down the road?"

"Here."

"Not sure I'd go to the new one," another guy says, "with what I've heard."

"Yep, think they're understaffed, still working the bugs outta the new one."

I'm trying to tune out the exchange and starting to settle in over my hot coffee. The stream rises as I take in the caramel overtones coming from the thick ceramic cup—it smells woody and sweet. An "ahh-moment-of-ecstasy" for me.

The door opens, and a group of six ladies walk in. They appear to be in their fifties and sixties, wearing muted casual dresses and matching hairdos. They all seem to be talking at the same time, over each other, as they make their way past the table of men, continue toward me, look around, and then select a table near my booth.

No more silence between the chatter of both groups. I don't usually eavesdrop on other people's conversations, but I couldn't avoid this one. They're talking loudly.

"I wish I could have seen my gallbladder after they took it out," one of the women says.

"You'd want to see it?" a puzzled friend asks in surprise.

"They said it's full of stones. I'd love to see what that looks like."

"What I wonder is," another said, "after they take out your gallbladder, how do you digest?" The question goes unanswered.

Another woman asks, "But what about the new stones? Where do the new stones go? You know if you don't have your gallbladder anymore...." That question also goes unanswered. The conversation switches to one of them buying a vacation home in Colorado. "So, Mary, how was your trip to Colorado? You get situated?"

"As you know, we bought a smaller home, as I told you about," Mary shares. "Really cute, just perfect for Ralph and me. And they told us it would be empty of the other people's furniture as soon as we closed on it. But when we took our first load, we couldn't believe it; their furniture was still there."

"Oh, my God, you got all the way there, and the people hadn't moved out yet?"

"Full house! What were we to do? We didn't know. I called the real estate lady, and she didn't know either. So, there we were with our furniture and nowhere to put it. The real estate lady called us back later, saying they needed another week." They continue talking about the furniture and how to handle such a calamity.

Then the conversation switches back to health issues with a twist. Someone named Walter is in the hospital. "He was all 'blowed' up," says a lady who visited Walter yesterday at the new hospital. "They had to get the swelling down."

"Is Walter going to be okay?"

"As long as he gets four hours of sleep, he's okay."

A lady who hasn't spoken yet says, "This is just between us, but I thought you'd want to know…." They lean in closer to each other, whispering. They are not talking about Walter now but about Walter's wife. It's some heavy gossip. To protect the innocent, I won't repeat it here.

I've observed that the more critical the gossip is between friends, the softer the voice relaying it becomes. Hushed tones continue as they share stories about Walter's wife and poor Walter in the hospital.

Of course, these ladies might as well shout into a radio station microphone, print it in the newspaper, or post it on social media. In a town this size, it'll be public knowledge before noon, passed person to person, each time with the warning: "This is just between us, but I thought you'd want to know."

Gossip, from the mouth of a skilled tittle-tattler, can gut someone they don't like, clean the meat off their bones, and serve 'em up stone-cold dead before the victim finishes their morning coffee.

I feel it's time for me to move on down the road. I leave a tip on the table and sling my backpack over my left shoulder. As I open the door to go, I see both the group of men and the women stop talking, look at me, and watch me walk away.

These morning coffee talk conversations are not peculiar to small towns. They go on every morning all across America. Probably around the world. Mostly retired types solving world problems, along with bitching and griping about their phone bill or whatever wrong they want to be righted.

To them, I'm just another stranger passing through town—a not-from-around-here guy.

NOTE TO SELF

Never underestimate the power of a clean windshield and a good cup of coffee. Both help you see clearer.

46

Road to Nowhere

The news and truth are not the same thing.

WALTER LIPPMANN

TODAY, I FIND MYSELF DRIVING through the very heart of America—geographically, at least. The landscape is a vast sea of farms and fields, stretching endlessly in every direction. The land seems to go on forever, and with that comes an oddly unsettling feeling. It's the same sensation I get when I gaze up at a star-filled sky on a cloudless night, far from the noise of city lights. Like I'm small. Insignificant. A fleeting moment in some far-greater plot.

As I make my way north along 83, my mind wanders. I think about everything I've seen so far and the impressions that have stayed with me. I can't help but laugh, an unrestrained chuckle escaping me. This journey, this quest to find the real America, is unfolding right here before me. It's all around me—alive and thriving.

But then, amid the expansive fields, the quiet stretches of road, I think of something else that's been on my mind. Everywhere I go, I hear it from people: news fatigue. At first, I thought it was just my exhaustion from the constant barrage of headlines, but it seems I'm not alone. According to Pew Research, nearly 70 percent of Americans are suffering from the same thing. "Freaked-out Americans Desperately Seek to Escape the News," Claire Suddath had written in *Bloomberg News*.

According to a study by the American Psychological Association, two-thirds of Americans say the state of the nation is their number one source of stress, even more than work or money. So, what's the answer? How do we escape?

There was a time when comedy could be a refuge. A good, hearty laugh was almost like medicine for the soul. That's still true, I suppose—but don't go looking for it on your television screen. Comedy today has evolved into something unrecognizable, a political battleground where late-night hosts are less funny and more angry, more divisive. What was once lighthearted banter is now bitter tirades. The laughter has been replaced by vitriol. These so-called "comedians" have traded in punchlines for hate speech, becoming nothing more than mouthpieces of ridicule and contempt.

It's tiring. Even when these angry jesters make jabs at people you may consider your political enemies, it's just exhausting to hear it over and over. There's nothing genuine about it— just laugh tracks and applause, making you think everyone's in on the joke. But we're not. Ratings tell the story. Late-night shows, once the gold standard for comedy, now draw less than eight million viewers combined. Johnny Carson, back in his heyday, could draw nine million. Jay Leno brought in six million. And yet, now, comedy and news have become one toxic mix, polluting the airwaves. The once-vibrant world of entertainment has been overrun by a political agenda. What happened to the laughs? What happened to the joy? The truth is, most prime-time entertainment is no longer about entertainment—it's about telling you what to think, mocking you if you disagree.

The culture of canceling those who disagree has seeped into every corner of our society. From entertainment to universities to boardrooms and living rooms, there's a constant tension that's hard to escape. And it's troubling.

I've had conversations with people from all walks of life, and a common thread has emerged: a deep concern about the country. Folks are worried about the biased news, the constant stream of divisive rhetoric. The elites, in their ivory towers, look down on what they dismiss as the "flyover" states, reinforcing the idea that anything outside their bubble is irrelevant. Yet, that very dismissal reflects their ignorance—because there's a vast, untapped wisdom in the places they overlook.

Perhaps those early humans who walked this land knew something we've forgotten. There's something about their connection to the Earth, their reverence for the world around them, that modern life doesn't seem to grasp. Our dependence on technology and our relentless pursuit of progress have created a veil, blinding us to the deeper mysteries of life.

Despite all our advancements, humans have barely begun to understand the vastness of our planet and the universe beyond. There are still mysteries yet to be discovered, things we can't even imagine. And remember, all the scientific discoveries we've made were already here before we figured them out. Maybe those ancient people, so connected to the rhythms of nature, had a better understanding of the unseen forces that shape our lives.

Archaeologists believe humans may have lived in North America as far back as 12,000 BC. Some suggest that as the Ice Age ended, the first humans crossed the Bering land bridge from Asia into what is now Alaska. Evidence of early settlements dates back approximately 1000 BC, with small villages emerging along the coast. The oldest Hopi Indian reservation, Oribi in northern Arizona, is thought to date back to 500 BC. And farming—corn, squash—has deep roots in North America, with evidence of corn cultivation in Mexico as far back as 5500 BC.

Corn—once a tiny, thumb-sized crop—has played an essential role in human history. Over thousands of years, it's been nurtured and cultivated, evolving into the hearty, towering stalks we recognize today. Some of the earliest evidence of corn's evolution was found in Mississippi, dating back more than a thousand years.

When the first Europeans landed in Jamestown, Virginia, in 1607, they were met by native villages already established along the East Coast. These people, living off the land, had a different understanding of time, of history, of connection.

And here I am, driving along this long, open highway, alone in the vast middle of the country. It's a beautiful escape, a welcome break from the noise. Out here, it's easy to see why so many of my friends back home, worn out by the twenty-four-hour news cycle, might envy this quiet, peaceful life.

The music on the radio plays louder now, filling the space inside the car. The land outside rolls by, a sweeping, beautiful panorama of fields and sky. Sunflowers wave in the breeze. The blue sky stretches on forever, and the open road calls me forward. It's peaceful here, in the middle of America.

Note to Self

If the world ever gets too loud—too angry, too certain, too smug—don't match its volume. Escape it. Find a patch of earth that doesn't have cell service and just sit there awhile.

Let the silence stretch until your soul settles. Remember that peace doesn't shout; it whispers. And the truths that shape you most don't always come from screens—they come from soil, sky, and the unhurried road that asks nothing of you except to keep going.

Rediscover awe. Rediscover stillness. Rediscover yourself.

47

MILLION-DOLLAR WATER

If you want to get rich, offer people something for free.

MARK CUBAN

IT'S THE FRIDAY OF LABOR Day weekend, and I realize I've forgotten about the holiday. It strikes me that I should just stay put at this pleasant little spot I've found, tucked beside the wide Missouri River. As I gaze at the water flowing gently by, it feels like I've stumbled upon a living history lesson, a kind of portal to a time when pioneers and adventurers ventured boldly into the unknown.

Perhaps I should linger here longer, lost in contemplation of Lewis and Clark, who camped on this very spot all those years ago. But then, a fleeting thought—if I don't leave now, the roads will soon be filled with carloads of families, all out to grab the last bit of summer before fall settles in.

On the other hand, Mount Rushmore is just a few hours away. And something inside me says I'll regret not taking this detour, especially since I've heard about that iconic sight my whole life. Those colossal presidential faces carved into the Black Hills have always called to me, a monument to American grandeur. The image of the granite busts in history books I read as a child is still vivid in my mind. Well, at least it was in the history books back when I was in school. These days, I'm not so sure they'd even make it into a modern textbook. The four faces —once revered as national heroes—are no longer considered heroes by those who see the past only through a lens of relentless revision.

But the Crazy Horse memorial is nearby, and I'm not about to pass up an opportunity to see both.

I give in to the urge to keep moving, even though part of me wants to stay. The rebellious voice in my head justifies it: "It's all just one big continuous road. All the Heartland Highway!" So, despite my better judgment, I pack up my cozy camp, leave the river's edge, and head toward those rock-faced Presidents—and Crazy Horse, too.

Leaving Pierre, the capital of South Dakota, I head west on Highway 14, away from Highway 83 and toward the Black Hills. The road is long, straight, and open, with only a sharp left and right turn to break the monotony as I make my way between Pierre and Wall. The landscape stretches out in waves of hay fields and rows of five-foot-tall sunflowers.

These sunflowers are something to behold, their brown centers standing tall with their yellow petals like a thousand little suns reaching for the sky. Farmers found they make a profitable crop—sunflower seeds for snacks and oil, all of it contributing to the world's food supply. They also have an environmental magic called phytoremediation, which is the fancy term for cleaning up polluted soil. The more you know!

Some might find this landscape monotonous, but I don't. There's something captivating in the simplicity of it all. The sky seems purer here, outlining every detail, every blade of grass, every sunflower, with a precision that feels almost too clear for words. I'm hardly able to keep my eyes on the road, so entranced am I by the ever-shifting colors of the landscape—abstract art laid out before me by nature itself.

But then, I notice something odd: homemade road signs everywhere, all advertising ... a drug store? I don't care about a drug store, but these signs, well, they've piqued my curiosity. They've been advertising for miles, some of them even giving the remaining distance to Wall Drug: "Just 100 miles ahead." Then fifty. Then twenty. Then two.

What could possibly be so special about a drug store?

Then I see it: "Free Ice Water." And another: "Five-Cent Coffee." Now, that's a throwback, especially the five-cent coffee. It's an old sign, surely long outdated, but it tells a story all its own.

And the signs? They're all over the place—sometimes hundreds of miles away from the actual store, in places as far-flung as China and Australia. I'll tell you this: Wall Drug has managed to make a name for itself, one sign at a time. And no, it's not affiliated with the "Wall" that you might be thinking of, that big-box retailer that ends in "mart." No, this is something different altogether.

By the time the sun sets, I've arrived in Wall, South Dakota. It's the crossroads of I-90 and I-240, a tiny town that, to all appearances, exists solely because of Wall Drug. There's not much else here, save for a couple of gas stations and a Dairy Queen. Wall Drug is the main attraction. It's the reason the place still stands.

As I park, a green dinosaur—a huge, eighty-foot-tall fiberglass creature looms over a couple of RVs and trucks parked by the gas station. The night sky is ablaze with sunset colors, and the fading light dances across the buildings of Wall Drug. The sunset's fiery blues and oranges swirl through the sky, an artwork made from clouds and light.

Of course, by the time I've fumbled for my camera, the scene has changed, as it always does with sunsets. I catch a fleeting shot, but it's nothing compared to the full, vibrant picture I saw just moments before. But, as always, that fleeting moment—like so many others on this journey—is safely tucked away in my mind, like a memory card in a camera that's never out of reach.

I decide to stay the night, but there are no motel rooms left. Not wanting to wander far, I turn toward the dinosaur where I saw the RVs parked. There's a small area for campers, and I'm hoping to find a spot to settle in for the night. In the morning, I'll have breakfast at Wall Drug Cafe, walk around, and then hit the road toward Rapid City and Mount Rushmore. It's a plan that's as good as any.

The next morning, the cafe's buffet line is packed with the usual suspects: eggs, sausage, biscuits, the kind of fare you'd expect. Nothing's too fancy in a place like this. But, it's cool. As I wander around, taking in the eclectic collection of artifacts on display, I pass a bathroom on the back side of the courtyard. It's one of those spots where, when you least expect it, you find something that sticks with you.

On the bathroom stall door, in bold black marker, some clever young soul had written: "I took a dump at Wall Drug." Not exactly groundbreaking humor, but after all the buildup from those road signs, it somehow made me smile.

And here's the oddest thing: that silly graffiti triggers a memory. It takes me back to my first days at the University of Texas. I remember walking into the UT Tower for the first time, stopping at the restroom near the north doors. And there, in a stall, someone had written: *God is love.*

Love is blind.

Ray Charles is blind.

Ray Charles must be God.

I hadn't even started my classes yet, but I was already being educated—by graffiti, no less. It felt like a whole new world, and that's what college was supposed to be. People thought differently here.

Back in Wall Drug, I'm still processing all this when my gaze shifts to the framed black-and-white photographs that cover the walls. Some of them date back to the late 1800s, when cameras were still a rare novelty. It's fascinating to see these snapshots of the past—moments frozen in time, capturing a world that's now long gone.

One set of photos, tucked in a corner, catches my eye. They show the grim moment of a hanging, the last legal one in Meade County. It's the story of Ernest Loveswar, a man of mixed heritage who was convicted of murder. The photos capture his final walk up to the gallows, the noose placed around his neck, and the tragic moment of his death.

The darkness of those images is jarring, but it's also history—stories of a time when things were different, when justice and retribution were dealt in ways we no longer consider. I turn away from the somber photos, seeking something lighter. And sure enough, there's a collection of vintage shots: Native American women washing clothes in the river, cowboys branding cattle, a young Scotty Phillips with his sons, General Custer with soldiers at the Gordon Stockade, Calamity Jane, Annie Oakley, Buffalo Bill. These are the images that capture the spirit of the Old West, the characters who made it legendary.

But soon enough, my stomach starts to grumble. I could go for something greasy. A little indulgence never hurt anyone, right? Satan, in the form of a greasy plate of food, beckons. And like so many others, I fall victim to temptation.

I've been eating better lately, but today, I throw caution to the wind. I stop by Zesto, a little ice cream stand in Pierre, South Dakota, with a slogan that reads: *Zesto is Besto*. The parking lot is full of people abandoning their diet as they approach the window. The girl behind the counter doesn't even blink when I close in. She's seen it all.

"What can I get you?" she asks, the question more of a polite formality than anything else.

I hesitate, trying to act like I know what I'm doing. "Uh ... I'll have the toddler size," I say, hoping my indecision doesn't show. She raises an eyebrow. "Okay. What flavor?" she asks.

"Vanilla and ... the flavor of the day, blackberry," I say, feeling the pressure of the decision mounting. "Got it."

As I stand there waiting for my ice cream, I think of the calories, the sugar, the guilt. But it's an indulgence. A treat. It's just a few minutes of joy, right? I resolve to savor every bite. The Zesto person hands me the cup, and I walk back to my truck. It's all so simple. And for a fleeting moment, it's enough.

Back at the gas station, I notice a shiny car pulling in. A convertible Mustang, its long, sleek lines making it look like it's moving even when parked. A young couple steps out, and they start pumping gas. It's odd, I think, to see such a fancy car in a place like this. But then again, it's Wall Drug. Anything can happen.

Maybe, just maybe, I should've followed my first instincts and stayed by the river. But then again, I'm here, and that's enough for now. Tomorrow, I'll visit Mount Rushmore and continue my journey through the heart of America. I'll take in all the beauty, history, and stories that this vast country has to offer.

Note to Self

Joy doesn't always show up how you expect it. Sometimes it's in a cheap cup of coffee, a silly sign, or a soft-serve cone on a hot day. Don't miss it while waiting for something bigger. The little stuff—that's the good stuff. Keep noticing.

48

STONE-FACED

Johnny Cash's face belongs on Mount Rushmore.

KRIS KRISTOFFERSON

CONTINUING MY DRIVE NORTH YESTERDAY, I rolled into Pierre, capital of South Dakota, just as night was settling in. I found a campsite next to the Missouri River, though in the dark, I couldn't see it, just heard the river rippling, like a whispered secret, as I drifted to sleep.

This morning, I woke slowly, stretching into the day with a yawn or two. I brewed my coffee, the smell of it rich and inviting, and stepped outside with my cup in hand. The air was fresh, September cool, and the sunshine begged to be savored. I walked around for a bit, soaking in the beauty before sitting down at a metal picnic table overlooking the steep, pebbly riverbank. Sipping my coffee slowly, I let the peaceful sight of the Missouri's swift waters wash over me. Birds swooped overhead, sparrows, crows, and grackles, all darting across the sky like a winged parade. A few pecked the ground nearby, unfazed by my presence—like I'd wandered into some kind of Hitchcock movie, only without the tension, just feathers.

South Dakota's also home to a good number of ring-necked pheasants. Argo and I watched a dozen or so dash across Highway 83 as we cruised along, their iridescent feathers flashing in the sun. Come hunting season, though, this landscape will change. Fewer pheasants, more hunters. That's how it works here. Farmers make a good chunk of money leasing their land for hunting. It's a land of opportunity—and pheasants don't get to enjoy it much longer.

Under the bright blue sky, I took it all in, breathing deep the September air. I'm just a humble traveler passing through, making my way across the Land of the Free and, occasionally, the Mildly Confused.

I wondered if, back in 1804, Lewis and Clark had enjoyed a similar moment when they camped near the confluence of the Missouri and Bad Rivers. No metal picnic tables, no coffee mugs, but perhaps the same cool breeze and birds. Though their stay was brief, the expedition ran into a bit of a misunderstanding with the Lakota. They didn't have an interpreter, and when weapons were drawn, it almost spelled the end of their journey. Luckily, Chief Black Buffalo stepped in, diffusing the situation before it escalated. A narrow escape.

When I first set out on this journey, I had Highway 83 mapped out all the way from Texas to North Dakota—that was the plan. Or at least, it was a plan. But plans and whims don't always get along. Wanderlust runs deep, and it doesn't wait for a road map to tell it what to do. I'm not the type to rigidly stick to a plan when something catches my eye. All of us who've got that wanderer's itch know how it feels when the call to see something—anything—becomes too strong to ignore.

There's a quote I've always liked from Charles Lutwidge Dodgson—better known as Lewis Carroll. He wrote, "In the end... We only regret the chances we didn't take, the relationships we were afraid to have, and the decisions we waited too long to make."

He might have written *Alice's Adventures in Wonderland*, but he knew what it was to take a leap—an invitation to curiosity. And sometimes, you have to follow that pull.

As I looked at the map, I realized Mount Rushmore was only a few hours to the west. The carved faces of the presidents—etched into the granite—have lived in my mind as icons. You've seen the photos, the school history books, but now, the real thing is within reach. I knew if I didn't stop, I'd regret it.

So, I turned Argo toward Keystone, South Dakota, the little town that sits at the foot of the mountain, and set my sights on the monument. It was a must-see, the perfect detour.

Mount Rushmore stands as a testament to human perseverance—carving four iconic figures from a rock wall with nothing more than hands, ropes, and vision. It's funny, though, the mountain wasn't even named after the men who worked tirelessly to carve it. Instead, it was named after a New York attorney sent to check land titles in 1884—an obscure reason, but as my European friend would say, "very American."

When I reached Rapid City, just a stone's throw from Mount Rushmore, the day was slipping toward evening. It's the long holiday weekend, and I knew it'd probably be packed, but I decided—why wait? I could always head back to Highway 83 tomorrow if the monument wasn't all it was cracked up to be.

I took Highway 16, winding my way through the trees to Keystone, passing over an arch of timber bridges and a tunnel built by the Civilian Conservation Corps, the CCC, during the Great Depression—an engineering marvel that fit snugly in this rugged, mountainous landscape. As I rounded a bend in the road, there they were: The faces of Washington, Jefferson, Roosevelt, and Lincoln. It's one thing to see a photo, but in person, it's real.

And it's big. I knew from the pictures that Thomas Jefferson's nostrils could fit a grown man or two, but standing there, the sheer size of the monument was hard to fathom. The granite heads look out across the land, silently guarding history.

Some people today call for these faces to be torn down, saying that they no longer represent the ideals we strive for. But for me, these faces are more than just figures in stone. They're symbols of who we were, what we've built, and what we could be. Change is important, yes, but don't erase the past—learn from it.

I sat down at a picnic table to absorb the awe of it all and, as the dusk settled, I ate buffalo stew from the park's restaurant, the steam rising in the cool mountain air—comforting, hearty, and perfect for the setting.

I stuck around for the lighting ceremony, a moment that was as patriotic and inspiring as you'd imagine. But I didn't stop there. The next day, I returned, knowing that one of the last living men who helped build the monument—Nick Clifford, a former CCC worker—would be there.

Clifford worked on Rushmore between 1938 and 1940, and though he was mostly there as a baseball player (he was recruited for his skills as a right fielder), he also helped build the wood studio for the sculptors.

I met him in the gift shop, and after a few words, I asked if he'd be willing to share his story. His response was short and sweet: "No."

I smiled politely, but he didn't budge. He wasn't having it. Ninety-seven years of questions probably left him less inclined to entertain another interview. I get it now—history's lived it, he's been there. And sometimes, living history doesn't need to talk about the past again. So, I left him be. I was talking to time itself, after all. I thanked him and moved on. He passed away a year later, and while I won't have the chance to hear his story firsthand, his presence was enough to feel the weight of history.

For three days, I was amid it all—the stone, the stories, and the people who lived them. Walking through Mount Rushmore, I felt like a little bit of Indiana Jones, a little bit of Forrest Gump—wandering through time with the clumsy grace of someone trying to make sense of the world.

And I'll tell you this—I feel fortunate to be the one lucky enough to walk these roads, see these sights, and feel it all firsthand. Sometimes, the greatest gift is simply being here.

JOHN W. BUTLER

Note to Self

Some things are best witnessed in person. The wind in your hair. The sky stretched wide. The granite faces that don't speak, but somehow still say everything.

In a world full of noise, there's something sacred about standing in stillness, shoulder to shoulder with history—not to worship it, not to whitewash it, but to understand what it meant, and what it still might mean.

Let reverence and curiosity hold hands.

And remember: awe isn't just found in stone—it shows up in silence, in story, in the way a mountain stands and doesn't flinch.

49

CRAZY HORSE

Happy indeed is the naturalist: to him the seasons come like old friends; to him the birds sing: as he walks along, the flowers stretch out from the hedges, or look up from the ground, and as each year fades away, he looks back on a fresh store of happy memories.

JOHN LUBBOCK

FROM MOUNT RUSHMORE, I MADE the seventeen-mile journey through the Black Hills to the Crazy Horse Memorial. This part of my quest to uncover the heart of America felt essential—like a thread that would pull all the disparate pieces of the puzzle together. After all, this carving, the largest of its kind in progress anywhere in the world, seemed to embody something raw and enduring about the American spirit.

Crazy Horse—his name itself evokes a sense of untamed energy. The carving, a colossal figure being chiseled into Thunderhead Mountain, symbolizes not just a historical figure but an entire people. The project was the brainchild of Henry Standing Bear, who wanted to create a monument that would stand as a testament to the strength and resilience of Native Americans. This was more than just a tribute to Crazy Horse himself; it was an assertion of the Native American presence, their history, and their future.

As I rolled through the winding roads toward the memorial, I thought about the diversity of Native American tribes—574 in total, each with its own customs, languages, and ways of life.

Even now, these tribes remain so distinct, yet united in their shared histories and struggles. I couldn't help but marvel at the irony: the first humans to inhabit this land, the original caretakers of this vast country, were treated like outsiders for far too long, their culture and contributions largely ignored.

My college professors used to write off early humans as primitive, almost cartoonish figures who knew nothing of the world beyond their immediate surroundings. But there was intelligence in that, wasn't there? Survival on this continent required a kind of genius—the ability to adapt, to read the land, to communicate without words. These were not people to be dismissed.

Every year, new discoveries surface, reshaping our understanding of who they were.

HEARTLAND HIGHWAYS

I thought about Crazy Horse as I drove, about his leadership in the Lakota tribe and his role in the Battle of Little Bighorn. His name, Tȟašúŋke Witkó—literally, "his horse is crazy"— speaks to the fierceness of his spirit, of his unyielding devotion to his people and their way of life. Born around 1840 in the Black Hills, he became one of the most revered leaders in Native American history. His image, now carved into the side of Thunderhead Mountain, is a reminder of both the power of the land and the power of a people determined not to be forgotten.

When I arrived at the site, the scale of the Crazy Horse Memorial took my breath away. The face of Crazy Horse, alone, is the height of several buildings, its contours still rough and unfinished, yet unmistakable in its majesty. It stands there, high above the surrounding landscape, as a symbol of perseverance, bridging the gap between cultures, between the past and the present.

This sculpture is not just a work of art—it's a living testament to a history that is still unfolding. The memorial is funded entirely by private donations and admission fees, which speaks to its importance to so many people who feel an unbreakable connection to this legacy. Henry Standing Bear's vision was clear: to honor Crazy Horse and to create something that would outlive any one generation. The project began in 1948, and when it's completed, Crazy Horse will be shown riding horseback, pointing toward the land his people held sacred. The vision that Henry Standing Bear had in 1939, when he first contacted Polish sculptor Korczak Ziolkowski to bring this idea to life, is still alive today. Ziolkowski died in 1982, but his work—and the work of his family—continues. I met with his daughter, Jadwiga, who now oversees the continued progress of the memorial. Sitting with her over a cup of coffee, I couldn't help but feel the weight of what she, her family, and the many workers here are carrying forward. She spoke with quiet pride about her father's relentless drive to carve Crazy Horse into the mountain. She remembered him on that first day in 1948, standing alone on that vast rock with nothing but a hammer and chisel, imagining what it could one day become. It's hard to imagine the commitment it must have taken, not just to start, but to continue such a monumental task. But Jadwiga made it clear: her family never considered stopping, even after her father's death. They carried on, generation after generation.

"The idea started with Henry Standing Bear, and Dad took it on," Jadwiga told me, her voice soft but full of conviction. "He believed in this so strongly. And even though he didn't live to see the finished sculpture, it's still happening. My dad thought ahead, made sure it would continue after him. It's a family mission now."

I sat there a while, listening to her stories about growing up on Thunderhead Mountain, the view from their home, and how her family was part of the land—and how the land was part of them. She talked about her mother's vision for getting people involved, for ensuring that this project was not just something for the past but for the future, too.

Her family's unwavering commitment to completing the memorial speaks to a larger idea: this is about more than just honoring one man; it's about honoring a people, a culture, and a history that deserves to be remembered. The Crazy Horse Memorial is one of the most ambitious and meaningful tributes to Native American history, but it's also a reflection of something larger —the pursuit of justice and the struggle for dignity in a world that has often overlooked both.

As we finished our coffee and the conversation shifted back to the future, I asked Jadwiga about her thoughts on America today. Her face softened, a mix of concern and hope in her eyes. "I think it's a great time," she said. "But I also worry. We all do. It's easy to forget where we came from. But we have hope. Without it, we wouldn't be here."

Her words lingered in the cold mountain air as I made my way back to Argo. We hit the road again, easing our way back to Highway 83, the heart of America, and the place where history—both tragic and triumphant—is still being made.

Note to Self

Don't let time or distance numb you to the stories that came before you.

You don't have to carve a mountain to carry someone's legacy forward. Sometimes it's as simple as listening closely, remembering well, and living in a way that honors the truth, especially the hard, complicated kind.

Reverence isn't about looking back with guilt or pride; it's about looking back with *honesty*.

And then looking forward with purpose.

50

GHOST PLANE

All our days are numbered, but only God knows the number. Pray there are many; dance like there are few.

UNKNOWN

I VEERED WEST OFF HIGHWAY 83, aiming for the quiet, final resting place of a plane that had once soared above America on a crisp October day in 1999.

Van Ardan and Robert Fraley were living the dream. They worked as agents for one of the most charismatic and beloved golfers of the time: Payne Stewart. Their world was fast-paced and dizzying, a whirlwind of media, triumphs, and endless travel, but there was a special bond between the three men. They all lived in Orlando, raising their families nearby. It was a time of joy, camaraderie, and success.

That October morning, the weather was perfect—mid-sixties, with the kind of crisp, clear sky that made every flight feel like an adventure. The men kissed their wives goodbye and headed to the airport, where a private jet was waiting to take them to the Tour Championship in Houston. Golf course designer Bruce Borland was aboard, there to review some project details during the flight.

What no one knew as they took off was that this flight would capture America's attention. Even the president would be pulled from a meeting with economic advisors to track its progress.

The Learjet roared down the Orlando runway just after nine. "Four-seven-bravo-alpha … you're cleared to the Dallas Love Field via the Jeff Six departure," the air traffic controller announced.

Captain Michael Kling was at the helm, a seasoned Air Force vet with countless hours of flight experience. His copilot, First Officer Stephanie Bellegarrigue, was young but capable, with a solid 1,700 flight hours under her belt, ninety-nine of those in the Learjet.

It was a special day for both pilots. Payne Stewart, the flamboyant golfer always clad in knickers and a flat cap, was a man they admired, and to be flying him was a treat. Payne's style was unmatched—his swing was fluid and effortless, his charisma unmistakable. He'd won eleven PGA Tour events and was known not just for his skills but for his signature flair.

But just minutes into the flight, things took a strange turn. The plane veered off course, heading north when it should have turned west. No response came when air traffic tried to reach them.

The minutes stretched into an uncomfortable silence, and concern started to creep in.

The air traffic controllers' voices were laced with confusion. Was it a technical malfunction? A medical emergency? Or something darker? As the minutes ticked by, it became clear that something was terribly wrong. The flight was now a ghost plane—on autopilot, with no one in the cockpit. The U.S. military was notified, and an F-16 was dispatched to investigate.

The fighter pilot, Chris Hamilton, was soon at the plane's side. "I got fifty to a hundred feet from the airplane," he recalled, "and I could see there was something wrong. The cockpit was frosted over, or perhaps it was condensed. I couldn't see inside."

That's when reality sank in: the plane's cabin had depressurized, cutting off oxygen and plunging the interior into frigid temperatures. It was flying on fumes, drifting through the skies, its destination uncertain. Military officials feared it could crash into a populated area, causing a disaster of unimaginable scale. Could they shoot it down to prevent that? As the ghost plane continued its course, the nation watched, riveted. The news stations interrupted regular programming, broadcasting updates as the aircraft drifted toward its unknown fate.

Somewhere in South Dakota, Nina Vilhauer, a nurse from Mina, was struggling with a migraine. She'd called in sick to work and was lying in bed, not feeling up to her usual creative pursuits. But when her husband called, the conversation quickly shifted. He told her to turn on the news—there was a plane falling from the sky.

Nina didn't believe him at first. She assumed he was making a joke. But when she finally tuned into the news, she understood his grave concern. As a nurse, her instinct kicked in. Could she help? Was there anything she could do if the plane came down nearby?

She went outside, looking up at the sky, but there was no smoke—just two fighter jets circling, perhaps helping authorities pinpoint the wreckage. She got in her car and headed west, but the road was blocked by fences and section lines, paths used by farmers to get to their fields. As she neared the area, she saw the Care Flight helicopter, confirming that medical professionals were already on the scene.

Still, her mind raced. What had she just witnessed? She would never forget the sight of that plane spiraling toward the ground, surrounded by a divine light, as if it were being guided to its final resting place.

"I just knew, in my heart," she told me, "that the Lord was with them."

Later that day, Nina felt compelled to write a poem for the families of the passengers on that flight, to tell them what she had witnessed. It wasn't easy, but the words came to her on a walk down a section line, and by the time she got home, the poem was complete.

Faith in Him

By Nina Vilhauer

My thoughts have been with your family so many, many times,

Knowing the heartache you must feel being the loved ones left behind,

But I want to tell you something about that final flight, I know the Lord was with them as He kept them in His sight.

I watched the plane glide silently across the South Dakota sky, I had a helpless feeling as I prayed for the helpless souls inside.

When the plane began its final descent, it spiraled toward the ground,

A beacon of light came through the clouds and followed the Learjet down,

I was startled to see this magnificent light,

And yet, in my heart, I knew the Lord had come to be their guide, My Heavenly Kingdom is waiting for you.

I can't take away your heartache, I can't take away your pain, but I hope I can reassure you the Lord was with their plane.

God's blessings to each one of you

May faith in Him not sway,

For He sends His unfailing love to guide us every day.

The poem hangs in the living room of my friends Rickly and Debbie in Colorado. Debbie is the widow of Van Ardan, who was on that plane.

And in the field near Mina, South Dakota, a granite memorial rock stands where the plane crashed. It bears the words of Psalm 40:2-3 and the names of those who perished that day.

As I stood at that memorial, I couldn't help but feel the weight of the lives that were lost. But I also felt an overwhelming sense of peace, knowing that, even in the chaos, the light of God had been there, guiding them all the way.

Note to Self

Some moments ask you to stop and feel everything.

To feel the weight of loss, yes—but also the mystery of peace that can somehow meet us there. I don't understand how light can show up in the darkest places. I just know it does. I saw it. Or maybe I just believe it that much.

And belief—that gentle kind—is sometimes all we're given.

And it's enough.

51

WALTER'S CROSS

If you carry your cross joyfully, it will carry you.

THOMAS À KEMPIS

A MAN WALKING ALONE APPEARS up ahead, on the opposite side of the road. A hitchhiker?

At first, I wonder if my mind is playing tricks on me. Driving for hours on this long, unending road with scenery that never seems to change has a way of messing with your perception. The steady hum of the tires on asphalt becomes a kind of hypnotic rhythm, and before you know it, the mind starts concocting odd, almost dreamlike visions.

I'm traveling north on Highway 83, straight up the middle of the country. On either side, there's nothing but miles of agriculture in motion, swaying gently with the winds—fields of corn, wheat, sunflowers, and cattle. It's like being trapped in a loop, the same scenes unfolding over and over again with each mile. This part of the country, this breadbasket of the nation, is defined by its farming. The towns dotting the landscape exist only to support the land that sustains them. I'm well north of Bismarck, North Dakota, headed toward Minot, and I haven't passed a town for miles.

So when I see this lone figure walking along the road, it seems odd. No car broken down in sight, not behind me, not up ahead. Nothing. There's just him, walking alone in the middle of nowhere.

As I pass, I get a better look, and my suspicion is confirmed—he's not hitchhiking. He's dragging a wooden cross, taller than he is, behind him.

Of course, I assume he's a little off his rocker. People don't walk alone out here in the middle of nowhere with a cross for no reason. Still, curiosity gets the better of me. I turn the car around, heading back to where he's walking. Something tells me this is either going to be a strange encounter or something more—though my active imagination warns me that I could be walking right into a setup. Robbery? Maybe worse? It doesn't matter. I have to know.

As I roll up alongside him, I lower the window just enough to speak without feeling too intrusive. "Just curious… what are you doing?" I ask with a grin, keeping the tone light. "I'm carrying the cross for Jesus," he replies, his smile wide and unbothered. "I'm Walter." He stretches out his hand to shake mine, and I take it, cautiously at first, then with more ease. Walter seems harmless enough. I get the sense he's genuinely on a mission, something I can respect. He's dressed simply—walking shoes, blue jeans, a red t-shirt, and a red ball cap with "Jesus Loves You" emblazoned on it, along with a drawing of a man carrying a cross. This is no joke for him. He's all in.

I have to know more. "So, I've been sitting here driving for hours, and you're… walking.

Carrying a cross. What's the story behind this?"

He seems ready for the question. "I wanted to do more," he begins. "My wife and I worked in a local church for twenty years. I kept asking the Lord, 'What more can I do? I want to do more.' And then I saw a man carrying the cross, and I thought, 'I can do that.'"

The man he's referring to is Arthur Blessitt, a traveling preacher who has carried a wooden cross in every nation around the world since 1968. As of 2019, he claims to have walked over 43,000 miles through 324 nations and territories, making it into the Guinness World Records for the longest walk in history.

"I tried it once," Walter continues, "and I collapsed on the couch after just a few miles. My wife reminded me she was there, that we were in this together. The whole family thought we were crazy, walking and carrying the cross like that."

"It's a reasonable assumption!" I laugh, relieved that he's not offended by my lighthearted response.

"But you know what?" he says, growing serious. "Then you get to that one person. You share Jesus with them, and it makes everything worth it. We were walking through Kansas once, and this lady stopped us. She said she had asked the Lord for a sign, and when she saw me carrying the cross, she just broke down in tears. She could barely even speak." "That meant something to her?" I ask, genuinely moved.

"It did," Walter says, nodding with quiet conviction. "It really did."

As I drive away, my mind lingers on Walter, dragging his wooden cross down the highway from Texas to Canada. There's something about that image that makes my heart skip. The cross—symbol of devotion, life, death, and resurrection suddenly seems bigger than the long stretches of empty road. A strange, powerful encounter with a man on a mission.

It makes me reflect on my own life and the times I've questioned my purpose, my journey.

That feeling of wondering if there's more than just the dust and the bones of living—it's something that has haunted me for a long time.

It came early. My first real existential crisis hit when I was just a kid.

Growing up, I spent a week or more each summer at my uncle's farm near Decatur, Texas. It was the kind of place where you could be a boy—doing farm chores, hiking through the woods, fishing, hunting with my trusty .22 rifle, and just staring up at the sky, trying to make sense of it all.

One of those blistering Texas summer days, when the sun felt like a hot blanket pressing down on everything, my existential crisis hit. The farmhouse, without air conditioning, baked under the relentless heat, the shade trees by the pond the only relief to be found.

It was late morning. The chores were done. I was ready for some peace, so I decided to go fishing, hoping to catch a big ol' catfish. Walking through a field toward the pond, I came upon an ant bed.

I'd seen plenty of ant beds in my time, destroyed more than a few, but this one stopped me in my tracks. I stood over it, watching the ants scurry about, each one on its mission. Some were carrying bits of food, others were returning to the mound, some heading out, moving in a kind of chaotic rhythm.

It was mesmerizing. Overwhelming, even. I thought, *This is what it must be like for God, looking down on us from above.*

Humans, like ants, marching around in circles, constantly moving—searching for something, building higher, always looking for more.

From the church lessons I'd heard growing up, I knew that God watches over us, sees every move before we even make it. I wondered: *Am I just one of those ants, scurrying about? Is this all there is?*

Psalm 121:1-8, from the Bible, came to mind: "The Lord watches over you—the Lord is your shade at your right hand; the sun will not harm you by day, nor the moon by night. The Lord will keep you from all harm—he will watch over your life; the Lord will watch over your coming and going both now and forevermore."

And there I was, casting my shade over the tiny ants, pondering whether this is how God sees us—so small, so busy, so unaware of the grand plan.

Why is there suffering? Why do the ants work so hard, only to be crushed beneath my boot or wiped out by poison? Why do we struggle so, when it feels like God could just make it all stop?

I'm sure I wasn't the first kid to ask these kinds of questions, but I also knew no one had the answers I wanted. My teachers didn't know. My family didn't know. They all brushed it off, saying I was just a curious kid. So, I stopped asking. But the questions stuck with me.

Over the years, though, I've concluded that it must be true—there is a God, and this life, as confusing as it is, is part of His grand design. How else could this complex world work?

I see evidence of God everywhere. From the tiny, seemingly insignificant ant to the magnificent elephant. From a microscopic cell to the most intricate of human beings. There's something beyond all of this, a force that holds it together, and I can feel it.

But, at some point, I had to accept that I wouldn't get all the answers—not now, anyway. One day, maybe. But for now, I believe.

Maybe it's not about knowing. Maybe it's just about trusting that there's an answer— even if I can't see it yet. Because sometimes, in this wild, unpredictable world, that's all I need to keep moving forward.

I pray.

I believe, even when I don't have it all figured out.

The storm will come.

I want to be ready for that storm.

JOHN W. BUTLER

Note to Self

Next time you think you're carrying a heavy load, remember Walter—dragging a full-sized wooden cross up the spine of America like it's just another afternoon stroll. And maybe don't be so quick to assume that the guy walking alone on a remote stretch of Highway 83 is out of his mind. He might just be walking in his purpose. There's something disarming about that kind of conviction—the kind that says, "God told me to do this," and then just ... does it. No Instagram. No GoFundMe. Just a guy, a cross, and a pair of well-worn shoes. Sometimes faith looks like a quiet prayer. Sometimes it looks like a hitchhiker with a gospel billboard strapped to his back.

Let the ants be ants. Let God be God. And maybe just try to be someone willing to keep walking—boots dusty, questions unanswered, faith intact.

Also, pack snacks. Revelation comes slowly on the open road.

52

Fargo

*And I guess that was your accomplice in
the wood chipper.*

MARGE GUNDERSON, *FARGO*

IT IS NEARING THE END OF SEPTEMBER. I am in Fargo, North Dakota. Yes, that one, the setting from the notorious and darkly comic movie of the same name. It is thirty-five degrees outside at around nine in the morning. I am sitting in Deana's Diner. The coffee is hot. The waitresses are friendly. The food is fast. Not wanting to be rude when my server keeps asking to top off my coffee, I agree and am buzzy in under thirty minutes flat.

I order my usual diner-basic breakfast but stop mid-order, taking note of what the locals are eating: "Instead of toast," I say, "I'll take the pancakes."

Lickity-split, my waitress sets before me a plate of eggs over easy, a separate plate with a short stack of two massive pancakes, and a third plate holding cups of butter and a six-ounce metal pitcher of hot maple syrup.

I have no idea how much coffee I have had already. All I know is that my mug is always full, and I keep sipping from that mug.

All the employees are wearing t-shirts with Deana's Diner logo on the front. On the back, each shirt has a different phrase: "Life is short, lick the plate." "I love you a waffle lot." "Mind your own biscuits." "Life will be gravy; put your fat pants on." "The soup of the day is tequila." After roaming about the city all afternoon, I realize it's high time I do my laundry. I steer toward a place billed as "Fargo's finest coin laundry." The name of the place is Fargo's Finest Coin Laundry. After throwing my clothes in the washer, I set the timer on my phone and headed out.

I pull Argo into a McDonald's parking lot and go inside for coffee. More coffee, you ask?

Don't judge.

The waitress is middle-aged, with a piercing on the right middle side of her lip. It's puffed up red around the small silver stud. I'm thinking it's infected. Her eyes are glazed over. Her manager is moving in slow motion behind the counter, walking back and forth. I make eye contact, and she looks at me but doesn't seem to see me—there is a vacantness in her facial expression.

The drug crisis is the dark side of America. But much is being done to help those who are addicted. One famous singer who survived the dark side and found his way to the light is Jelly Roll.

Jelly Roll, the singer and rapper known for his blend of country, rock, and hip-hop, has become an unlikely yet impactful advocate in the fight against addiction and the broader drug crisis in America. His journey of overcoming addiction has made him a powerful voice in raising awareness and providing hope to others battling substance use disorders.

Jelly Roll's music often reflects his struggles with addiction, mental health, and the harsh realities of life, which resonates deeply with fans who are going through similar challenges. Beyond his music, Jelly Roll has taken concrete steps to support the recovery community and raise awareness about the drug crisis, and support organizations that provide addiction treatment and recovery services like The Bridge Ministries, which helps those recovering from addiction.

Meanwhile, I am still standing in line behind a girl in a long flowing dress made of thin material, dark green, mixed with various shades of gray and burgundy. In her left hand, she holds strings looped through two compact sleeping bag sacks. Her long hair could be beautiful if it were given some attention and a brush. Her face is almost attractive. Again, with a bit of care, it could be. Sadly, her loveliness is pocked with the early stages of meth addiction.

I can't be far off, as she is not ordering anything to eat. She is talking in and out of a slurring tone to the lady behind the cash register. I overhear her asking for directions to a local rehab center. The waitress knows precisely where it is and proceeds to give directions. But it is a comedy of miscommunication.

"So, then I … well, do you mean, I … take a left," the girl repeats the instruction, but points right. She wants to understand, while something inside her is racing too fast for her. She can't seem to slow her mind down to comprehend the simple directions.

The manager is listening and appears frustrated that her clerk is taking so long to give directions, and no orders are being taken at the cash register. I'm about to walk out to find another place for a coffee.

The manager interrupts, taking over and giving directions to the poor, lost creature.

The lady takes my order. I thought about getting some food with my coffee, but looking around, I don't think it would be a good idea. It's a sanitary issue. She makes my coffee, which was okay until she put her hand across the lip of the coffee cup. I can't drink it after that. But I paid for it, so I took it. Some flowers will benefit from the acidity of it, I hope, as I pour it into the side of the landscaping mulch.

This is not a problem peculiar to Fargo. It is nationwide. Every city of any size. Drugs of one type or another. Legal and otherwise. Chemical escapes. But the path of the escape is into a spider web that doesn't let go.

The meth and oxycodone plague is decimating our nation and many nations worldwide. In 2015, 33,000 people in the United States died from overdosing on opioid drugs. Of those, 13,000 were caused by heroin; opiate medications caused the remaining deaths. Those who are addicted come from all races, all socioeconomic levels, and all geophysical locations. Addiction makes no exceptions in those who are vulnerable to its hellish call. Data from 2018 shows that 128 people in the United States died every day after overdosing on opioids. The Centers for Disease Control and Prevention estimates that the total "economic burden" of prescription opioid misuse alone in the United States is $78.5 billion annually, including healthcare costs, lost productivity, addiction treatment, and criminal justice involvement. The cost of lives lost is incalculable.

I read a local free magazine while waiting for the dryer to finish. There is a write-up on a farm-to-market restaurant. It's just a few blocks away.

After the clothes are dry, I return them to their designated places in the overhead compartments in Argo. Then, Argo and I drift together toward the site I read about. I say drift because even though it was very close, we detoured through Roger Maris Park, along the side of the river, taking in the winding, narrow-lane drive.

Roger Maris, for any non-baseball fans, was one of the great baseball players, setting a new Major League Baseball single-season home run record with 61 runs in 1961, breaking Babe Ruth's 34-year record of 60 home runs. That record remained unbroken for 37 years until 1998, when the era of drug-enhancement and overtraining became a thing. Maris achieved his feat through sheer raw talent.

Maris moved to Fargo at the age of four, so they still consider him a hometown hero.

I finally made it to the restaurant I read about, Luna's. It doesn't look like much from the outside, set in a strip of shops between a liquor store and a nail salon. But that's my kind of place: local, small, off the beaten path. A place like this adds to the adventure. These spots are the wild cards of the dining world—either a hidden gem or a total bust.

And while I've had my fair share of both, there's something about that uncertainty that keeps me coming back for more.

Note to Self

Some towns hum with quiet ache. Not loud or showy—just a low-grade thrum you feel if you sit still long enough. You can try to drown it in noise, or sugar, or screens, but the ache's still there, under the linoleum floors and flickering fluorescent lights.

And yet, people stay. They smile. They sweep the sidewalks.

Even here, grace persists. Not glamorous, but gritty. Not loud, but real. And maybe that's enough.

53

Main Street

The nice thing about living in a small town is that when you don't know what you're doing, someone else does.

IMMANUEL KANT

THERE'S A "MAIN STREET" IN just about every town, but this Minnesota prairie town boasts one that stands out—it's not just a street; it's almost a celebrity in its own right. And all thanks to one mischievous misfit of a kid who grew up just a few blocks away and penned a biting novel that laid bare the lives of the people who walked these very sidewalks.

Sinclair Lewis, the son of the town doctor in Sauk (pronounced "sock") Centre, grew into a literary maverick with a knack for poking fun at the very things America held dear— capitalism, materialism, and small-town life itself. He was the Gandalf of American literature— except his magic wasn't wands and rings, but words that unmasked the quirks and absurdities of life between the world wars. And when it came to small-town life in Minnesota, Lewis had more than a little fun.

Sauk Centre was founded in the mid-1800s, named after the Sauk people, who once lived along the St. Lawrence River. Picture a sleepy afternoon here, where life moves slower than molasses in January. I found myself in a dusty corner of the library, where the books seemed like they might start chatting amongst themselves. And there, on a shelf, I spotted it—*Main Street*. It looked like it had lived through a hundred adventures, worn and weathered.

This wasn't just any book. This was Sinclair Lewis's *Main Street,* published in 1920. It was his seventh novel, a satire that wasn't exactly well-received by the locals. They didn't take too kindly to his portrayal of small-town life. But instead of being chased out of town with pitchforks, the book became a kind of odd attraction, drawing in curious visitors eager to see if the real-life town matched the fictional Gopher Prairie.

As I cracked open the pages of *Main Street* in that quiet library, it felt like stepping into a time machine—one that whisked me back to an earlier, simpler Sauk Centre, where gossip flowed like syrup at a pancake breakfast. It was like staring into a hall of mirrors, with reality and fiction reflecting each other in curious harmony.

Lewis wasn't just a writer—he was a literary trailblazer. He wasn't afraid to call out the absurdities of American life, and his words still pack a punch today. The man who snagged the Nobel Prize in Literature wasn't just telling stories; he was shaping the American literary landscape, and his legacy lives on in the pages of books and in the town he never really left. It just so happened that the Sinclair Lewis Writers' Conference was happening in town that very weekend. The event gathered aspiring writers, seasoned authors, and book enthusiasts in a Midwestern celebration of words. Picture a space where creativity flowed as freely as the Mississippi River, and where the written word carried a kind of magic all its own.

Excitement was in the air, and as I joined the event, Sinclair Lewis's spirit seemed to hang in the corners of every conversation. Writers shared their stories, swapped editing war stories, and gave advice on everything from crafting plot twists to surviving the dreaded first draft.

The workshops were a whirlwind of ideas and inspiration, a place where we all grew a little wiser, a little braver, and more connected to the world of storytelling. At lunch, literary discussions ranged from the world of science fiction to romance, as if we were all feasting at a banquet table where every genre had a place.

Leaving the conference, I felt like I'd just stepped off a boat into the river of American letters, ready to add my own story to the mix. It was a day of laughter, learning, and a reminder that in the world of stories, there's always room for one more adventure.

And now, as I head down the highway, with the Minnesota night setting in and the temperature dropping to a chilly twenty-nine degrees, I can't help but smile at the snowbirds preparing to flee. They'll pack up their trailers and campers and head south to the warmth, avoiding the frigid northern winter like seasoned pros.

As I walk out of the market, I overhear a conversation between two locals. "We'll catch up with you down there next week," one says, "I'm not leaving for another ten days."

A man walking beside me chuckles, "More room for the rest of us when they head south."

I smile, "So, you stick around for the winter?"

"Oh sure," he says with a grin. "Been doing it forever. I laugh at them—they can't take a little cold."

I figure from his red-weathered face that he's the type who's ready for ice-fishing. Before long, he'll be on a frozen lake, cutting holes and waiting for the first walleye of the season. As for me, I encounter another man, bundled up and heading for a truck.

"You getting ready for an adventure?" I ask.

"Yep, heading to McAllen, Texas, for some sunshine," he replies. "Gotta get out of here every year for a bit of warmth."

Places like McAllen are already swelling with his type, ones who head south to find the warmth of the sunshine and the easygoing charm of Southwesterners, with their ever-present "howdys" and "y'alls." Two climates.

Two ways of life.

We somehow make room for us all.

Note to Self

A small town's heartbeat can be loud if you lean in to listen. What looks like stillness from the outside is often brimming with stories, contradictions, and a stubborn kind of charm. Humor and heartache tend to share the same table here. And whether folks are weathering winter or chasing warmth, something is comforting in the way America makes space for both.

Sometimes, the most surprising insight comes not from racing down the highway, but from walking slowly down Main Street.

54

SWEET HOME CHICAGO

One of the hallmarks of Chicago is that we do so many things in an original manner. What other city has made a river flow backwards? What other city makes traffic flow backwards?

MIKE ROYKO, PULITZER PRIZE-WINNING JOURNALIST

THE FOLLOWING AFTERNOON, ARGO AND I took the long way around Chicago, the radio blaring "Sweet Home Chicago." It's funny how I can belt out songs while they're playing, but can barely remember the lyrics five minutes later. Still, that Chicago anthem hits me every time. The city, with all its grit and grandeur, always stirs something in me, even from the confines of the car.

Chicago, of course, is famous for more than just its blues. There's the Great Chicago Fire, for instance. Legend has it that poor Mrs. O'Leary's cow knocked over a lantern while being milked. What the newspapers didn't mention was the dry summer, the drought, and the wooden city that was bound to catch fire. The O'Leary house survived, and Mrs. O'Leary spent her life hiding from the media frenzy, victim of a sensationalized myth that even a city-sized tragedy couldn't compete with. The fire, like Krakatoa, is one of those disasters etched into history, full of rumors and wrong turns.

As Argo and I pass through the sprawling city, I reflect on my near move to Chicago years prior. I skirt through parts of the town trying to avoid the suffocating congestion, but that is impossible to do. It's tough, unrelenting. Chicago was given the labels of "murder capital" and "mass-shooting capital," and though I might dismiss them as exaggerations, I'm not taking any chances today.

I'd once considered making Chicago home, nearly moving there as a teenager. WLS, the powerhouse station, offered me a gig. Imagine me, DJing in the city that gave birth to so many legends—Paul Harvey's voice coming from those same walls. I stayed at the Palmer House Hotel, steeped in history and old-world charm, where even Ike and Tina Turner brushed past me on their way through the lobby. It was the stuff of daydreams—a shot at greatness, a taste of what could have been.

But as much as I loved the idea of Chicago—the energy, the history, the music—I turned it down. Every visit was cold and windy. I wasn't ready for that. Maybe I should have been.

Maybe I was just too young and naïve to see the opportunity.

The city had its allure. It's a city that has fought hard to define itself, caught between a long history of crime, corruption, and resilience.

It's a city of big personalities and even bigger hearts. People in Chicago don't hold back—they'll tell you exactly what they think, get in your face with a scowl. Then show you love and compassion just as fiercely. The Cubs win? The entire city feels like a giant parade. The Bears lose? Same energy—just more grumbling. The passion for sports here, for the history, the culture—it's infectious. Chicagoans are proud. And while they might make fun of you for your accent, they'll offer you a drink, show you around, and maybe even give you a few tips on how to survive the Windy City.

I'll be back for the city's energy, its unyielding drive, and the beautiful chaos. I'll return to see the towering architecture, get caught up in a conversation about "da Bears" over a cold beer, and yes, probably share a deep-dish pizza with someone who claims in a gruff, assertive voice, "There's no other pizza like it."

Note to Self

Some cities you pass through. Others pass through you. Chicago's the kind of town that leaves smudges on your windshield, your memories, your soul. It's loud and loyal and doesn't care if you like it. But if you do? Well, it might just let you stay awhile.

It's a city that doesn't ask for approval. It's too busy moving, building, surviving. The people here know how to weather storms—literal and otherwise. They've seen it all and still find a way to show up for each other, grumble together over sports, and celebrate like champions even when their team hasn't won in years. There's a rhythm to this place—a backbeat of blues and bus horns, of deep-dish debates and frozen breath on winter mornings.

You can't fake your way through Chicago. You either mean it, or you don't.

And if you're lucky enough to stand still long enough to feel it? The unshakable sense of hometown pride —you'll leave with more than just a snapshot. You'll carry it with you, in your voice, in your walk, in the way you learn to love the complicated things a little deeper.

55

HEADING EAST

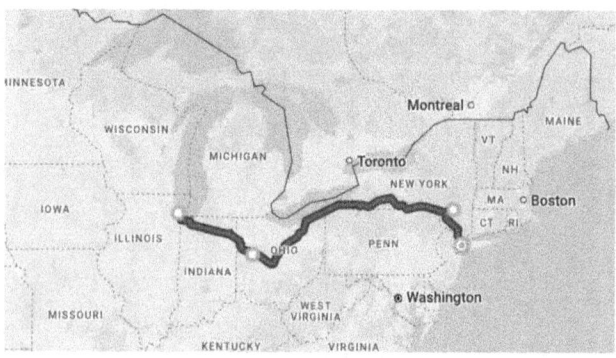

*Two roads diverged in a wood, and I— I
took the one less traveled by.*

ROBERT FROST, THE ROAD NOT TAKEN

FROM CHICAGO, I HEADED TO Jackson Center, Ohio, where the Airstream factory gives birth to its famous silver-skinned trailers and motor-coach vans, such as Argo.

The story began in the 1930s when Wally Byam, an inventive advertising man from Oregon, built a tiny teardrop trailer for himself and his wife to travel comfortably. Wally wanted to sleep under the sky, but not on the ground. It was stylish camping. Honest and easy. Others saw it and wanted the same. His prototype drew so much curiosity on the road that in 1931, he founded Airstream.

While many early trailer manufacturers vanished during the Great Depression and World War II, Airstream endured. By the postwar boom, Airstream had become synonymous with freedom on the American highway — stylish enough for Hollywood stars and practical enough for families exploring the national parks.

Over the decades, Airstreams have found fame as NASA quarantine vehicles for returning astronauts, pop culture icons in movies, and cherished vintage collectibles. Airstreams still carry Wally Byam's spirit of endless road trips, reflecting an American dream of roaming wherever the open road leads, with the comforts of home always rolling behind you. Airstream remains an enduring symbol of American adventure, instantly recognizable by its sleek, riveted aluminum shells and aerodynamic curves inspired by aircraft design.

I took a tour of the Airstream factory and thanked the people I had called from the road for helping me find a switch or solve a problem with Argo. Then, I scheduled Argo to get a checkup the next morning.

It was after six and I was hungry. Places to eat are limited in Jackson Center. The population is only around 1,300. The choice was taking a chance on the gas station food, choosing between a stiff sandwich in plastic, a pizza under a lamp, or a half-warm sub. Chuck at Airstream said I could walk about two minutes down the road to a dive called the Heidout. "It's mostly a bar, but has food that won't kill ya," he said. I felt uneasy when I pulled the door open, leaving the old Ohio night air behind me. Inside, I was greeted with the smell of beer and stale malt. The sharp edge of old whiskey in the air, and maybe spilled cola.

Nine people sat at the U-shaped bar. A few high-top tables were scattered around, with smaller tables clinging to the walls. A man and a woman sat at one. Married, you could tell.

Married people don't need to speak much.

The room was dim, except for the neon lights behind the bar and a TV that showed cops at a crime scene. Another screen ran lottery balls and numbers that no one had won.

I stepped toward the bar. They all turned. They looked for a friend but found me instead. I was nobody they knew. Nobody from here. The woman behind the bar stops talking midsentence, like a record catching a scratch, then keeps going, just a little louder.

One man, older, with a face like an unpaved road, stares straight on at me. Not hostile, not friendly. Just looking. Judging. Remembering—he's seen men walk in before. Some stay quiet. Some don't.

I wanted to leave, but my legs held. The old man at the end raised his arm and said,

"Come on in."

"Thanks," I said. "Need to hit the head first." You have to gauge a place before you sit down. It's how we stay alive.

"It's back there," the woman behind the bar said. She pointed up and behind me, laughing. They always laugh about the bathroom. It's how we remind ourselves we're all just bodies in the end.

I found it. Came back. They didn't look up. Some talked. Some drank and thought their thoughts. A young guy in a ball cap stirred his whiskey like he wanted to drown something in it.

I took the last stool near the door.

"What'll you have? Beer?" the waitress asked. She didn't care much, but she was kind in her tired way. She had a shirt with a beer logo on it. Clean enough. She looked thirty, going on forty. She ran this place like she didn't want to be here.

"No beer," I said. "Just food. What's good?"

She bent down and handed me a menu. "Burgers and pizza. That's what we have."

The fellow next to me half turned my way. "Where-ya-frum?"

"Texas. Just making a stop at the Airstream factory." He nodded, returning to nursing his beer with a low, sour ache of loneliness.

There were bars along the road. Cheap signs. Paint peeling. Some wood. Some tin. Bars for the lonely and the glad, where people drink for joy or drink because something hurts.

The Heidout was one of those. Folks knew each other. They'd played ball together once, or fought each other, or kissed behind barns.

The next day, I point Argo east, taking the scenic route. It starts with farmland—wide skies, flat roads, silos, and cornfields. Passed an Amish buggy somewhere along one of the twolane roads. The road hums under Argo's tires like it has nowhere better to be.

I took the route that cuts through the southern edge of the Catskills, which are located in southeastern New York, north of New Jersey, and northwest of the Hudson Valley. It took more time, but the trade-off is highway monotony for winding roads, wild deer, and gas stations that sell fly rods and maple syrup. I stopped once for gas and black coffee that tasted like metal. No one talked. That was fine.

In the Catskills, pines line the highway like soldiers. The clouds hung low and slow across the ridges. The air smelled like moss and woodsmoke and a kind of clean you couldn't buy. Old towns with empty hotels. Places where people had come to dance and swim and eat and forget their names. That was long ago.

By the time I hit the bridge, the city was rising ahead of me like a fist—steel and glass and noise.

Note to Self

The road doesn't hand out epiphanies like souvenir magnets. It gives you blisters and windshield gunk and directions that may or may not be accurate.

But eventually, after enough gas station coffee and side-of-the-road prayers, it gives you a strange peace, the kind that sneaks in once you've finally stopped trying to make the trip mean something big. Maybe the meaning isn't in the grand revelations. Maybe it's in the repetition. The packing. The unpacking.

The way the land flattens, then rises. The way strangers say, *"Safe travels,"* like it's a blessing they still believe in.

I didn't find the America I see on screens. I found the real one instead.

56

ALL-AMERICAN STATE OF MIND

> We shall not cease from exploration. And the end of all of our exploring. Will be to arrive where we started. And know the place for the first time.
>
> T. S. ELIOT

ARGO AND I INCH OUR WAY BACK into New York City, where the traffic moves with all the speed and grace of a tranquilized sloth. Radio 1010 WINS is abuzz about politics. It's comforting, in a weird, apocalyptic way, to know that absolutely nothing has changed. Both sides are flinging insults like monkeys during a banana shortage.

Standing in Times Square, I reflect back two years ago. I stood in this exact spot, ready to go in search of America. Thirty-three thousand three hundred twenty-one miles later, I did it. After two years, an endless raft of asphalt miles, and countless conversations, I understand the great big, beautiful country a little bit more. The road has a way of revealing truth to you—the truth beneath the noise. In small towns and big cities, I met a diverse range of people. And, surprise, we are not as divided as some would have us believe. We have much more in common than what divides us. The people I came across were kind. They were curious. They wanted to help. They wanted to connect. Most of us are simply trying to get through the day.

Make it to the weekend.

There were also the lonely people. The forgotten people. The left-behind people. And those living on the street corners, under bridges, and in the nooks and crannies of America.

I walked down into the nearby subway tunnel. The air was heavy, filled with the scent of old metal and old rain. A man lay there, half-hidden beneath a worn brown coat. His face was lost in the folds of it, beard tangled, eyes closed, just too tired to open. I dropped some dollars into his coffee can. Not much. But it felt like something that mattered. People rushed past. No one saw him. Maybe they did once, and then they stopped.

I moved along the platform near the suicide pit of the trackway with the fast people. Voices bounced off the tiled walls, sharp, clipped, hurried, waiting on the train. It starts as a distant rumble, like thunder trapped underground. You feel it more than you hear it. The sound swells into a roar as the train approaches, its wheels shrieking against the steel rails. A rush of air is pushed ahead of the cars. The doors slide open with a pneumatic hiss. People spill out. A mosaic of humanity—sleepy-eyed students, suited professionals, restaurant workers, and tourists. I surge with the fast people into the open doors.

◀ ▲ ▼ ▶

Exiting near Central Park, I take a slow walk down the paths, out onto a side street. A neighborhood coffee shop is tucked into the tight confines of an old building. Restless souls come to escape the city's relentless noise. The scent of deep, dark coffee blends with the lingering aroma of old leather and aged wood. The walls, heavy with faded photographs of a city long past, offer a glimpse into a New York that no longer exists.

I settle into a chair, once a rich mahogany, now bearing the marks of time. Varnish, cracked, and faded. I sit, gently stirring my coffee, while chatting on the phone with a friend about my trip.

A young man, looking twenty, is sitting at the table next to me, listening to my side of the phone conversation. His textbook is open. Sneakers, worn thin from the endless city streets. In his grey hoodie, he looks like someone who hasn't slept. The coffee in front of him sits half-full, the steam long gone. He glances out the window, his eyes scanning the world but never seeming to find what he's looking for. When I hang up, he turns to me.

"Sorry, I couldn't help but overhear you talking about your road trip," he says.

"Something I've been thinking about doing. Mind if I ask you about it?"

"Sure, ask away." He leans forward, curiosity lighting up his face. "It's something I'd like to do, but would be afraid to do it. Isn't it dangerous out there, especially all alone? Didn't you feel afraid?"

"No." I thought for a moment. "Well, maybe once or twice. Some strange noises at night put me on alert while I was camping a few times. And, yes, there are some weird people here and there. But my sixth sense lets me know when to keep my distance. All in all, America feels safe. People are kind. Friendly. When I asked for directions, they were helpful. Both in the big cities and the small towns."

He frowned. "But driving alone? The desert. The forest."

I sipped my coffee, reflecting. "This may sound strange, but I felt a force was with me. A spirit. A guide. God."

"So, you believe there is something bigger than us out there.

"I believe there is something bigger than us out there. God."

He looked at me, puzzled. Then he softened. "Okay. But there must've been a moment when you thought about turning back?"

This kid was a serious student type, so I offered up more than I usually would. I lean back, feeling the weight of memories. "There was a night, lost in the forest in Maine. Standing among the giant redwoods in California. And then there was this night in Arizona, driving through the darkness, the sky thick with stars, the road empty. I didn't see a single car for hours. I kept driving, the headlights cutting through the blackness. I stopped. Got out to stretch my legs. There was a brush of air against my face. A big gust followed. Then the sound of nothing. I felt a sense of respect for the night sky filled with stars. The land. It'll be here long after we are gone. And I'll be just another speck of dust swept away in the wind?" "Umm," he said.

I polished off the last, lukewarm sip of my coffee and tossed a smile over my shoulder as I headed out. "Kid, here's the best secret I've got after my decades of living: half the stuff you're terrified of won't happen. The other half will happen, but you'll survive it. And will make a damn good story someday. So breathe, be kind to yourself and others, and wear comfortable shoes."

◀ ▲ ▼ ▶

Later, I wander along 42nd Street ending at Bryant Park in the heart of Midtown Manhattan. It's sort of the backyard of the New York Public Library. The library, of course, is that massive building with the two intimidating stone lions out front, crafted from Tennessee pink marble. Patience and Fortitude are their names. They are stone. They are strong. I feel sure that if they could spring to life, they would not hesitate to devour you. Not in the metaphorical sense, I mean, they would literally eat you.

I walk past them and enter the library. The doors are heavy. The floor is cool. Walking into the vast Rose Main Reading Room, I find an empty seat at a table about halfway back. There is a faint scent of old paper and leather bindings. The Beaux Arts-adorned room is library-quiet.

That's a good thing, considering it's a library.

It's a place to think, a place to reflect—right in the heart of Manhattan. Books line the walls. Old books. Books that have been read and reread. Standing silent, and knowing, with the wisdom of the ages. This place has a way of making you feel both brilliant and dumb at the same time.

There is a stillness, a calm that makes you acutely aware of every creak of someone's wooden chair, every rustle of a page turning. That kind of silence that makes you hyper-aware of your thoughts. I started making notes in this room before I left two years ago. Now I return to review my road trip notes and write about it. I start writing, but I have a hard time focusing, and I begin to wonder if my thoughts and reflections could disturb the delicate equilibrium of intellectual introspection among the dozens of anonymous neighbors around me—a stupid thought. I start writing again till my mind drifts.

I wonder what the guy sitting two tables over is reading. His brow is furrowed, like he's trying to solve Fermat's Last Theorem. That's New York for you—even the library feels like a spectator sport.

Starting to write once again, I pause. Look up at the ornately scroll-framed mural on the ceiling. A painted sky with reddish sunlit clouds. It reminds me of some of the skies on my road trip. Natural light is streaming in through the grand, arched windows. It dances off the stained oak wood tables, casting a golden, dreamlike glow through the air.

On the long oak table where I'm sitting, there is a book. It is open face down against the table lamp. My curiosity is piqued. I reach for it. The book was opened to a poem by Walt Whitman. He connects back to my high school years. Whitman was required reading in Mr. Coltharp's English literary class. I remember a sunny day when he held class under a shade tree on campus to read poetry. He was one of those rare teachers.

I read from the page that the book is open to Walt Whitman's "Song of the Open Road."

"You road I enter upon and look around! I believe you are not all that is here;

I believe that much unseen is also here."

I look left and right. Is someone playing a joke on me? Whitman reflects on the unseen aspects of a journey. The road holds more than meets the eye. Perhaps this is the synchronicity phenomenon that psychologists Carl Jung and Jordan Peterson write about, where meaningful coincidences often arise during significant moments. An underlying order that links a person's inner thoughts to the external world. Not by direct cause and effect, but by their simultaneous occurrence. Coincidence? God sending me a message? Then I read more of Whitman's poetry:

"Allons! whoever you are come travel with me!

Traveling with me you find what never tires.

The earth never tires;

The earth is rude, silent, incomprehensible at first—

Nature is rude and incomprehensible at first;

Be not discouraged—keep on—there are divine things, well envelop'd;

I swear to you there are divine things more beautiful than words can tell."

Okay, this spooks me. There it was, "Song of the Open Road." And Walt Whitman, on the unseen in travel, the "divine thing more beautiful than words can tell." It felt providential, like a sign that my journey was an ongoing, unfolding story whose whole meaning would only reveal itself later—if ever.

Hopefully, you're inspired to embark on your journey to some of the places I visited. Find new roads. Find winding roads under endless skies. Chase your dream with that same reckless excitement I felt. Meet locals who start their conversation with, "So, you're not from 'round here, are you?" And you'll respond, "No, I'm just passing through... and possibly lost."

Sure, all the truth might've been in plain sight back home, hidden under a pile of one of my Chinese takeaway cartons, crumpled snack wrappers, or lost socks, but it was on this trip that I found the beautiful truth of America.

If I told all the stories, this book would be a Megillah—a Yiddish term for a long story.

We're talking ancient scroll levels of storytelling here. You'd need snacks—and possibly a support group to finish it. When I first typed up my road notes, the manuscript was roughly the size of War and Peace—and I don't mean a casual beach read, I mean the full Russian epic that could double as a foundation for a small shed. It was hundreds of pages of pure, unfiltered brilliance, by which I mean a lot of rambling about gas stations, detours, small town gossip, and questionable diner stops. I heroically hacked it down to about 650 pages, at which point a person with actual editorial talent—and access to sharp instruments—stepped in and trimmed it to something you could lift without injuring yourself.

So, many stories are left out. Many I never wrote down, but I carry them in my memory —as long as my memory still works.

I set out without expectations, at least, or tried to. It's impossible to completely empty your mind of all your biases and the world's noise, but I did my best. And in trying to go without preconceived notions, I found beautiful places. Beautiful people. Beautiful moments.

I connected with real people. Listened to their stories. And came to understand that to truly connect with another human being, you must enter their world.

HEARTLAND HIGHWAYS

I have been tested. I have tested myself. I have learned. It's as if I've undergone a mental renovation—a software update I didn't ask for, but now I can't live without. I am returning home. I am not the same.

◄ ▲ ▼ ►

America is the land of endless highways and more self-discovery than a year's worth of therapy sessions. The flat expanse of the plains, the jagged peaks of the Rockies, and those endless stretches of road that seem to go on forever—they call to you, beckoning with the promise of something more. I collected more than just memories; I came away with a newfound understanding of what it means to embrace the journey—potholes, detours, and all.

It wasn't just about the sights; it was about the people. The characters at roadside diners, and those surprisingly philosophical sages who currently have no home. Each encounter was a reminder that America is a melting pot of personalities, and every person has a story to tell.

It put me more in touch with the innermost parts of America's Heartland—both the heart of the land and the heart of its people.

Studies show that 62 percent of Americans do not travel away from home for leisure or business in any given year. Some can't afford it. The hassle and fear of it simply paralyzes others. But there's a price to this kind of isolation—losing sight of the world outside and only seeing it through a selectively distorted lens of mass media.

We've become a nation of Chicken Littles, continually shouting that "the sky is falling," and it may very well be one day. But today is not that day. (Wait, let me look out the window. Nope, we're good.) So, I urge you to step away from the screen. Put down the phone. Take a road trip. Embark on an adventure. If it can't be thirty-three thousand-plus miles, could it at least be one?

Go with an open mind. Go without expectations.

Just go. Let the world surprise and delight you again.

My road trip gave me so many gifts. I arrived at the end of my journey, profoundly grateful, wondering where I would go next. Perhaps a journey of even greater importance will soon unfold, leading me down roads of even deeper meaning. Maybe this is just the beginning. Who knows? Only God. (And possibly my GPS, but mostly God.)

Note to Self

People think the noise is what matters—getting attention. The shouting, the banners, the applause. But out there on the long road? I found the silence. And in the silence, I found truth.

I return home not the same person I was when I left. The road remade me, mile by mile, into someone who listens more closely, walks more gently, and believes more deeply. I found kindness in strangers, beauty in desolate places, and truth in voices I might never hear again. America is vast, restless, imperfect—and yet, profoundly alive, constantly moving forward like a great river.

Life rarely sticks to the map, and that's the beauty of it. Detours may feel like delays, but they're often where the real stories live—the unplanned conversation, the unexpected friendship, the hidden road with the better view. Welcome the detours.

The highway may end, but the journey does not. It carries forward, within my spiritual life, with every step I take. I'll keep listening. Keep looking. Talking to people I don't know. Taking time to help a stranger.

MEET THE AUTHOR

John W. Butler is an award-winning broadcaster, author, speaker, and podcaster—a storytelling road warrior with a country soul and a sharp wit, blending equal parts Texas radio charm and Maine forest mystery. He began working in a TV newsroom at the age of fifteen, spun records as a radio DJ, and hosted a weekly interview show while working his way through high school and college in television and radio.

He graduated with honors from the University of Texas at Austin and earned a master's degree from SMU in Dallas. He's deeply embedded in the Texas media scene, serving on the Texas Association of Broadcasters board and as the past President of the Golden Mic Club. As President of Butler7media, he and the Texas-based radio stations he operates have garnered awards for broadcast excellence.

John is a tireless advocate for community service. He has recorded books for the sight-impaired and disabled and has dedicated over 2,000 hours to supporting cancer patients in memory of his late wife. He is a devoted single dad to his son and daughter, and now affectionately known as "Papa John" to his five grandchildren. John thrives on travel, exploring by automobile, train, foot, boat, and bike. He is still working on his golf skills in the never-ending quest for a hole-in-one, but jokes he spends more time in the rough than on the green.

If you enjoyed this book, please consider leaving a review on Amazon and on your social media, unless those sentences are "This book ruined my life" or "I only used it to prop open a door."

At the very least, let me know if it inspires you to celebrate America and take a road trip.
www.HeartLandHighway.com